Managing to discriminate

Despite the introduction of anti-discrimination legislation and significant changes in the character of gender relations throughout the twentieth century, men and women continue to be segregated into different kinds of jobs within the UK labour market. This book provides a theoretical and empirical analysis of the recruitment process and the ways in which it can sustain and reproduce sex discrimination. It also examines the rationalisations provided by those who perpetrate these unlawful practices and indicates some forms of resistance which are often mobilised in attempting to challenge, or in seeking to eliminate sex discrimination.

Managing to Discriminate is a theoretical development of a research project sponsored by the Equal Opportunities Commission designed to examine whether, and if so how, the recruitment process can contribute to the continuation of gender divisions and inequalities in employment. The EOC was acutely aware of the absence of evidence concerning the specific methods and procedures of organisational recruitment and of the particular ways in which sex discrimination could characterise this process. The recruitment process is especially vague, nebulous and indeterminate and can be shrouded in secrecy. Equally, since sex discrimination is illegal, its empirical identification can be very difficult. By examining particular recruitment exercises as they actually occurred, and every stage of their process, this book presents rich, detailed qualitative material that makes it a landmark in the research of the recruitment process and sex discrimination in employment.

Managing to discriminate

David L. Collinson

David Knights

and

Margaret Collinson

London and New York

First published 1990
by Routledge
11 New Fetter Lane, London EC4P 4EE

Simultaneously published in the USA and Canada
by Routledge
a division of Routledge, Chapman and Hall, Inc.
29 West 35th Street, New York, NY 10001

© 1990 David L. Collinson, David Knights, Margaret Collinson

Typeset by LaserScript Limited, Mitcham, Surrey
Printed and bound in Great Britain by Mackays of Chatham

British Library Cataloguing in Publication Data

Collinson, David L., *1957–*
  Managing to discriminate.
  1. Great Britain. Employment.
  Equality of opportunity
  I. Title II. Knights, David, *1940–*
  III. Collinson, Margaret, *1950–*
  331.13′30941

Library of Congress Cataloging in Publication Data

Collinson, David.
  Managing to discriminate / David Collinson, David Knights,
  and Margaret Collinson.
    p. cm.
  Includes bibliographical references.
  1. Sex discrimination in employment—Great Britain.
  2. Employees—Great Britain—Recruiting. I. Knights,
  David. II. Collinson, Margaret, 1950– . III. Title.
  HD6060.5.G7C65 1990
  331.13′3′0941—dc20   89-71348
                                                           CIP

ISBN 0-415-01816-1
     0-415-01817-X (pbk)

Contents

Illustrations

Acknowledgements

The research on which this book is based could not have been completed without the co-operation of a great many managers, employees, trade unionists and jobseekers. The analysis of the data benefited initially from the advice of staff in the Research Unit and Employment Section of the Equal Opportunities Commission (EOC).

Further analysis was then greatly enhanced by the comments and encouragement of David Morgan at the University of Manchester. In particular, however, the production of the EOC research report, a doctoral thesis, and finally this book owes a great deal to Doris Collinson who, as the mother and mother-in-law of two of the authors, spent long hours typing, amending and correcting these separate texts.

Abbreviations

APSM	Assistant Advertising and Promotional Services Manager
BIFU	Banking, Insurance, Finance Union
CRE	Commission for Racial Equality
CSE	Conference of Socialist Economists
CSR	Consumer-service representative
EAT	Employment Appeal Tribunal
EILM	Extended internal labour market
EOC	Equal Opportunities Commission
HND	Higher National Diploma
IDS	Incomes Data Services
ILM	Internal labour market
IPM	Institute of Personnel Management
LEA	Local Education Authority
MSC	Manpower Services Commission
MSF	Manufacturing, Scientific and Finance Union
NGA	National Graphical Association
ONC	Ordinary National Certificate
OND	Ordinary National Diploma
SDA	Sex Discrimination Act
STC	Short-term contract

Part one

Theoretical studies of sex discrimination in the recruitment process

Introduction

The post-war period in the UK has seen significant changes in gender relations. There has been an increase in: the employment levels of married women; the number of women returning to work after maternity; dual-career families; later marriages; divorce rates; contraceptive controls and delays to the starting of families. Equally, during the 1970s and 1980s, legislation outlawing sex discrimination has been introduced. Yet despite these changes, occupational segregation by sex persists as a primary characteristic of the UK labour market. This book considers the findings of a research project which was financed by the Equal Opportunities Commission (EOC) between 1983 and 1985 to explore whether, and if so how, the recruitment process can contribute to the perpetuation of these traditional segregated patterns of 'men's' and 'women's work'. While early socialisation, both in the family and the educational system, may help to shape the sex-segregated supply of labour, the research was primarily concerned with establishing how demand-side practices might *reinforce* these pre-given labour-market patterns. The project's objective was therefore to provide detailed case-study evidence concerning recruitment and promotion practices with special regard to equal opportunities for both sexes.

The EOC, in exercising its legally defined responsibility for reviewing the workings of the equal-opportunities legislation, wished to sponsor research into the recruitment process not only because of the relative ineffectiveness of the 1975 Sex Discrimination Act (SDA), but also because little substantial evidence on the nature of sex discrimination in recruitment had been forthcoming in the few cases that had reached the tribunal stage. As the Employment Appeal Tribunal judgment in Khanna v. the Ministry of Defence (1981) concluded, tribunals have had to rely upon inferential evidence because 'direct evidence of discrimination is seldom going to be available'. Accordingly, this project was designed to secure 'direct evidence' by observing both formal and informal recruitment practices and by interviewing all participants at the various stages of selection.

Case-study evidence was drawn from forty-five private-sector organisations, representing five separate industries across the North West of England. The research was conducted in the early 1980s against a backdrop of economic recession, high levels of (male) unemployment and significant increases in female employment, especially in part-time work. This book outlines the main findings of the research. Yet, rather than merely duplicate the presentational approach of the EOC research report (Collinson 1988a), where the findings were outlined in relation to the various stages of recruitment, the following analysis seeks to provide a more theoretically informed examination of the empirical data.

The primary objective of the book is to explore the asymmetrical power relations of the labour market and recruitment process by focusing on the forms of control and resistance which were found to characterise sex discrimination in selection. Seeking to reflect the changing and dynamic nature of the social practices which constitute the labour market, the book draws on the empirical material to reveal how sex discrimination can be *reproduced, rationalised* and *resisted* by those in positions of both domination and subordination within the recruitment process. By contrast, such issues of control and resistance were of little direct interest to members of the EOC Research Unit, whose terms of reference were severely circumscribed by the equal-opportunities legislation.[1]

Several problems had to be confronted in conducting the research. First, how were sex discrimination and, conversely, equal opportunities to be defined, understood and identified? Second, what was the nature of the recruitment process and what was the most appropriate methodology for its exploration? Third, what possible measures could be prescribed in order to eliminate sex discrimination from selection procedures? These analytical, methodological and prescriptive issues are addressed throughout the book.

Before presenting the research findings in Part II of the book, the way in which the available literature deals with these three central problems is critically appraised. Whilst Chapters 1–4 inclusive review the explanatory framework of Marxist feminism and labour-market sociology, this introductory chapter discusses conventional studies of sex discrimination in the recruitment process. Whether adopting a legal, psychological or economic perspective, this literature has proved to be of limited assistance in addressing the three foregoing questions. Concentrating on description and prescription, conventional studies fail to *analyse* how and why sex discrimination is reproduced in recruitment practices. It is a central contention of this book that in the absence of a thorough analysis of how sex discrimination is produced and reproduced, adequate solutions to the problem are unlikely to be advanced. Nevertheless, as a background to later discussions, the legal, psychological and economic perspectives will now be outlined in turn.[2]

The legal perspective

This perspective is rigidly adhered to by the EOC and is essentially derived from the 1970 Equal Pay Act and the 1975 and 1986 SDAs. Within the broad area of recruitment practices, contraventions of the legislation can take a variety of forms. Section 6 (1) of the 1975 Act states that apart from minor exceptions, it is unlawful for employers to discriminate on the grounds of sex and marriage:

– in the arrangements made to decide who should be offered a job;
– in any terms of employment;
– by refusing or omitting to offer a person employment.

Direct discrimination occurs where a person is treated less favourably on the grounds of sex or because he or she is married. *Indirect discrimination* might be the outcome of applying a condition or requirement to all candidates, which is more difficult for one sex (or married people) to meet. If the employer cannot justify the condition as 'acceptable to right-thinking people as sound and tolerable' (Ojutiku v. Manpower Services Commission 1982), then a ruling of indirect discrimination is likely to emerge.

As the 'guardian' of the legislation, the EOC has the power to commission research to discover whether these Acts are being implemented. Equally, it can instigate 'Formal Investigations' of those organisations that have been the subject of complaint from the public. Thus, for example, the Commission's Formal Investigation into the Leeds Permanent Building Society (EOC 1985a) revealed evidence of direct and indirect sex discrimination in the recruitment process. In 1978, approximately 150 young men were recruited on to the company's management trainee programme. Although 25 per cent of the applicants were women, none were recruited. From an analysis of the records (application forms and interview notes) it was found that the Society had discriminated *directly* against women either by refusing them interviews, or in affording them less favourable interview treatment, particularly through the disproportionate emphasis placed on the requirement to be geographically mobile. Drawing on a retrospective survey of applicants which revealed that women (50 per cent) were less able than men (65 per cent) to comply with the requirement of total UK mobility, the Commission ruled this condition also constituted *indirect* sex discrimination.[3]

On the whole, however, formal investigations are conducted very infrequently. Most of the literature concerned with selection emanating from the EOC is overwhelmingly prescriptive in character and is usually designed to highlight the organisational benefits of 'good practice'. The detailed recommendations found in this literature can be summarised under the three subdivisions of the recruitment process that will be used throughout the book, namely: the *criteria, channels* and *procedures* of recruitment.

Selection criteria

The EOC's booklet 'Fair and Efficient Selection' (EOC 1986) highlights 'two major myths' about selection criteria. The first myth of *sex-typing* relates specifically to the definition and description of jobs, while the second myth of *stereotyping* concerns the person specification and the evaluation of candidates. Job sex-typing is characterised by the taken-for-granted assumption that it is 'normal' and 'natural' for particular jobs, tasks and skills to be the province of only one sex. Sex-typing can also reflect and reinforce exaggerated requirements in either internal or external job vacancies. Unnecessary conditions concerning, for example, age, mobility, length of service or experience might have a disproportionate impact on women and so constitute indirect discrimination. Requirements should only be retained if they are relevant to the job.

Stereotyping occurs when sex differences in physical and temperamental characteristics and abilities are exaggerated and generalised. Stereotyping is also facilitated by ill-defined, impressionistic person specifications, particularly those that overstate their requirements. It is recommended that all applicants should be assessed on their individual merits, according to their personal ability to perform a given job. They should not be treated primarily as members of a group with specific and separate aptitudes. When evaluating candidates' commitment, particularly by reference to leisure pursuits, it is important for selectors to remember that many women have less opportunity for these than men because they combine work with greater domestic responsibilities. Conversely, selectors ought not to assume that precisely because of these familial commitments, women are less reliable employees.[4] These processes of sex-typing and stereotyping must be avoided at every stage of recruitment.

Recruitment channels

It is advised that job advertising should neither present men and women in stereotyped roles nor restrict applications from either sex. Equally, recruitment solely or primarily by word of mouth might unnecessarily limit the choice of applicants. This method should be avoided in a work-force of predominantly one sex, if in practice it prevents members of the opposite sex applying. Failing to advertise vacancies internally may also constitute unlawful discrimination.

Selection procedures

Application forms should not include questions pertaining to families, ages of children or marital status, since these are unlikely to be relevant to job performance. Male and female applications should be processed in exactly the same, systematic way. Interview questions should focus on the requirements of the job. If this necessitates asking personal questions, relating for example to hours of work, overtime or mobility, these should be asked equally of *all* applicants in order to avoid accusations of unlawful practice. Selection tests must be fully validated to ensure that they contain no sex bias. Recruitment decisions should be formulated by systematically matching job requirements with candidates' relevant characteristics. General selector impressions, hunches and intuition must be eradicated because they might be influenced by prejudices. In addition, all those handling applications and conducting interviews should be trained in the avoidance of unlawful discrimination. These prescriptions are informed by the argument that equal-opportunity practices will enhance organisational efficiency and profitability since selection will be based on competence, rather than irrelevant characteristics such as sex.

The psychological perspective

Like the legal perspective, the psychological literature also emphasises that lawful selection will have economic benefits. This literature originates predominantly from the US since sex discrimination has received 'scant attention' (Anderson and Shackleton 1986: 21) from UK psychologists. Focusing primarily on laboratory experiments of simulated selection procedures, these studies have consistently highlighted the limited reliability and validity of the employment interview (Mayfield 1964; Webster 1964; Ulrich and Trumbo 1965; Wright 1969; Schmitt 1976; Dunnette and Borman 1979; Arvey and Campion 1982; Reilly and Chao 1982). It has been argued that the interpretative nature of the interview is especially vulnerable to the personal prejudices of selectors, which often result in the adverse treatment of women and minority groups (Arvey 1979).

Unstructured interviews, in particular, have been criticised as unreliable and inconsistent 'predictors' of future performance (Mayfield 1964). They have been found to be dominated by interviewers, who are themselves susceptible to the 'halo effect'. Here the interviewer is over-impressed by one single characteristic of the applicant which then informs his or her judgement of the whole person. The halo can also operate in a negative way (Smith and Robertson 1986: 59). Research has found that selectors often make their interview judgements and decisions within the first four minutes of the session (Webster 1964) and then spend the remainder of the interview selectively confirming their original preconceptions. Dipboye's (1980) findings suggest that selection decisions may even be made from the little information available prior to the interview. Here the preconceptions of interviewers were found to be self-fulfilling since they shaped the structure of the interview, which in turn conditioned the original pre-interview assessment.

As a consequence of these findings, it has been proposed that where a great deal of job-related information is supplied, the impact of 'irrelevant stereotyping' on interview decisions is reduced and a greater consensus between interviewers emerges (Makin and Robertson 1983). Other studies suggest that reliability and validity are enhanced by structured (Schmitt 1976) or situational interviews (Latham and Saari 1984), or board and panel interviews (Arvey and Campion 1982). The latter, it is argued, force interviewers to share their perceptions, thus enabling them to acknowledge and eradicate irrelevant inferences and stereotypes (Rohstein and Jackson 1980).

In an exhaustive 'state of the art' account of 'unfair discrimination' in the recruitment process, Arvey (1979) outlines the three prevalent methodologies of psychological research, each of which is confined to the laboratory setting. First and most common are those experiments that present bogus curricula vitae of hypothetical candidates, which research participants are then asked to evaluate. By manipulating the sex of these 'pencil and paper' candidates, whilst trying to keep other variables constant, experimenters have suggested that women tend to be evaluated lower than men, even if they possess similar or identical qualifications (for example, Dipboye et al. 1975, 1977; Zikmund et al. 1978). This has been found in particular, where: the job is predefined as masculine (Cash et al. 1977); women constitute less than 25 per cent of the pool of applicants (Heilman 1980) and where personnel officers are classified as 'authoritarian' rather than 'democratic' (Simas and McCarrey 1979).

In an attempt to increase the 'realism' of the experimental setting by presenting more detail about the hypothetical organisation and the job vacancy, 'in-basket' studies have emerged as an alternative methodology. Participants are asked to assume the role of a personnel manager who has to produce written decisions on a tray of pressing matters. The sex of candidates and issues about hiring are two variables that have been manipulated in order to test for selector prejudice. A third methodology uses videotapes or controlled interviews, which contain standard questions and answers but vary the sex of the interviewee. Observers are asked to evaluate the different candidates presented. The overriding conclusion from these simulated experiments in recruitment is that women will suffer disproportionately from prejudiced interviewers, whose stereotypes are ill-founded and built on ignorance. On the basis of these findings, occupational psychologists have prescribed a whole series of ameliorating selection techniques designed to diminish the likelihood of company violations of anti-discrimination legislation. These prescriptions can take a variety of forms, such as cognitive and personality tests (Robertson 1985); biographical data (Reilly and Chao 1982); work sample and (job-related) simulation tests (Robertson and Kandola 1982); supervisor/peer evaluation (Schmitt et al. 1984); self-selection (Makin and Robertson 1983) or assessment centres (Robertson 1985).

As the numerous textbooks on selection techniques for personnel managers indicate (for example, Plumbley 1974; Thomason 1978; Finnegan 1983; Torrington and Chapman 1983), some of these psychological prescriptions have been incorporated into personnel managers' areas of 'expertise'. This has been reflected in attempts to formalise recruitment procedures generally and to introduce selection tests in particular. Occupational psychologists claim that their prescriptions will be more efficient than current organisational practices because they are based on validated and reliable scientific evidence.

The economic perspective

By contrast with the legal and psychological literature, the economic perspective highlights the *rationality* of sex-discriminatory practices. Orthodox economic analyses are primarily informed by human-capital theory (Becker 1957). Central to this perspective is the assumption that women will 'choose' to develop less human capital (in terms of academic qualifications, employment, experience and of motivation, stability and ambition) than men because of their role in the domestic division of labour. Since the conventional sexual division of labour, with the male as the bread-winner and the female as the housekeeper, is assumed to be consistent with maximising economic utilities and since women are deemed to be less productive in employment as a result of accumulating less human capital, then sex discrimination is seen to be economically rational. Accordingly, women's 'choice' not to accumulate human capital and to concentrate on their familial responsibilities is a rational one, as is employers' decisions to select labour on the basis of productivity.

As the main UK economists to have conducted research in this area, Chiplin and Sloane (1976, 1982) provide a more sophisticated version of human-capital theory by considering in greater detail demand-side factors, rather than simply concentrating on the supply-side 'choices' of both sexes. They suggest that the recruitment process is inherently problematic for management because a great deal of unavailable information is expensive to secure. Accordingly, screening on the basis of group characteristics such as sex is likely to be favoured by the 'rational recruiter' (1976: 79) who wishes to minimise costs. In their second book (1982: 88) they assert that the potential gains for employers of sifting and identifying those females who do not comply with stereotypical group norms have to be compared with the costs of obtaining this information. While the authors recognise that cost minimisation is no defence under the law, they acknowledge the pervasive influence of economic rationality upon managers. They (1976) are therefore sceptical of the impact of anti-discrimination legislation to eliminate, rather than merely to force underground, sex-discriminatory practices.

In each of their two books, Chiplin and Sloane devote a full chapter to the role of recruitment in the reproduction of occupational segregation. Their later work outlines a research project into recruitment in the East Midlands and West of Scotland. Exploring those vacancies notified to Jobcentres (largely just before the 1975 SDA), they found that sex was a pervasive cheap screening device in the context of marked occupational segregation. Work sex-typed for men tended to be found in higher-paying jobs and where overtime and shift work was required, while 'women's work' was often defined as part-time. When men were required, other indirect signals included the specification of apprenticeships and good health. For women, typing skills and appearance were often stipulated.

This study is useful because it was conducted in large part before the 1975 SDA, thus making it possible to identify exactly how many job advertisements were openly sex-typed. After the Act became law, the researchers noted a tendency for pay and overtime to become increasingly prevalent covert signals for male candidates. On the basis of their research findings, Chiplin and Sloane highlight the importance of statistical monitoring as a primary organisational mechanism for establishing equal opportunities.

Power and the liberal perspective

Each of the above perspectives has some descriptive and prescriptive value for this analysis. They reveal how sex discrimination may be based on perceived economic vested interests (economics) informed by deeply taken-for-granted sex prejudice (psychology) and have self-defeating consequences (legal). Moreover, by providing practical prescriptions for the elimination of sex discrimination, this literature implicitly insists that change is possible and that individuals have the power to transform historically deep-seated practices. Nevertheless, they share common theoretical and methodological weaknesses which reflect a general concentration on description and prescription to the neglect of a detailed analysis of the conditions and consequences of sex discrimination in the recruitment process.

More specifically, what is missing from these three perspectives is any analysis of the *power structures* and *dynamics* which characterise the social relations and practices of organisations and of labour markets. This neglect reflects and reinforces assumptions, methodologies and prescriptions that identify either intentionally or unwittingly with the concerns and interests of management in the recruitment process. The structures of organisational power (for example, hierarchy, class, gender and racial inequality) are therefore taken for granted and are consequently embedded in this conventional perspective.

Thus, each of the foregoing perspectives subscribes to a liberal and individualistic conception of equal opportunities, in which the primary concern is to eliminate obstacles to free competition at work. As Jewson and Mason (1986a) argue, the liberal perspective seeks to ensure the 'fairness' of procedures, whilst ignoring the unequal conditions and consequences of these procedures. It therefore embodies an individualistic and meritocratic emphasis on the need to unshackle personal talent and ability without regard to irrelevant group characteristics such as sex. Unlawful discrimination is treated as a distortion of free competition and as a reflection of traditional practices and values. In order to fine-tune the market and eradicate such imperfections which hinder individual development, the state must intervene as an impartial arbitrator between competing individuals. The legal, economic and psychological prescriptions of training, monitoring and testing respectively, reflect this concern to follow legally prescribed procedures that are bureaucratically impartial in their attempt to eliminate sex discrimination from the recruitment process.

In so far as this liberal meritocratic perspective tends to be 'power-blind', then the principle of equal opportunities is always in danger of being reduced merely to a legitimatory *ideology*, which, in concentrating on the 'fairness' of procedures and the success of individuals, actually provides a plausible justification for vastly unequal outcomes. When reduced to an ideology of competitive individualism, the consequence of equal-opportunity programmes is likely to be the appointment of a few women into comparatively senior positions in the capacity of 'honorary men'. The introduction of 'token women' (Kanter 1977: 207; Morgan 1981: 102) can provide a superficial veneer of legitimacy to the claim that equal opportunities are being implemented.

As Legge has commented, 'If some women succeed, the illusion of equal opportunities is maintained as the unsuccessful may be portrayed as inadequate, rather than discriminated against (1978: 55). When used in this ideological fashion, claims by companies to be 'equal-opportunity employers' can legitimise inequalities based not only on gender but also on class (see, for example, Offe 1976; Willis 1977; Collinson 1981).[5] As Lee and Loveridge warn, 'Equal opportunity is a principle to which lip-service is easily paid' (1987: 1).

The conventional literature is therefore characterised by 'manager-ialist' assumptions which have the effect of reinforcing the status quo. For example, the absence in human-capital theory of a critical analysis of the asymmetrical power relations of paid and unpaid work facilitates its use as a rationalisation for the perpetuation of gender inequality and as a 'powerful legitimation for the lack of success of women' (Crompton and Jones 1984: 144). Equally a tension often exists in occupational psychology between prescribing for a managerial audience and the elimination of sex discrimination. It is common, for example, for psychologists to advocate the use of word-of-mouth recruitment as an 'efficient' form of selection because this provides greater information about candidates (for example, Smith and Robertson 1986).[6] And yet, the EOC's Code of Practice specifically recommends that such informal recruitment channels be avoided because their use can facilitate direct and indirect sex discrimination.

'Power-blind' voluntarist and liberal assumptions also pervade the research methodologies adopted by the conventional literature. These methodologies do not facilitate a detailed examination of the recruit-ment process. Many of the foregoing studies rely exclusively upon retrospective managerial accounts of recruitment to the neglect of observing *formal and informal practices*. This indirect methodology contains several weaknesses which may distort the research findings:

(1) At best it provides only an incomplete picture of events, like accounts exclusively from trade unionists or interviewees.

(2) It ignores, or is unable to explore, the possible discrepancy between accounts and actual recruitment practices. Respondents do not always say what they mean, mean what they say or even do what they say. This is particularly so with regard to equal opportunities, where formal policy statements may not be implemented at grassroots level (see, for example, Torrington et al. 1982).

(3) Attitudinal surveys of this kind tend to disregard the problems of interpretation and possible distortion that characterise their methodology.

(4) The quantification of opinions can take on the appearance of

'hard fact', where, for example, the expressed intentions of respondents are confused with actual practices. Equally, aggregation
can provide statistics with a percentile significance that belies
their actual numerical strength. The measurement of discrimination is often thereby limited to a statistical summation of the
(sometimes hypothetical) stated intentions and accounts of
managers.

(5) The way in which initial criteria might change over time, in
accordance with the perceived qualities of actual candidates,
cannot be analysed when specific vacancies and practices are not
examined.

To overcome these weaknesses some studies, such as that by Chiplin
and Sloane (1976), have cited the experimental evidence of occupational psychology on interview processes (for example, Arvey 1979;
Arvey and Campion 1982). Yet the assessment of hypothetical
candidates for decontextualised jobs in simulated laboratory interviews
by volunteer evaluators has produced, and could only ever produce,
artificial conclusions. The concern to establish the scientific credibility
of psychological studies leads to increasingly controlled laboratory
conditions and highly abstracted, quantified studies which have much
less applicability to actual recruitment practices than managerial
accounts. To infer actual organisational practices from artificial laboratory conditions is highly problematic. This is particularly so since the
participants in these studies are usually students who have little
experience of organisational recruitment and who are aware of the
experimental nature of the project (but usually not its precise objective)
and that no job vacancy actually exists. The applicability of these studies
to the UK context is further weakened by the fact that the vast majority
were conducted in the USA. Hence in examining this research, the
'Ambrit fallacy' (Littler 1982: 50) of fusing the cultures of the USA and
the UK needs to be avoided.

The failure of the conventional literature to examine the recruitment
process in any detail is also reflected in the neglect of internal
recruitment practices. Yet promotion is a key consideration; for even if
women are selected, they might in fact be channelled into low-grade
'dead-end' jobs. Hence it is important to explore whether organisational
barriers exist to women's upward mobility. Relatedly, by examining the
nature of the job for which women (and men) are appointed, the
relevance of selection criteria can then be assessed. Equally, job descriptions and job tasks can be observed and compared. Yet here again, the
conventional literature is wholly deficient.

In sum, the legal, economic and psychological literature is characterised by an over-reliance, at best on managerial accounts of practices,

and at worst, on laboratory experiments. The failure of this literature to provide a full analysis of the way in which sex discrimination is reproduced in the recruitment process is reflected in a theoretical, methodological and prescriptive approach which is inherently 'power-blind'. Yet, as we have already stated, without a detailed understanding of the conditions and consequences of the reproduction of job segregation, it is very unlikely that adequate solutions to sex discrimination will be advanced.

Managerial and male power

The two primary sources of power which tend to be ignored and thereby reinforced by conventional liberal perspectives are managements' power over labour and men's power over women. First, liberal perspectives fail to recognise the problematic nature of management's fundamental role in capitalist organisations; namely the *control* of the enterprise (Braverman 1974). This is the primary means by which labour's productiveness is increased, surplus value is appropriated and capital accumulated (Marx 1946: 309, 576). Central to managerial control is the insistence that the function does and should have the power and prerogative to make decisions surrounding the 'differentia specifica' (Braverman 1974: 52) of capitalist production, namely the purchase and sale of commodified labour power. Recruitment is obviously the key aspect of managment's purchase of labour power. And, as Braverman (ibid.) highlighted in his critical appraisal of Taylor's 'Scientific Management' principles, quantified and 'scientific' recruitment techniques are crucial elements in the deskilling of work which in turn is a key aspect of management's exclusive control of the capitalist labour process. 'Scientific' selection techniques are designed to individualise and objectify workers in order to render them predictable and controllable.

Second, conventional studies tend to neglect the way in which power is inherently *gendered*. Thus, for example, they fail to consider how some groups of male workers have organised to restrict women's entry into employment (Barrett 1980; Walby 1986). Men's power in employment is illustrated by the prevalence of occupational segregation by sex. Hakim (1979) has distinguished between horizontal and vertical job segregation by sex. Horizontal segregation describes the complete separation of male and female occupations, while vertical segregation refers to the way in which men typically occupy more highly graded jobs than women. In addition, the conventional literature tends to ignore that men's power over women is not confined to employment, but is also crucially based in the domestic sphere (Burton 1985). Liberal prescriptions usually omit to consider how the conventional domestic division of labour might constitute a further barrier to the establishment of equal opportunities. Hence conventional perspectives on sex discrimination in recruitment fail to incorporate managerial and male power within their analyses.

However, whilst seeking to adopt a power-sensitive approach, we are also concerned to avoid an overly deterministic response to the voluntarism which characterises the foregoing conventional literature. Accordingly, the analysis seeks to demonstrate that the actions and consciousness of human beings cannot be wholly determined by the asymmetrical power relations through which they live their lives. For, as Brown has argued, 'Over-determined views of human history and society leave no room for and assign no weight to individual or group, experience, meaning and action; structure predominates over agency' (1984: 317). The perspective adopted in this book seeks to reject an overly deterministic and structuralist approach to managerial and male power within the labour market and recruitment process. It is concerned to retrieve the agency of human beings and the dynamic and changing character of their social relations from the all-pervasive and invariably static forms of analysis which afford conceptual priority to social power, control and structured inequalities.

The conceptualisation of power in the labour market and recruitment process utilised here assumes, following Giddens (1976, 1979), that power relations, no matter how asymmetrical, are always two-way and to some extent interdependent and reciprocal. The interdependent nature of all power relations means that they invariably involve elements of autonomy and dependency for both the dominant and the subordinate. Whilst domination may seek to reduce interdependence to dependence (see Roberts 1982), this objective can never be realised because subordinates always retain some control over their actions. As Giddens writes, 'Those in subordinate positions in social systems are frequently adept at converting whatever resources they possess into some degree of control over the conditions of reproduction of those social systems' (1979: 6).

Giddens therefore rejects deterministic versions of social power by emphasising human agency and by insisting that 'Every social actor knows a great deal about the conditions of reproduction of the society of which he or she is a member' (ibid.: 5). He argues that human beings must be treated as skilled and knowledgeable social agents. Since human beings are self-conscious, they can reflexively monitor and rationalise their own and others' behaviour and thereby construct their social world and render it meaningful. Central to this idea of human agency is a recognition that within their social relations individuals retain a relative autonomy and a capacity to act differently than they do: that is to say, human beings always have the capability of 'acting otherwise' (1979: 91) – for example, either to intervene in the course of events or to refrain from so doing. In emphasising the agency of human beings, Giddens seeks to present an analysis of power which reflects the dynamic rather than the static nature of social life. He thereby recognises that 'the seed of change is there in every act which contributes towards the reproduction of any ordered form of social life' (Giddens 1976: 102).[7]

The most strikingly 'ordered form of social life' with regard to gender inequality in the labour market is the pervasive way in which jobs are segregated by sex. The following analysis seeks to explain the persistence of job segregation through an examination of power and agency in the recruitment process. In so doing, it addresses what Burton has called the 'crucial point' which is to try to explain 'the tenacity of sexual asymmetry, while at the same time according to individuals an active role in the construction of their own lives' (1985: 123). Our central concern is therefore to examine the persistence of this tension between, on the one hand, the relatively stable and often taken-for-granted structure of job segregation and, on the other hand, the dynamic nature of the social relations and practices within the recruitment process which reconstitute and transform this structure. We seek to highlight how the asymmetrical nature of managerial and male power relations in the recruitment process is a reflection of, may be reproduced by, and even transformed through, the active agency of men and women.

Against the background of this theoretical emphasis on power and agency, the book draws on empirical material to illustrate the way in which job segregation is *reproduced, rationalised* and *resisted* within the recruitment process. It will be argued that the persistence of job segregation is a result primarily of these three labour-market practices. The final section of this introductory chapter now presents a brief outline of the methodology adopted in the EOC project, the nature of the industries researched and the overall structure of the book.

Managing to discriminate

The data from the EOC project was collected over a period of two years commencing in September 1983.[8] Five employment sections were covered and a total of forty-five companies and sixty-four work-sites visited. The sections were: banking; mail order; insurance; hi-tech and food manufacturing. Research focused primarily on large companies, with only five employing less than one thousand staff nationally. The 1986 change to the Sex Discrimination Act, which no longer exempts businesses of five or less employees, is applicable to only one of the companies researched. The vacancies explored ranged from low-grade manual, clerical and maintenance jobs to sales, scientific/technical and managerial occupations.

In large part, the primary objectives of the research project were defined by the requirements of the EOC steering committee. With little available evidence of the typical processes by which sex discrimination can be reproduced in recruitment, the Commission was concerned to secure case-study data of potentially unlawful sex discrimination in ongoing selection exercises within a variety of industrial settings. It was envisaged that this information would facilitate the formulation of EOC policy in relation to recruitment. In order to satisfy these requirements, it was therefore necessary for the project to secure access to the whole of the recruitment process and, where possible, promotion practices as well.

Because of the sensitivity of the subject matter and the concern that access would be extremely difficult, initial attempts to balance the quantity and quality of cases within each sector were soon discarded. It became clear as the research progressed, first, that uniformity in the number of companies researched could itself be misleading since the organisations varied in size and market penetration. Some industries were dominated by just a few companies, while others contained literally hundreds. Second, recruitment levels also varied enormously. Insurance sales, for example, proved to be a particularly productive area for research because of its high and consistent demand for labour. Third, and perhaps most important, the uneven number of case-study companies was a consequence of the quality and quantity of the access afforded to the researcher. Again, this varied considerably between the industries, organisations and even within the same company.

When seeking access to organisations and information, three particular barriers had to be faced, each of which reflected the asymmetrical power within organisations. The first was management's primary concern to maintain control of the organisation. The second was the sex-segregated nature of jobs as well as the gender of the researcher and respondents, whilst the third was the highly impressionistic, nebulous and indeterminate character of many recruitment exercises. Hence, managerial control, job segregation and the recruitment process, the very subjects under study, constituted the major barriers to collection of data. Indeed, they impacted on all four stages of the research process, namely: contacting the companies; interviewing managers; observing job interviews; and interviewing other participants. The way in which the negotiation of each of these access stages helped to shape the research findings can be discerned by turning to the Appendix, where a more detailed and quantitative account of the research process is provided.

Despite these barriers, the quality of the access secured in some cases allowed the research not only to record accounts of recruitment and promotion, but also to uncover actual practices as they occurred.[9] A

17

large number of people gave generously of their time, often for much longer than they had originally agreed, in order to contribute to the project. The result is that the research was able to secure extensive evidence concerning internal and external recruitment practices and sex discrimination. Although in the final analysis, only an Industrial Tribunal or Employment Appeal Tribunal can declare recruitment practices to be illegal, the complaints and resistant practices of staff and job applicants, the sometimes openly discriminatory statements of recruiters and the observation of their practices all combined together to provide a firm basis from which to present the empirical material.

Having said that, we recognise that these sixty-four work-places in forty-five private-sector organisations are not necessarily representative of British industry as a whole. However, the research was neither funded nor designed to quantify and measure the incidence or amount of sex discrimination in these five sectors. Rather, it was concerned to produce case-study evidence of how recruitment practices might contribute to the reproduction of job segregation. Accordingly, the selection of industries, companies and particular recruitment exercises was primarily access-driven. Moreover, the selection of the specific case-studies presented in later chapters is largely informed by the key theoretical issues which are either raised or found to be neglected in the conventional and critical literature. The examination of feminist and sociological studies in Part I is therefore important as a means of developing the theoretical perspective on power and agency which informs the selection and interpretation of the empirical material.

In consequence, the question of the representativeness of the data is subordinated in the following chapters to a central focus on the analysis and explanation of how recruitment *can* reinforce job segregation. At this level, there is no reason to believe that the detailed evidence secured is untypical of the social processes involved in sex-discriminatory recruitment practices. In each of the sectors and in all of the organisations where access was provided, job segregation was a central characteristic. Whilst this is clearly not an adequate indicator of the persistence of unlawful practices, the research revealed that none of the participating organisations could be said to have fully eliminated sex discrimination from their recruitment practices. The extent to which all of the sectors researched were characterised by a highly segregated labour force, will now be illustrated in the following brief background to each industry.

Banking

Banking is dominated by a few large companies. Evidence from three of the four big London clearing banks is used in this book, combined with case-studies from a smaller bank. Since the Second World War, banking has undergone rapid social and technological upheaval. Dramatic increases in personal customers and the services offered to them have stimulated a sharp rise in banking recruitment and employment. In 1948, for example, the London clearing banks employed 84,869 people (71.9 per cent male), but by 1970 this had risen to 176,875 (Heritage 1983: 132). These statistics contain a significant shift in the sex composition of the work-force. While the male labour force grew by only 40 per cent during this period, women's employment expanded by 270 per cent (Heritage, ibid.). This pattern continued up to 1980, by which time women comprised 64 per cent of the labour force in the English clearing banks (BIFU 1985). By March 1985, the banks employed 301,000 women (Department of Employment, July 1985).

Despite the feminisation of many banking functions, men's traditional domination has persisted because the vast majority of female recruits have been incorporated and confined within the lower-clerical grades. For example, technical services, messengers, engineers, security and branch and assistant managers still remain largely sex-typed jobs for men, whereas tellers, secretaries and part-time work continue to be the preserve of women. At Midland Bank, for example, although 56 per cent of staff are female, they comprise 60 per cent of the clerical grades, but only 16 per cent of appointed staff and 1.8 per cent of group managers (IDS 1985). In 1983, at the National Westminster Bank less than 2 per cent of the 40,000 women employed were in administrative or managerial posts, contrasted with 37 per cent of men. Similarly, in Lloyds Bank, of the 3,153 managers, only forty-three were women (BIFU 1985). Within the first five years of service at Barclays Bank, 30 per cent of men compared with 10 per cent of women had reached grade three or above (BIFU, ibid.).

During the 1980s, three of the four big London clearers have appointed head-office managers with responsibility for equal opportunities in relation to sex, race and disability. As a result, some progress has been made, for example, in the monitoring of recruitment, the introduction of career-break schemes, the circulation of policy guide-lines and the introduction of training. Yet it remains to be seen whether these initiatives will be able to challenge and transform the deep-seated and historical nature of job segregation in the industry.

Mail order

The origins of the UK mail-order industry lie in the working-class 'Turns clubs' that provided a collective means of purchasing goods which were otherwise too expensive. Mail order is now the fastest growing method of retail distribution. Its sustained growth in the twentieth century has been stimulated by the potential profits to be gained from bypassing shop outlets and supplying information and goods straight from the warehouse. Selling is conducted either direct to the customer or via self-employed 'agents' who work from home. The vast majority of employees and customers in the mail-order industry are women (Cockburn 1986).

The two companies in which research was undertaken are major employers in the north of England that operate within the indirect agency market. Each functions with a team of agents co-ordinated by agency offices and serviced by warehouses (where merchandise is received, stored, allocated to orders and dispatched to customers) and a head office (which houses specialist management functions). Both companies had embarked upon a restructuring of employment practices in their warehouses. One had reduced recruitment because of a fall in market share and the impending introduction of new technology. The other was breaking all records on pre-tax profits and consequently was recruiting extensively. It is these selection practices on which the evidence from this industry concentrates. Although only two mail-order companies were explored, the nature of the industry is such that their joint market share is much greater than the combined share of the twenty insurance companies into which research was conducted.

Insurance

Women have entered the insurance industry in increasing numbers throughout the twentieth century. By March 1986, 107,000 women worked for insurance companies, with another 43,000 employed in auxiliary organisations (Department of Employment, August 1986). Women thereby constitute 42 per cent of the total insurance work-force and 54 per cent of the auxiliary. Since most of these women are employed in clerical occupations, whereas many male employees work in other functions, females constitute a much higher proportion of insurance office workers, as Storey (1986) has noted. However, these women do not enjoy the status, salary and career prospects of the nineteenth- century insurance clerks, the vast majority of whom were men (Supple 1970). Rather, they tend to occupy secretarial and clerical grades, while men almost exclusively hold supervisory and managerial posts. In addition, part-time, temporary, switchboard/reception, office services/typing and assistant-administration-manager jobs are usually sex-typed female, whereas selling, surveying, claims inspection, motor engineering, data processing and branch-manager grades remain the province of men. 'Women's jobs' inevitably offer low pay, status and autonomy, while men's are conferred high salary and status as well as extensive autonomy since a great deal of their time is spent outside the office.

It is in the area of insurance sales that the greatest employment difference between this industry and banking presently exists. The research findings in Chapter 7 concentrate on two distinct ways of selling life insurance. The first and longer-established involves the selling of policies through intermediaries such as insurance brokers, bank, building-society and estate-agency managers, solicitors and accountants. The second approach sells policies direct to the public. In each case the evidence reveals significant barriers to women's access to selling.

Hi-tech

As the 'Women into Science and Engineering' initiative of 1984 emphasised, scientific and technological skills have been the traditional preserve of men. Accordingly, a shortage of skilled female labour has been the conventional explanation for the perpetuation of job segregation in science generally. However, the hi-tech sector promises a new era for equal opportunities. First, shortages in female and male skilled labour in this sector (MSC 1984) might stimulate employers to discard outmoded and potentially unlawful recruitment practices. Second, many hi-tech companies have emerged since the 1975 SDA and are therefore well placed to integrate equal opportunities into their personnel policies and practices. Third, the transition from heavy electro-mechanical to electronic engineering which is cleaner, lighter and safer could provide work more compatible with conventional stereotypes for women (Cockburn 1985).

A progressive approach is found in some companies. In 1983, for example, IBM UK introduced a scheme allowing up to twenty women each year to return part-time after maternity leave. Of the 850 employees at F International, 94 per cent are women (Upton 1984) and 700 are hourly paid freelance homeworkers. They work an average of eighteen to twenty hours per week as secretaries, administrators or programmers (Simons 1981). In 1986, ICL formed the 'Contract Services Unit' of home-based workers, as a result of severe shortages in programmers, analysts and technical authors. The Unit enables the retention of staff with at least five years' experience who would otherwise resign to have children.

Despite these initiatives, research in the computing industry (for example, CSE 1980; Dasey 1980; Simons 1981) has revealed that job segregation remains a primary characteristic. While women predominate in data processing and control, they constitute only 15–20 per cent of programmers and 5–10 per cent of systems analysts in the UK. The hi-tech case-studies will examine recruitment in research and develop-

ment, manufacturing, software and hardware sales, maintenance engineering and data processing.

Food manufacturing

Of the 601, 200 workers who are employed in the food, drink and
tobacco manufacturing industry, 41 per cent are women (Department of
Employment, September 1985). Many of these are employed in low-
grade work and few are promoted to managerial positions. The food-
manufacturing industry comprises a great variety of organisations
producing a diversity of products. The case-studies are drawn from three
organisations.

The first company, which produced a whole range of convenience,
dehydrated and tinned foods, provided the most detailed access to
selection that was secured in the research. Here, recruitment practices
were examined at three separate work-places: head office, catering
division and manufacturing division. In total, seventeen recruitment
exercises, together with all of the relevant documentation, were
observed. This included the observation of twenty-seven job interviews.
The second company specialised in the manufacture of a complete range
of breakfast cereals. Here, selection practices were examined at the
head-office complex and a manufacturing division. Largely because of
the introduction of new technology, manual workers were being laid off,
rather than recruited, in both these companies. In consequence, the
vacancies explored are primarily clerical and managerial. By contrast,
the third company, which is a small bakery, owned by a larger
confectionery group, was regularly recruiting manual workers for
temporary vacancies.

Each of these companies reflected the same patterns of occupational
segregation by sex that were characteristic of all the organisations
researched in the project. In all five sectors where research was
undertaken, a substantial number of women were employed but they
were working primarily in subordinate positions. These segregated
employment patterns were also highly typical of those found throughout
the UK economy.

The book is divided into two parts. The first part is a review of
theoretical and empirical work on sex discrimination in recruitment.
This examination of the critical literature not only constitutes an
important form of research (Kanter 1977: 298), but also facilitates the
elaboration of the theoretical basis through which the empirical cases
from the EOC research can be presented in Part II. Chapters 1–4
inclusive examine those studies which, in contrast to the conventional
liberal perspectives, do seek to illuminate how power operates in sex-

discriminatory recruitment practices. While the first two chapters consider the reproduction of gender inequality in the labour market generally, the second two focus more closely on the recruitment process in particular.

Chapters 1 and 2 present a critical appraisal of Marxist feminist explanations for women's subordination in the labour market. In particular, they highlight the failure of the 'reserve army', 'labour-market segmentation' and 'patriarchy' theories to provide an adequate analysis of the agency of management, labour and men and women. These two chapters illustrate that although the three main Marxist-feminist theories of gender inequality in the labour market are centrally concerned with asymmetrical power relations, they tend to neglect human agency and resistance in favour of an overly deterministic perspective.

The following two chapters then draw on labour-market sociology to focus more specifically on the recruitment process. Chapter 3 outlines the degree to which informality has been found both to characterise the channels, criteria and procedures of recruitment and to result in the reproduction of job segregation. Chapter 4 considers whether it is possible to formalise the recruitment process and if so, how far this might help to eliminate sex discrimination. In particular, this chapter highlights research evidence of the marginal role of personnel managers in recruitment and the implications of their organisational subordination for the establishment of equal-opportunity practices.

In Part II of the book we then examine the empirical material by exploring the key themes of managerial control, job segregation and informal recruitment practices. Drawing on evidence from all five sectors of the EOC research, Chapters 5 and 6 focus primarily on *managerial control*. In particular, these chapters describe the practices, ideologies, contradictions and divisions which were found to characterise the managerial function.

Chapter 5 explores the attempts by personnel managers to initiate formalised and accountable equal-opportunity practices and the resistance of line managers to such interventions. The research findings in Chapter 6 illustrate that personnel specialists do retain some agency, autonomy and influence in specific recruitment exercises. However, despite their professional role as the advocates of equal opportunities, some of these managers still operated informal and/or sex-discriminatory practices. This tension between professional policy and personal practice is explored through an examination of the ways in which personnel managers sought to rationalise their potentially unlawful practices.

The second two empirical chapters provide a more context-bound account of recruitment practices and job segregation by concentrating on a detailed case-study of both external and internal recruitment practices in the insurance industry.

Chapter 7 illustrates how the selling of life assurance is widely perceived to be a male preserve and to be work which is only appropriate for organisational and family 'bread-winners'. Conversely, Chapter 8 reveals that in contrast to external vacancies such as selling, internal clerical work in insurance largely remains the domain of women. This point is reinforced by a series of case-studies which indicate the extensive internal barriers to women's career progress. The chapter also considers the different ways through which women and trade unions were found to resist the reproduction of job segregation.

In the final chapter, we conclude on the basis of the empirical evidence that an adequate explanation for the vicious circles that characterise the persistence of job segregation requires a more sophisticated analysis of human agency and therefore of power relations than has been presented heretofore. Such an analysis involves a focus on the contradictions which also characterise human agency and in particular the search to secure socially validated forms of identity. By highlighting the contradictions embedded in current forms of social domination, the possibility of, and potential for, social change can begin to be assessed and envisaged. Against this background, the final chapter concludes by prescribing the organisational changes that seem necessary if sex discrimination in the recruitment process is to be eliminated.

Chapter one

Managing the labour market

Introduction

In contrast to the conventional legal, economic and psychological perspectives discussed in the Introduction, the available literature which does contribute to an understanding of how power operates in sex-discriminatory labour-market and recruitment practices will now be reviewed. Before exploring studies that focus specifically on the recruitment process in Chapters 3 and 4, the following discussion considers wider analyses of power and gender inequality in the labour market as a whole.

What follows in this chapter is an evaluation of those Marxist-feminist perspectives that highlight how capitalist power structures in particular can help to shape the social reproduction of women's labour-market subordination. These approaches emphasise that women can be used as a reserve army of labour and/or be segregated into dual or segmented labour markets. Whilst the reserve-army thesis concentrates on the historical tendency in capitalist society towards the homogen-isation of labour, segmentation theory explores the opposite pressure to stratify and segment the labour market and therefore the work-force. These theories establish a more power-sensitive account than is found in conventional liberal perspectives of how and why sex discrimination can persist in the labour market.

None the less, it will be argued that these Marxist-inspired analyses are problematic primarily because, in focusing on the structural imperatives of capital accumulation, the agency and resistance of both labour and capital are neglected. In this particular chapter we are concerned to highlight the absence in these perspectives of any analysis of management as agents within the labour process and labour market. Hence, the final section of the chapter seeks to outline a more sophis-ticated approach than is found in the foregoing literature to the conceptualisation of managerial power and practices. The implications of these arguments for the analysis of sex-discriminatory recruitment practices will then be outlined in the conclusion.

Women as a reserve army

This perspective developed out of the early feminist focus on domestic labour. In brief it had been argued that women's unpaid, domestic labour produced goods, services and people in a way that benefited and sustained the class structure and the capitalist pursuit of profit. This approach valuably demonstrated that housework, on the one hand, was productive labour, yet, on the other, severely curtailed women's experience to that of servicing men and rearing children within the home. It emphasised that an adequate understanding of gender inequality required a broad analytical focus stretching beyond recruitment, the labour process and employment to take account of the conventional domestic division of labour and how these structures and practices interconnect with employment.

However the domestic-labour debate was side-tracked by a doctrinal Marxist dispute about whether housework created use or surplus value (for example, Dalla Costa and James 1972; Harrison 1973; Seccombe 1974) and whether the privatised household was necessary for the reproduction of capitalism.[1] It also tended to relegate women exclusively to the domestic sphere and to neglect their contribution as paid workers. Nevertheless, the Marxist assumptions which underpinned this perspective formed the basis of a subsequent feminist analysis of women's position as a unique section of the reserve army of labour.

In its original form, the reserve-army thesis argued that a continuous surplus of labour was an inevitable and essential condition and consequence of capital accumulation (Marx 1946). It was argued that an industrial reserve of labour facilitated the accumulation of profit by reducing the power of employees to demand higher wages. This was because, as the economy expanded, the surplus population could be drawn into employment with the need to increase wages to attract other workers. The reserve army was a pre-condition of capital accumulation since it was essential for employers to be able to recruit at speed for their new machinery and enterprises.

In the absence of a reserve pool of labour, expansion would raise wages to the point where profits were undermined and the entire accumulation process endangered. In periods of contraction, the unemployed in the reserve army increased, and this intensified competition for jobs within the ranks of the unemployed and between them and the employed. Consequently, the latter would seek to protect their employment by accepting lower wages and increasing productivity. As production expanded, more workers were thereby displaced. Hence, the existence of the reserve army exerted enormous competitive pressure on the employed work-force, thus maintaining profit levels. The industrial reserve army therefore constituted the internal disciplinary mechanism *par excellence* for the regulation of wages and the maintenance of profits within the capitalist system.

The feminist version of the thesis is that women constitute a specific section of the reserve army because of their unique flexibility and disposability (Benston 1969). Married women in particular were identified as a unique segment of the reserve army because of their domestic role, and the familial ideologies surrounding it, in which they were dependent on the male bread-winner wage for part of the costs of reproduction (Beechey 1977, 1978). Women's labour power could be paid at a price below its value, that was lower than men's labour power, and which reduced the value of labour power overall. It was predicted that due to women's distinctively flexible position within the reserve army, they were likely to act as a cheap substitute for male labour (Benston 1969; Beechey 1978) in the process of the self-expansion of capital and the deskilling of work. The wartime employment of women in traditionally male jobs was a common example used to support the view that women could act as a substitute for men (Beechey 1978). Other studies (for example, Braverman 1974; Connelly 1978; Bruegel 1979) all contributed to this general perspective which argues that female workers were used as a cheap, available and disposable reserve army of labour by employers who could exploit 'the elasticity of housework' (Thompson 1983: 196).

The reserve-army debate was undoubtedly important in displaying a link between women's subordination in employment and capitalist practices and in refusing to relegate women to the home. However, as an overarching explanation of women's employment patterns, the thesis has been found to be theoretically and empirically inadequate. The difficulties with the thesis are derived primarily from the attempt to apply pre-existing Marxist categories to the analysis of women's employment. By adhering to the economistic framework of traditional Marxism, much of the debate is unable to overcome the highly abstract and sexually undifferentiated character of the original gender-blind version of the reserve army.

This point is elaborated by Anthias (1980) in an extended critique of Beechey's (1977) approach, which, she argues, is economistic, functionalist and teleological. Anthias suggests that it is untenable for Beechey to explain women's employment with reference to the economic advantages accruing to capital. These benefits are not so much reasons as merely descriptions of consequences. Similarly, in arguing that women are a cheap reservoir of labour because of their dependence on the male bread-winner wage, Beechey fails to recognise how the latter may also be a consequence of the former. In addition, Beechey is unable to explain why, given women's cheap labour, they are not *always* preferred by capitalist employers. Yet, as Anthias insists, the substitution of women for men is by no means an automatic process.

This raises a crucially neglected issue in the reserve-army debate – that of 'gender typing' (Anthias 1980: 59) or job segregation by sex (Hakim 1979). The persistence of job segregation in both the UK and the USA constitutes a major challenge to the validity of the female-reserve-army model and the economistic analysis which usually accompanies it. Indeed, the two major dimensions of the thesis, namely the cheap substitutability and disposability of female labour, are eroded by empirical evidence concerning sex-typing and job segregation.

On the first question of disposability, there is now considerable evidence to suggest that the sex-typing of 'women's work' creates a rigidity in the labour market preventing their expulsion (Milkman 1976; Barrett 1980; Yanz and Smith 1983). Increasingly throughout the twentieth century, women have been integrated into wage labour. Whilst they have often been segregated into low-paying clerical and service jobs, there is no indication that this work is temporary.[2] Indeed, as Barrett (1980: 161) emphasises, it is implausible to suggest, for example, that all typists and cleaners will simply be dispensed with when the economy contracts.

On the second question of women's substitutability, these changes in the sex composition of the labour force are readily translated into a thesis on feminisation which assumes a direct intention on the part of employers to replace male workers with a reserve army of female labour. Premissed on the assumption that the cheapness of female labour is a function not only of their sex but also of the ease with which the jobs they fill can easily be deskilled, the thesis on feminisation appears plausible; that is until an empirical examination reveals that the deskilling imperative is overstated[3] and that substitution is limited by the sex-typing of jobs and other discriminatory forces which are deep-rooted and taken for granted in contemporary life.

Braverman's (1974) focus on capital's general tendency to 'deskill' and degrade work by transforming the labour process has been heavily criticised for its disregard of worker agency and resistance to managerial control (Friedman 1977; Wood 1982; Knights et al. 1985).[4] The deskilling thesis tends to assume that managements always seek to homogenise and feminise the work-force. This reflects a taken-for-granted view of capitalism as a cohesive, reified and disembodied structure. Consequently, managerial power, intentions and practices tend to be merely 'read off' as the wholly determined outcome of the generalised tendencies of the capitalist totality with its underlying functional imperatives of surplus-value extraction and the competition to accumulate capital. Managers are simply treated as the 'unproblematic agents of capital' (Storey 1985: 195).

In addition, it has been demonstrated by Liff (1986) that the large numbers of women who have entered the labour force in the post-war boom have not, on the whole, replaced men, but have been employed in new or expanding areas of the economy. Moreover, she argues that if managers were really seeking to feminise the work-force at every opportunity, the sexual division of labour should be a 'very live issue' (ibid.: 90) between management and labour. Yet in practice, this is rarely the case. When questioned on the subject, managers often struggle to explain job sex-typing because it is so deeply taken for granted. Liff suggests that managers' contorted and unconvincing justifications demonstrate that 'female and male workers are not seen as undifferentiated substitutable groups'.

It can be concluded that assumptions about employers' automatic preference for women as cheap labour or their inevitable search to homogenise the work-force through deskilling strategies are likely to be inconsistent with empirical findings in many localised settings and in different historical periods. The theoretical and empirical evidence concerning women's disposability and substitutability thus reveals the reserve-army concept to be too abstracted, monolithic and one-dimensional. A reserve-army analysis may retain some validity for particular categories of labour such as part-time and temporary work where managements do enjoy extensive control over the labour process and labour market[5] (see, for example, Perkins 1983; Grieco and Whipp 1986; Collinson 1987b, 1988c). However, as a universal conceptual tool for explaining the general interrelationship of women's paid and domestic work, the resilience of job segregation and the power and practices of management, the thesis proves inadequate. Its failure to focus on these issues can be explained as resulting from the tendency of the reserve-army thesis to reproduce a functionalist and overly deterministic analysis which reduces labour-market practices to the wholly determined outcome of the disembodied structures of capitalism with its relentless inner logic of capital accumulation. By contrast, the second major explanation of women's labour-market subordination incorporates an account of job segregation and managerial power into its analytical framework.

Dual and segmented labour markets

In response to the focus of conventional economic theory upon individual difference and rational choice as an explanation of the sexual division of labour (see Introduction), more critical economists have highlighted employers' power to structure their demand for labour by operating either dual (Doeringer and Piore 1971; Barron and Norris 1976) or segmented labour markets (Edwards 1979; Reich et al. 1980). Doeringer and Piore (1971) argued that because firms wished to retain those workers with specific knowledge and scarce skills, they would offer them higher wages and long-term careers. These privileged employees were referred to as primary-sector workers, while those who a company could 'afford to lose' were defined as secondary-sector workers.

Barron and Norris (1976) sought to apply this perspective to explain gender divisions in the labour market. They argued that employers try to divide the labour market between 'primary' and 'secondary' jobs in order both to retain workers whose skills they require and to buy off the best organised employees. Secondary-sector jobs were primarily characterised as unstable, low-paid, and offering poor conditions of employment. Barron and Norris distinguished five attributes which employers believed were peculiar to women that resulted in the latter's confinement to the secondary sector. These were: dispensability, social differences (i.e. clearly distinguishable group characteristics), a low interest in training, indifference to economic rewards and an aversion to employee solidarity.

However, dual-labour-market theory has been subjected to heavy criticism. As an ahistorical and largely descriptive and static theory it treats all women in an undifferentiated way by conflating the various forms of female employment into a single unified category of 'secondary'-sector work (Beechey and Perkins 1987: 137). Moreover, as Walby (1986: 82) argues, Barron and Norris are incorrect to assume that the dual-labour-market model applies universally to all jobs in Britain. Whilst it might be appropriate to manual work in manufacturing, it is totally incompatible with, for example, clerical work.

A second criticism, again outlined by Walby (1986: 81), which can be applied to the female reserve army as well as the dual-labour-market thesis, is that sexual differentiation is treated as a function of the domestic division of labour and thus as predetermined outside the labour market. Patriarchal structures within the labour market are thereby neglected. In particular, the way in which gender is implicated in the social construction of skilled definitions is completely omitted in this perspective (Beechey and Perkins 1987: 137).

These difficulties are partly overcome by an alternative, more historically sensitive, approach which views internal and external labour markets as segmented. Radical economists argue that labour markets are segmented by monopoly capitalists into the secondary, subordinate and independent primary markets (Edwards 1979) as a means of securing control over labour. These segments correspond to a threefold typology of simple, technical and bureaucratic managerial control. Accordingly, it is argued that women's entrapment within the secondary sector of low paid, unskilled and insecure jobs, facilitates capital by sustaining gendered divisions within the work-force. This 'divide-and-rule' policy of stratification which informs labour market segmentation prevents any working-class solidarity that might otherwise emerge out of the homogenisation of labour. Accordingly the thesis claims that segmented labour markets are functional for employers. As Reich et al. put it, 'Labour market segmentation arose and is perpetuated because it is functional – that is, it facilitates the operation of capitalist institutions' (1980: 239). In addition to highlighting management's power to control labour-market practices, early segmentation theory was valuable for its recognition of many women's confinement within the secondary or peripheral sector in part-time and temporary jobs or those which are insecure, low paying with poor prospects.

However, like the reserve-army model, early versions of this perspective remained at too high a level of abstraction which resulted in a tendency to reify labour markets (Jewson and Mason 1986b) and a failure to differentiate among employers (Wharton 1985), industries (Beechey 1978) or women (Walby 1986). Power tended to be reduced to questions of class and women were merely welded on to a Marxist perspective in a mechanical way. As a result, segmentation theory ignored class differences between females, conflated the consideration of gender *relations* with the position of women and, most crucially, neglected the importance of the domestic division of labour for the economy (Armstrong 1984: 31). Consequently, as Thompson (1983: 187) notes, although radical economists describe discrimination and stereotyping, they cannot fully explain it.[6]

One major problem with radical segmentation theory is its tendency to attribute to managers a power and intentionality that is unwarranted and to assume that their central interest is the erosion of potential labour solidarity. As Hyman (1987: 30) contends, labour-market segmentation is not primarily *intended* to divide the work-force. Rather, these class and gender divisions reflect a fundamental concern to establish a greater stability of employment, particularly for those workers with scarce skills and knowledge who are strategically placed in the labour market. Segmentation is thereby expected to reduce recruitment and training costs. Equally, the use of peripheral workers in the secondary sector is a convenient way of accommodating to unstable and unpredictable product markets. Consequently, the ensuing divisions within the work-force may be an *unintended consequence*, rather than a primary motive of managerial attempts to accommodate to the expectations and disruptive potential of strategically placed occupational groups in the labour market and the fluctuations of demand in the product market.

31

Moreover, segmentation theory constitutes a demand-side perspective that fails to consider the way in which such factors as trade-union organisation, legal controls or broader social forces help to shape and segment the supply of labour (Craig et al. 1985). Accordingly, segmentation theory is characterised by the same deterministic approach as the reserve-army thesis, for it treats management as omniscient and the labour force as passive and submissive. Managerial domination is theorised as a smooth, highly intentional and unproblematic process, free of contradictions and unintended consequences.

To summarise, the two major theoretical frameworks discussed so far, which seek to explain women's labour-market subordination, tend to assume that management is primarily concerned either with job deskilling and feminisation and/or labour-market segmentation and work-force divisions. In the pursuit of surplus value, it is argued, managers must concentrate their efforts on increasing the divisions between conception and execution and between male and female workers. Yet these approaches provide little concrete empirical evidence of how the female reserve army or the segmentation of labour markets is *reproduced* through particular recruitment and redundancy practices.

These empirical omissions in turn reflect a theoretical tendency in the reserve army and segmentation theory to provide an overly deterministic analysis. As a consequence, managers are treated as the unproblematic agents of capital and their practices are 'read off' as the wholly determined outcome of the capitalist imperative to secure surplus value. Inevitably, the result is a functionalist form of analysis which assumes that management is, first, all-powerful and omnipotent in its ability to control at will both the labour process and labour market and, second, concerned exclusively with deskilling and the control of labour. Third, these perspectives take for granted that management is a highly cohesive, and undifferentiated, monolithic and homogeneous class or function which is united in its pursuit of labour control and the extraction of surplus value. Both these approaches, then, can only contribute to our understanding of labour-market practices if we modify their tendency to collapse into crude functionalist determinism. Accordingly, it is plausible to argue that in certain restricted employment conditions, a reserve army of cheap and flexible labour proves extremely useful to employers. Similarly, it is possible to recognise how management can benefit from segmented labour markets without arguing that this is simply the result of a divide-and-rule strategy designed to prevent the development of collective solidarity in the work-place.

In the final part of this chapter, we now seek to retrieve the agency of management from an exclusively structuralist analysis of capitalism. In so doing, assumptions of management's omniscience, unity and cohesion are rejected by highlighting two central contradictions of managerial control, which are embedded; first, in the relationship between capital and labour, and second, within capital itself.

Managerial strategy and agency

There is now considerable evidence in the literature of widespread shop-floor resistance (see Beynon 1973; Nichols and Beynon 1977; Willis 1979; Collinson 1981; Pollert 1981; Westwood 1984; Thompson and Bannon 1985). The persistence of this worker resistance indicates that managerial control through deskilling (Taylor 1947) has in many cases either not been implemented or has failed to reduce labour merely to the robotic appendage of capitalist technology (as Braverman 1974: 194 pessimistically predicted). In consequence, it has been argued that workers cannot be reduced to the commodified objects of managerial control (Storey 1985; Hyman 1987), for as knowledgeable social beings, they inevitably retain a subjective sense of themselves as socially and technically skilled agents with a degree of discretion and power to resist the controls placed upon them. Accordingly, management must ultimately depend upon the skill, particularly that of a 'tacit' nature (Manwaring and Wood 1985), voluntary initiatives and the co-operation, consent or at least compliance of employees (Burawoy 1979; Knights and Collinson 1985). Hence, alongside the *antagonistic* relations between capital and labour, based on the material conflict between wages and profits, is a coexisting and contradictory *interdependence* (Cressey and Macinnes 1980; Bradley 1986).

Since deskilling will now result in the total elimination of conceptualisation and discretion from labour-process tasks, management might in certain market conditions relax its control and seek a co-operative relationship with labour. As Hyman notes (1987: 41), management must not only attempt to limit worker discretion, which might be applied against its interest, but also harness the willing application to profitable production of that discretion which cannot be eliminated:

> The function of labour control involves *both* the direction, surveillance and discipline of subordinates whose enthusiastic commitment to corporate objectives cannot be taken for granted, and the mobilisation of the discretion, initiative and diligence which coercive supervision far from guaranteeing is likely to destroy.
>
> (original emphasis)

This tension between the concern to control and co-ordinate reveals

33

that management is not all-powerful within both the labour process and labour market. Indeed, as Hyman elaborates, the contradictions for management in seeking to coerce, yet also secure consent, are ultimately irreconcilable. Employers' contradictory demands for both dependable yet disposable workers result in a changing emphasis, first upon managerial prerogative and coercion (scientific management) and second upon worker co-operation and consent (human relations). These managerial practices reflect the 'direct-control' or 'responsible-autonomy' strategies outlined by Friedman (1977), who argued that *competitive labour markets* may force management to abandon direct control strategies. A coercive approach could prove counter-productive particularly where 'central' (Friedman, ibid.) groups of workers either possess scarce skills or knowledge, on which management rely, or have great organisational strength in collective resistance.

Responsible autonomy might also be adopted because of management's concern not just with labour-process control, but also with the realisation of surplus value in competitive *product markets*. Since employers place great priority on the continuity, reliability and quality of production, the flexibility of labour and on the competitiveness of its products in the market-place, their strategy might not be directed primarily at the conflict between capital and labour or the control of the labour process.

Yet having said that, deskilling and direct control could still be an unintended consequence of pursuing product-market objectives. Thus, for example, investment in new technology is often geared to the manufacture of new, improved or standardised products and its deskilling implications are largely secondary (Jones 1982; Child 1985). This raises the question of managerial intentionality and highlights the need to locate managerial practices within the 'full circuit of capital' (Kelly 1985: 32) which encompasses the buying and selling of goods and products as well as of labour power.

Thus, for a variety of reasons, employers might replace, or combine, deskilling and direct control with a strategy of segmentation and responsible autonomy. Here, employees are given status, discretion and responsibility in their job tasks and are subject to an 'enlightened' managerial philosophy of 'participation', 'co-operative teamwork' and 'employee commitment'. Yet like direct control, this alternative or additional strategy could have self-defeating consequences. Employees may well dismiss this managerial approach merely as dishonest propaganda (see Collinson 1981; Knights and Collinson 1985; Knights and Collinson 1987) designed to conceal the insecurity of workers' jobs and the capitalist pursuit of greater production and the extraction of surplus value. An attempt to construct an image of harmony and consent in industrial relations may thus be counter-productive for management, where it hardens rather than dilutes worker cynicism and resistance based on the 'us-and-them' polarisation of capital and labour. Shop-floor perceptions of the real and expected discrepancy between managerial policy and practice can have the effect of reinforcing and legitimising worker resistance.

Hence, neither of these managerial strategies can fully reconcile the central contradiction between control and co-ordination in the capital/labour relation because they themselves are internally contradictory. Whilst the first strategy emphasises managerial prerogative, it neglects management's continued dependence on labour for the production of goods and services. Although the second strategy stresses mutual interest and interdependence, it disregards the antagonisms and power inequalities between capital and labour. Yet the presence of such contradictions does not result in the abandonment of these strategies. Rather, as Friedman (1987: 291) has argued, the likely consequence is that fundamental tensions will continue to characterise the labour process.

In sum, managerial power is often circumscribed by the contradiction between capital and labour and by the competitive pressure of shifting product and labour markets. Equally, managers are by no means exclusively concerned with deskilling and labour-process control for in practice, they are just as likely to prioritise production, product quality and competitiveness respectively. Yet even these arguments tend to exaggerate the intentionality of managerial agency. As Storey suggests, managers cannot be assumed to be 'fully programmed rationalistic units who simply read off market dictats' (1985: 195). Indeed, recent research (for example, Nolan and Edwards 1983; Child 1985; Rose and Jones 1985) has demonstrated that managers are not all-knowing, wholly rational or necessarily far-seeing agents in their strategies for managing both labour and product markets. Drawing on six empirical case-studies, Rose and Jones (1985: 31) conclude that with regard to labour relations, managerial policy-making and practices tended to be 'piecemeal, unco-ordinated and empiricist'.[7]

Child (1985: 108) also argues that senior managers' decision-making has been found to be characterised by 'vacillation, the pursuit of factional interests and even randomness....Rationality often appears to be bounded and focused on the next step rather than on the long term.'

As Child suggests, one of the reasons for this level of irrationality in managerial strategy is the fragmentation *within capital* itself. Indeed, managers' contradictory and shifting attempts to discipline, yet secure consent, reflect and reinforce contradictions between and within the various managerial specialisms (Hyman 1987: 35). For the purpose of this book, three major contradictory divisions within the managerial hierarchy are particularly relevant: these refer to the way in which management is functionally, spatially and hierarchically differentiated.

Several writers have pointed to the extensive nature of intra-managerial competition and functional rivalry (see, for example, Dalton 1959). Armstrong (1986) has explored the battle between the managerial professions of accountancy, engineering and personnel to secure ascendency for their own approach to the control of the labour process (see also Hopper et al. 1984). Strategic solutions to management's 'control problem' might therefore be competing and internally fragmented. Similarly, Hyman (1987: 32) suggests that Taylorism is best seen as an engineer's ideology which was designed to challenge not only worker discretion but also the functions and status of other managers.

Equally, internal divisions within the managerial structure can also emerge in the possible attenuation between the formulation of corporate policy and its implementation at grassroots level. Child (1985: 109) has argued that the successful implementation of managerial strategy cannot simply be inferred from policy statements (see also Torrington et al. 1982). The practices of middle management, supervisors and workers may be inconsistent with corporate policy, either in subverting the formal control structure, or in contributing to efficient working without the intervention or knowledge of senior management.

Finally, the view of management as an integrated totality, even within the same function, is undermined by the highly sensitised orientation to career advancement displayed by individual managers (Hyman 1987: 30) within managerial hierarchies. The use of career as an indirect form of control over managerial behaviour is intended to induce conformity, co-operation and identification with the organisation. However, it can also generate contradictory consequences.

This is first because career as a form of control often fuels extensive grievances as a result of the scarcity of openings due to the pyramidal shape of hierarchies. Second, by 'promoting' an individualistic orientation in aspiring managers, it can generate counter-productive competition within the managerial structure. Hence, a contradiction may emerge between the need for communication and co-operation within the managerial function and the simultaneous retention of the individualistic success ethic in organisations (Luckmann and Berger 1964; Offe 1976). Careerism and competition can reinforce divisions, power struggles and communication breakdowns through the individualistic concern to differentiate and elevate self and/or to defend self and deny responsibility.

In sum, the following conclusions can be drawn from this final section. First, managerial power and practices cannot simply be 'read off' from their structural position within capitalist society. Second, the contradictory relationship between capital and labour leads managements to adopt a variety of strategies, each of which may have unintended and negative consequences for them. Third, managers are not exclusively concerned with the organisation and control of the labour process. However, their pursuit of other objectives could reinforce control in the labour process and labour market. Fourth, managerial practices are not always coherent, rational or co-ordinated. Finally, the managerial function is often internally fragmented, not only between different organisations in the competition to hire labour and sell products, but also between and within different managerial specialisms. While these arguments are largely gender-blind, their implications for the analysis of job segregation and management's role in its reproduction will now be discussed in the conclusion.

Conclusion

This chapter has discussed two central Marxist-feminist theories of women's subordination in the labour market. While useful for an understanding of how sex discrimination is reproduced in specific circumstances, this literature was found to contain major difficulties, many of which were a direct consequence of adhering too closely to an overly economistic, functionalist and deterministic Marxist critique of capitalism. Although the female reserve army and early labour-market segmentation theories are more power-sensitive than those discussed in the introduction, they were criticised for treating management as a monolithic, omnipotent and homogeneous class or function which can control the labour market and labour process at will. This reflects a highly structural analysis in which it is assumed that managerial practices are the wholly determined outcome of the inexorable capitalist imperative to secure surplus value. Yet in practice, it is often the case, first, that neither deskilling nor feminisation will be a viable strategy and, second, that segmentation is not usually intended to divide and control the work-force.

We therefore conclude that job segregation and management's role in its reproduction continue to be inadequately explored either at an empirical or theoretical level. This book is concerned to present a much more detailed analysis of managerial practices than is available in the above theories. It does so by examining: the strategies and practices of management in organising and selecting employees; the ways in which managers justify and rationalise sex-discriminatory practices and the tensions, divisions and conflicts that often characterise and fragment the managerial function. In order to explain the reproduction of job segregation in the recruitment process, it is important, we contend, to analyse each of these aspects of managerial practice.

Equally, a central concern of the book is to highlight some of the contradictory consequences of operating managerial control through sex-discriminatory recruitment practices. The foregoing Marxist-feminist literature treats feminisation and segmentation as wholly functional for the extraction of surplus value. Yet this approach neglects the negative unintended consequences which management might suffer from pursuing such strategies. By confining female labour to low-grade work, for example, management will not be utilising women's experience and potential to the full. Equally, if women resign because of the absence of opportunities, management again loses women's skill and 'experience and suffers the increased costs of recruitment and training.

Relatedly, the persistence of job segregation could be an entirely unintended consequence of employers' primary concern to ensure the stability and reliability of production. In seeking to protect production, employers might, for example, wish to avoid a challenge to deep-seated gender divisions within the work-force and the local community. Alternatively, managers themselves may simply take gender differentiation for granted as 'natural' and 'inevitable'. Hence, rather than being solely the result of a highly deliberate policy either to feminise or to divide and rule, the reinforcement of job segregation could equally reflect an unquestioning acceptance of conventional gender differentiation.

This point raises the final major difficulty with the foregoing Marxist-inspired theories of women's labour-market subordination – namely, their failure to address the question of gender differentiation. In the absence of a theory of men's domination both in employment and at home, crucial issues concerning the taken-for-granted nature of job segregation tend to be neglected.[8] These difficulties are partly offset by a growing feminist literature which has focused on the exclusionary practices of organised male workers. We therefore turn to a selective examination of this literature in the following chapter.

Chapter two

Gender and the labour market

Introduction

The previous chapter highlighted the theoretical and empirical dangers of economistic, functionalist and deterministic accounts of managerial control in the Marxist-feminist literature. It also argued that this literature failed to theorise the male-dominated nature of labour-market practices. In this chapter we examine a series of feminist studies that focus on the practices and ideologies of male workers in resisting the entry of female labour. On the basis of their detailed historical and empirical evidence, some feminist theorists have argued that a separate power structure of patriarchy, in addition to that of capitalism, is a necessary analytical prerequisite for the understanding of gender inequality in the labour market.

Indeed, there is now considerable evidence to support the view that male domination cannot be treated as synonymous with, nor merely subsumed within, an analysis of capitalism. This is demonstrated for example by: the sexism which characterises internal union relations (for example, Pollert 1981; Westwood 1984); the continued subordination of women in apparently 'socialist' societies such as Cuba (Thompson 1983) and Eastern Europe (Molyneux 1981); the way that gender divisions and women's domestic oppression predate capitalist society (Barrett 1980); and the importance in employment of sexuality (Weekes 1977; Burrell 1984; Wilson 1984; Hearn 1985; Hearn and Parkin 1987; Hearn et al. 1989); masculinity (Willis 1979; Gray 1987; Hearn 1987; Collinson 1988b; Morgan 1988) and sexual harassment (Mackinnon 1979; Sedley and Benn 1984).

In the first section of this chapter we examine several feminist studies of patriarchal labour-market practices. With reference to the work of Walby (1986) we then explore the underlying question of how to theorise patriarchy. The remainder of the chapter presents a critique of her proposals designed to overcome the problems that she identifies in the existing feminist literature. As in the previous chapter, we conclude by arguing that any theory of gender inequality in the labour market must acknowledge not only the asymmetry of power relations, but also the agency and resistance of the men and women who reproduce and transform these structures of domination.

Patriarchal practices

Increasingly, feminist writers have argued that men, both as workers and in male-dominated trade unions, are equally if not more responsible than management for both the exclusion of women and their segregation into secondary labour markets. By focusing on patriarchal labour-market ideologies and practices, these studies highlight the way that organised groups of male workers have been able to oppose the entry of cheap female labour by demanding the 'bread-winner wage' and by controlling both the provision of training and the definition of skill. They disclose how male workers have contributed to the segmentation of labour markets and to the way in which 'skill has become saturated with sex' (Phillips and Taylor 1980: 85), wherein men are associated with skilled work and women are automatically regarded as unskilled labour. Hence, far from work-force divisions being a source of weakness for labour, as radical economists argued (see previous chapter), feminist studies suggest that a heterogeneous work-force can be a condition and consequence of the solidarity and power of male labour.

This debate also demonstrates that the contribution of organised male workers to the reinforcement of labour-market segmentation and job segregation appears to transcend the class barriers between 'mental' and 'manual' work. Research suggests that middle-class 'professional' men have been able to exaggerate and mystify their own 'mental' skills so as to secure labour-market closure and job demarcation. For in medicine (Hearn 1982; Witz 1986; Lawrence 1987), the civil service (Walters 1987), personnel management (Legge 1987), the law (Spencer and Podmore 1986, 1987) and pharmacy, dentistry and accountancy (Crompton and Sanderson 1986), women have been shown to be excluded altogether or confined to low-grade tasks deemed 'appropriate' to their sex. Women GPs, for example, are found to be 'ghettoised' by their male principals and partners into gynaecology and obstetrics, family planning, psychiatric problems and paediatrics (Lawrence 1987). Similarly, women lawyers are often restricted to low-status desk work such as wills, probate and matrimonial affairs (Spencer and Podmore 1986).

In addition to this focus on middle-class professionals, skilled and semi-skilled working-class men have been shown to pride themselves on their differentiated, 'masculine' manual skills (see, for example,

Willis 1977; Collinson 1988b) and to seek, albeit from a weaker power base, to resist female entry (Humphries 1977; Hartmann 1979; Barrett 1980; Phillips and Taylor 1980; Rubery 1980; Cockburn 1983; Walby 1986; Baron 1987). These studies provide further confirmation that women's oppression cannot be understood merely as a consequence of the economic pressures of capitalism.

Craft unions, in particular, have been the object of extensive feminist historical critique. This has exposed the attempts of organised labour to reproduce and protect segregated work patterns and the family wage by sustaining labour-market control and a self-serving masculine ideology of skill. Cockburn's (1983) examination of the exclusionary practices of the printers in the UK provides a cogent and detailed illustration of how male-dominated craft unions have operated to sustain their relative economic privileges and high status. The print unions are perhaps untypical given their 'aristocratic' position within the labour movement. The ephemeral nature of newspapers has traditionally provided extensive industrial muscle to the printers.

Cockburn shows how union officials of the National Graphical Association (NGA) were able to exercise great influence over recruitment and training and therefore had the power to define the skill content of jobs and to control a single-sex labour supply. She reveals how the NGA has acted as a recruitment agency, retaining a list of available printers, and thereby supplying (male) labour to employers in the newspaper industry. These practices were not merely a consequence of a materialist concern to protect high wages by pre-empting any attempt to 'feminise' printing or to recruit non-union labour. For, as Cockburn demonstrates, the compositors also subscribed to a deeply masculine ideology which elevated men and their typesetting skills, while denigrating women and their keyboard skills.

Similarly, Baron (1987) has explored the way that gender and skill have been constructed in the US printing industry. She shows how nineteenth-century printers treated work as a source of masculinity, first, in their role as family provider, and second, through the physical and intellectual nature of the work itself. Male printers saw female labour as an unsuspecting tool of the employer to reduce the breadwinner wage (ibid.: 12). They also argued that women would lose their 'modesty' and femininity in the masculine shop-floor culture with its aggression, sexism, swearing and drinking. This masculine ideology reflected and reinforced men's dominance of printing skills.

The foregoing studies illustrate that feminist research on patriarchal labour-market practices has overcome much of the functionalism and determinism of Marxist economism. By retrieving the agency and resistance of labour, these studies present a stringent critique of deterministic and economistic demand-side analyses of managerial practices, as exemplified by the female-reserve-army and labour-market-segmentation theories. That gendered definitions of skill and men's labour-market control practices have been shown to transcend class boundaries provides an added impetus to analyses which reject the view that women's subordination can be subsumed within a critique of capitalism. This debate has begun to establish a more detailed and empirically informed understanding of organisational power relations and of the concrete social, economic and ideological forces which govern the interwoven and sex-segregated labour-market practices of supply and demand.

Theorists such as Cockburn (1983), Witz (1986) and Walby (1986) have drawn on their empirical data on patriarchal labour-market practices to argue for a perspective that has come to be known as 'dual-systems theory'. Whilst this approach has been less well articulated than the Marxist analysis of class and capitalism, which it seeks to critique (Cockburn 1983: 194), Walby (1986) has recently provided a more thorough explication of dual-systems theory. Her work is particularly valuable because she concentrates on establishing a definition of 'patriarchy' which avoids some of the pitfalls of earlier feminist approaches. The following section briefly reviews her central thesis.

Dual-systems theory

Walby criticises many writers concerned with women's subordination for their failure to acknowledge the full significance of the role of trade unions in the reproduction of job segregation. She presents a detailed historical account of how the policies and practices of both skilled and semi-skilled trade unions have been detrimental to women workers. Her evidence from engineering, cotton textiles and clerical work demonstrates the diversity of patriarchal labour-market strategies designed to maintain and reinforce job segregation in a variety of industrial contexts, labour and product markets, historical periods and economic conditions.

In cotton textiles, for instance, she records how male spinners in the nineteenth century excluded women from trade-union membership, training and jobs. The entry of women into the highly skilled work of mule spinner was resisted fiercely and effectively through industrial sabotage and strikes (Walby 1986: 99). By contrast, the failure of cotton weavers to organise resulted in female entry and low wages. Alternatively, the craft basis of the male-dominated engineering union facilitated an exclusionary strategy that controlled the provision of training to the detriment of women. In clerical work, Walby suggests that the segregation of women in new clerical subgroups throughout the twentieth century was the negotiated outcome of balancing male clerks' fears of female substitution with employers' preference for women as cheap labour. Overall, Walby insists that the labour-market strategies of trade unions, as they have shifted from total exclusion to the compromise of segregation, are essential for an understanding of the historical reproduction of job segregation.

On the basis of this empirical analysis, Walby seeks to establish a definition of patriarchy which, unlike earlier models (for example, Mitchell 1975; Delphy 1977; Hartmann 1979) is neither monolithic, nor descriptive and imprecise. Walby defines patriarchy as an interrelated system of different social structures through which men exploit women. She identifies the following autonomous structures of patriarchy: domestic labour, paid work, the state, male violence and sexuality.[1] The structures attributed most importance by Walby, particularly in explaining the articulation of capitalism and patriarchy, are the divisions of labour in the household and in employment.

Drawing on Delphy's (1977) materialistic analysis, Walby highlights the 'patriarchal mode of production' (ibid.: 52) in which housework is treated as a form of production, both in the generational sense of producing children and in the day-to-day sense of replenishing the husband's labour power. She contends that since all the tasks comprising domestic labour can be purchased in the market, where they are considered to be production, it is mistaken to treat them as reproduction, for 'they are all work, socially useful and should be seen as production' (ibid.: 36). Walby argues that the exhausted husband does not fully compensate his wife for the domestic labour which he expropriates. Hence, women share a common class position as the exploited labourers of husbands. This extraction of surplus labour is perpetuated through highly personalised and privatised relations within the home.

For Walby, the major reason why women have not resisted this exploitation by leaving the home is because of the way that the patriarchal relations of both waged work and the state prevent female entry on the same terms as men. By insisting that patriarchal labour-market structures constitute the 'primary mechanism' (1986: 54) that determines women's subordination, Walby subscribes to a one-way causal relationship from paid work to home: 'Women's position in the family is largely determined by their paid work rather than vice versa' (ibid.: 70).

This point reflects and reinforces her central concluding argument that an antagonism and tension exists between capitalism and patriarchy which is often neglected by other dual-systems theorists (for example, Hartmann 1981). According to Walby, the presumption that capital benefits from women's subordination to men and that men utilise capitalist relations in their subordination of women underestimates the conflict between patriarchy and capital over women's labour power.

This coalescence of interest between capital and men is compromised, for example, by capital's preference for female workers because they constitute cheap labour, which, in turn, threatens men's position both as workers and as expropriators of female domestic labour. Conversely, in so far as organised male labour is successful in confining women to the home, then capital's interest in unskilled female labour is thwarted.

Walby refuses to subsume the analysis of patriarchy within a critique of capitalism. She is also concerned to highlight the need for a broader, more coherent and historically specific understanding of both male domination and its articulation with capitalism (and racism). Accordingly, her work constitutes a valuable analysis and development of the feminist literature. Nevertheless, in spite of her focus on labour resistance, which partly overcomes the deterministic tendencies of earlier Marxist-feminist theories, Walby's analysis is in danger of merely replacing one form of historical determinism (capitalism) with another (patriarchy). In other words, her emphasis on the asymmetry of gender relations in the labour market is purchased only at the cost of producing an overly economistic and deterministic theory of the patriarchal division of labour in the household and in employment. This is demonstrated first by the analytical priority which she affords labour-market structures as the primary source of women's subordination. Walby thereby underemphasises the significance of women's domestic subordination which she argues is merely a consequence *but not also a condition* of patriarchal labour-market practices. By contrast, in seeking to explain the recursive character of job segregation, we wish to restore the importance of women's domestic subordination.

Second, the deterministic nature of Walby's approach is revealed by her theoretical intention to concentrate exclusively on social structure (1986: 71). By so doing, she fails to examine how these structures of domination are not only the medium but also the outcome of active agents within definite social practices. Only by treating patriarchy and capitalism as sets of interwoven social practices will an unwarranted determinism be avoided. Each of these difficulties will now be examined in turn.

Ideology and biology

Walby adheres to a highly economistic analysis of the domestic division of labour which highlights the way that husbands routinely exploit the domestic labour of their wives. We contend that this economistic theory of patriarchy underestimates the significant and interrelated role of biology, familial ideology and gender identity for the perpetuation of male domination, not only in the domestic environment but also in paid work. To support our argument we will now present a brief discussion of the feminist debate concerning biological reproduction and familial ideology.

In their early attempt to argue for a separate theory of patriarchy, radical feminists (for example, Millett 1971; Firestone 1972) focused on biological reproduction as the source of gender inequality. This approach has been heavily criticised for reducing complex gender relations to questions of biology (for example, Beechey 1979; Barrett 1980; Walby 1986; Connell 1987). Biological reductionism tended to be ahistorical and static since it treated male power and interests as monolithic and universal. It lacked an awareness of both cross-cultural variations in the social organisation of reproduction and also artificially separated patriarchy from capitalist relations. Equally, its emphasis on biology precluded the possibility of *social* transformations in gender relationships. Indeed, despite its more critical edge, this focus on the 'natural' inevitability of male domination paradoxically tended to mirror 'common-sense' rationalisations for sex discrimination.

In sum, by treating the two sexes as single, distinct and homogeneous groups, early radical feminists engaged in the false universalism of categorical thinking, which subscribed to biological determinism (Connell 1985). This resulted in a failure to explore the contradictions and specific forms through which the overall system of male domination has been reproduced, rationalised, resisted and transformed. It therefore precluded the possibility of change and emancipation.

Later theorists sought to emphasise the social construction of gender difference and to explore the way that male domination is perpetuated through capitalist society. Focusing on the self-perpetuating *vicious circles* between home and employment which reinforce women's subordination, these writers have sought to overcome early dual-systems theory. In so doing, a fruitful debate concerning ideology and biology has emerged.

Rejecting biologistic accounts, Barrett (1980), for example, argues that the concept of patriarchy is only ever applicable at the ideological level. She suggests that while gender inequality predated capitalism and is not a functional necessity for its reproduction, it 'has acquired a material basis in the relations of production and reproduction of capitalism today' (ibid.: 249). In seeking to display how women's oppression is now embedded within and reinforced by capitalism, Barrett highlights the importance of familial ideology, with its emphasis on the inevitability of the 'natural' bread-winner/homemaker dichotomy, in the reproduction of oppressive structures.

Unlike Walby,[2] Barrett recognises that the material relations of the privatised structure of the household, and the ideology of the family surrounding it, play a crucial part in shaping women's subordination in paid work: 'The family-household system of contemporary capitalism constitutes not only the central site of the oppression of women but an important organising principle of the relations of production of the social formation as a whole' (ibid.: 211). She argues that the categories of work undertaken by women often reflect a family-based ideology of gender which treats the tasks of servicing and caring as pre-eminently 'feminine' (ibid.: 157). Equally, women's involvement in part-time and homeworking reflects their responsibility for child care. Thus, she argues, the family-household system constitutes both the ideological and material basis of women's oppression in capitalist society. Moreover, Barrett ascribes primary significance to familial ideology, which she treats as relatively autonomous from the material structure of the household. Historically specific manifestations of familial ideology are particularly important for Barrett in accounting for the way that men and women come to understand themselves and each other: 'Gender identity and the definition of masculinity and femininity that pervades our culture are pre-eminently constructed within the ideology of the family' (ibid.: 205). Accordingly, she perceives the contemporary ideology of familialism to play a crucial role in structuring the agency and identity of human beings as gendered individuals. Hence, familial ideology is a crucial factor in explaining the deep-seated and taken-for-granted nature of gender differentiation. Barrett concludes that these hegemonic gendered definitions of self and 'other' which are based on, but distinct from, concrete biological differences, inform interconnected social practices not only in the home, but also in paid work. In the nineteenth century, for example, both male craft unions and the state drew on teh ideology of female domesticity to ensure women's subordination in paid work, even though in practice few working-class households were able to rely solely on the family wage of the male bread-winner. As a result of these taken-for-granted ideological processes, the sexual division of labour has become deeply entrenched in the relations of capitalist production.

Barrett's approach is valuable in displaying how labour-market practices and women's domestic subordination are best seen as mutually reinforcing. She presents a sophisticated attempt to assert the importance of gender ideology for women's oppression and to provide an alternative to biologism (radical feminists) and economism (domestic-labour theorists).

However, the analytical primacy which she ascribes to ideology has been rigorously contested by Brenner and Ramas (1984). Despite Barrett's assertion that ideology cannot be severed from material reality, Brenner and Ramas criticise Barrett's focus for its idealism, because ultimately it 'fails to identify any material basis for women's oppression in capitalism' (ibid.: 38). Explaining the historical material hardships of working-class women as a combined condition and consequence of biological reproduction and employers' concern with cheap labour, Brenner and Ramas seek not to reject, but to ascribe a secondary role to, gender ideology. While recognising the importance of eschewing economistic Marxism, they argue that Barrett is unable to explain precisely why and how gender divisions have evolved historically to become embedded in the material structure of capitalist social relations.

They seek to display that behind every manifestation of gender ideology outlined by Barrett are more deep-rooted and determining material realities embedded in both capital accumulation and the exigencies of biological reproduction and lactation. According to Brenner and Ramas, the incompatibility between profit-seeking and child-bearing and child-rearing has left women facing significant material vicious circles in nineteenth- and twentieth-century capitalism. These material vicious circles have rendered women unable to change their work situation because of their domestic conditions and their home situation because of their employment conditions. Like Barrett's analysis, Brenner and Ramas therefore begin to display, in their case at a material level, the mutually reinforcing relationship between labour-market structures and women's domestic subordination.

Brenner and Ramas argue that it was not so much ideology, but the *realities* of biological reproduction and family responsibilities which meant that women were disadvantaged in the labour market. While a contributory factor to these social patterns, 'ideology alone could not have forced women to accept lower wages' (ibid.: 56). Conversely, so long as women earned less than their husbands, it would be difficult for them to overcome their domestic role as homemaker: 'The more desperate women are to work, the more burdened they become by home responsibility, the more difficult for them to organise against their employers, the more intractable income inequalities between men and women remain' (ibid.: 63). Accordingly, they insist that material conditions often shape ideological practices and argue that gender ideology is 'rooted in and shaped by women's and men's actual experience and practice in everyday life' (ibid.: 70). The ideas of male bread-winner and female homemaker 'retained their force precisely because they were underpinned by an inescapable social reality' (ibid.). The unrelenting logic of a seemingly inescapable and inevitable family-household system conditioned the ideological understandings that men and women formed of each other and their social relations. Brenner and Ramas present a convincing argument that Barrett underestimates the significance of material and biological realities in the construction and reproduction of gender ideology. They argue that capitalist employers have always refused to support the continuity of women's employment by providing child-care facilities.

This brief review of the debate between these authors demonstrates the analytical importance of *both* biological reproduction and gender ideology for the perpetuation of the sexual division of labour at home and in paid work. It thereby challenges Walby's economistic theory of patriarchal exploitation in two ways. First, it suggests that Walby underestimates biology and ideology as contributory factors in men's domination of women at home and work.[3] Second and relatedly, it demonstrates that Walby's approach fails to acknowledge the mutually reinforcing nature of patriarchal labour-market practices and women's domestic subordination[4] – that is to say, women's domestic subordination is not merely a consequence *but also a condition* of patriarchal labour-market practices. Nevertheless, in their respective ascription of analytical priority to ideology and biological reproduction, neither of these studies has resolved the ensuing problem of determinism which also characterises Walby's account.[5] It is to the critique of structural determinism that we now turn.

Agency and practices

Walby defends her view that women's position in the family is determined by their participation in paid work by arguing that she is concerned exclusively with the historical analysis of social structures:

> I would not dispute that for any individual woman today her position in relation to the family significantly affects her view of paid work and her participation in the various forms of work. However, the explanation of an individual's work strategy is not the same as an explanation of the structures which constrain her choices. It is with the explanation of these social structures that I am concerned.
>
> (Walby 1986: 71)

Yet her indifference to the practices and 'motivation of individuals' (Walby 1983: 165) means that she is unable to explain how these social structures are constituted, and this inevitably results in a theory of patriarchy which is heavily deterministic as well as economistic.

Although Walby insists that women must be treated as 'significant actors in resisting their exploitation' (ibid.: 1), she does not incorporate this empirical insight into her theoretical perspective. Indeed, her primary theoretical concern is to explain why women do *not* resist their domestic exploitation by securing employment and why housework is 'as good as anything else a woman is likely to get' (ibid.: 248). Here Walby is in danger of superimposing her own interpretation on to the 'motivation of individuals'. Women's pursuit of paid work cannot be treated merely as a form of resistance to their dependence on men. For example, it may quite simply be a means of bringing more money into the household. In the absence of an examination of consciousness and agency, it is impossible to present an adequate exploration of resistance. Indeed, Walby's deterministic approach neglects vast areas of subtle forms of agency and resistance which are available to women in the social relations that comprise domestic work, labour markets and organisations.[6]

The importance of combining an analysis of structure with that of agency in relation to gender was emphasised ten years before Walby's study: 'The relationship between structure and consciousness is a key issue in sociology and it is critical for the understanding of women as employees' (Brown 1976: 49).

The critique of determinism and the importance of consciousness and agency in gender relations has also been outlined by other theorists. Thus, for example, in developing the criticism by Brenner and Ramas of Barrett's neglect of biological reproduction, Armstrong and Armstrong (1985a, b) seek to highlight human agency and to locate it within the requirements of biological reproduction and the historically specific conditions of capitalism. On the one hand, they are concerned to recognise biological difference but without falling into the radical-feminist trap that difference necessarily means inequality. For them, it is not only very difficult to distinguish between what is socially assigned (gender) from what is biologically determined (sex), but it is also crucial to recognise that biology is not somehow outside society and history as the use of gender implies. Yet on the other hand, they demonstrate that biology is not fixed or immutable and that its history is characterised by contradictions, class divisions, resistance and women's search to control their own biological capacities, not least through various contraceptive technologies. As they write:

> Women have not passively accepted the dictates of the state, the church or men. Indeed, childbearing itself may be a form of resistance against imposed standards and against powerless conditions. Women may gain power from bearing children – power over children and men. It should not be seen only as a passive response. Women are not merely vessels. They are active in making their own history.
>
> (Armstrong and Armstrong 1985a: 31)

Hence, the Armstrongs avoid biological reductionism and determinism by recognising the importance of human agency within the historically specific conditions of capitalism (1985b: 66). However, at the same time, they wish to retain a sense of sexual difference and to reject the idea, often implicit in the use of gender, that women are capable of being the same as men. They therefore refuse to accept a simple deterministic cause-and-effect relationship between natural and socially constructed sex differences: 'That women have babies, albeit under a variety of conditions, does not necessarily mean that they will rear the children or clean the toilets. Nor does it mean that they must live in nuclear families' (ibid.: 32). Neither does it mean that women must be recruited only for segregated, insecure, poorly paid and low-status jobs. In focusing upon the agency of men and women, the Armstrongs seek to demonstrate how natural difference is drawn on, exaggerated, challenged and transformed in gender relations.

A similar argument is proposed by Connell (1983, 1985, 1987) who also discusses the way that gender is socially constructed out of biological difference through the agency of human beings. Connell rejects biological reductionism: 'The naturalisation of gender is the basic mechanism of sexual ideology' (1987: 290). He also rejects the view of society as a cultural elaboration of biological difference (for example, sex-role-socialisation theory). Instead, Connell argues that the natural world is appropriated, negated and transformed by human beings through their labour to produce a social world that is 'radically unnatural' (1987: 78). Nature and society are connected through the *practice* of human beings. This connection is not one of causation, as biological reductionists suggest, but one of 'practical relevance'. Connell argues: 'The social practices that construct gender relations do not express natural patterns, nor do they ignore natural patterns; rather they negate them in a practical transformation' (ibid.). According to Connell, since natural differences are negated and transformed through social practices, it is to the latter that research must look for an understanding of the social construction of gender relations in specific historical contexts. It is therefore necessary to focus not only empirically, but also theoretically, upon human agency, which the concept of practice necessarily presupposes. This, in turn, requires an exploration of how human beings both think and act.

Connell contends that a social theory of gender relations must go beyond a narrow focus on social structures, no matter how constraining they may be – for otherwise, analysis will inevitably lead down the path of determinism and functionalism. Instead, the power structures of capitalism and patriarchy must be analysed 'in terms of the practices that compose them' (Connell 1983: 64), which in turn, requires an exploration of subjective experience, agency and resistance. From this perspective, social structures can be seen to be constituted by, as well as a limitation on, social practice. Since all practices necessarily respond to and transform social situations, structure is merely a way of specifying how practice, over time, constrains practice (Connell 1987: 95).

In emphasising the constitution of social structures through human practice, Connell seeks to acknowledge the fluidity and recurrent potential for social transformations in gender relations that are the result of the agency of men and women. Equally, he is also concerned to explore how 'class and patriarchy are forms of structuring that can be discovered in the same practices at the same time' (Connell 1983: 77).

In asserting the importance of theorising how these different structures of power can be present simultaneously within one set of practices, Connell argues that the structures of capitalism and patriarchy are best seen as interwoven and interpenetrating.[7] Accordingly, whilst 'in theory' it is possible to conceptualise two separate power structures, 'in practice' they cannot be examined independently.[8]

Hence we can conclude that an understanding of gender inequality must incorporate a central focus on human agency and social practice. For no matter how asymmetrical, the relations of power between men and women are never completely closed or predetermined. Despite the mutually reinforcing nature of patriarchal domestic and labour-market practices, social relations between men and women and within various labour processes are always subject to renegotiation, change and possible transformation.

By remaining exclusively at a structural level, however, Walby's conceptualisation of men's domination misses the way that asymmetrical gender relations are also built on a contradictory interdependence between men and women (Burrell 1984). Her economistic focus on patriarchal exploitation results in a deterministic and exclusive focus on social structure. Male domination is thereby treated as a largely unproblematic process, which is only diluted by the countervailing pressures of capitalism. From this perspective it is impossible to explain how male domination is experienced, understood, challenged and reproduced both by men and women.

Although Walby's approach to theorising patriarchy is comparatively sophisticated, it does reflect a common problem found in feminist studies, as Hollway has commented: 'One of the puzzling things about feminists' analyses is that they stress men's power and women's lack of power as if they were immutable principles' (1983: 134). Equally, Beechey and Perkins note that recent feminist analyses present 'a gloomy depiction of women, who appear as passive victims of a series of interconnected institutions – the family, the state and the labour market' (1987: 123). These comments apply equally to the three primary analyses of gender inequality in the labour market discussed in this and the previous chapter.

Conclusion

In this chapter we have explored several feminist approaches to men's domination of the labour market. By focusing on the resistance of male-dominated labour organisations to female entry, these studies provide a valuable counter to the deterministic tendency of the Marxist-inspired theories discussed in the previous chapter. In particular, we have been concerned to examine Walby's distinctive approach to dual-systems theory in which she argues that patriarchy cannot be subsumed within capitalism, nor treated as monolithic or merely embedded in the family structure. Her view of men's power as based on six relatively autonomous structures, located historically and spatially in differentiated social and political contexts, allows for the possibility of empirical variation in the form, extent and nature of patriarchy.

However, we have criticised Walby's theory of patriarchy for its underemphasis of familial ideology and biology and for its theoretical neglect of social practices, human agency and resistance. Paradoxically, while offering a gender-sensitive critique of earlier explanations of women's labour-market subordination, Walby's approach to patriarchy produces a parallel analysis which is overly economistic and deterministic.

In seeking to avoid these problems of economism and determinism, the analysis of sex-discriminatory recruitment practices presented in this book will focus on how and why asymmetrical power relations are reproduced, rationalised and resisted through the *social practices and agency* of men and women in positions of both domination and subordination. This approach therefore will seek to examine the way that the capitalist and patriarchal concerns to control the labour process and labour market through exclusion and segregation are often embedded in the same social practices. Hence, our objective is not with establishing priority for class or gender, material or ideological analysis, but rather it is to disclose how and why managerial control and job segregation are often simultaneously interwoven and interpenetrating in the social reproduction of contemporary recruitment practices.

We are also concerned to consider how far and why, the reconstitution of job segregation through recruitment practices is a taken-for-granted and unquestioned process, for this issue remains underexplored in the Marxist-feminist literature. Suffice it to say at this point that it is important to examine the complex interrelationship between sex-discriminatory recruitment practices and the structure and ideology of the family-household system. This relationship may often be mutually reinforcing, but it is only reproduced through the agency and resistance of both men and women. Even in the context of recruitment where managerial power is usually extensive, resistance to unlawful discriminatory practices is an important factor to be explored. By retrieving the agency and resistance of both men and women from the determination of capitalist and patriarchal power structures, some of the contradictory class and gender consequences, which might arise both from male and managerial domination and from male and female resistance, can begin to be identified.

In sum, this and the previous chapter have reviewed the major theories within the Marxist-feminist literature which seek to illuminate how gender inequality in the labour market is reproduced. While revealing the importance of power relations, each of these perspectives was found to be overly deterministic in a way which neglected a full examination of the agency of management, labour, men and women. A major difficulty in examining the foregoing theories is the relative absence of empirically informed studies of the contemporary practices and ideologies of managers generally, or of concrete recruitment practices specifically. This neglect is partly a reflection of the abstract levels of theorising carried over from Marxist economism which tends to preclude empirical research.

In addition, whilst some feminists have focused on the exclusionary practices of trade unions and the male ideologies which are their condition and consequence, little corresponding attention has been given to the exclusionary practices of managers or their justifications and rationalisations. This reflects the greater priority given by some feminists to the examination of trade-union practices in controlling the supply of labour. Indeed, certain writers (for example, Thompson 1983; Brenner and Ramas 1984; Armstrong and Armstrong 1985b) have been critical of a tendency in the feminist literature to overestimate the power of organised labour in the recruitment process.[9] Such criticism suggests that, just like radical economists who overstated managerial power in the reinforcement of segmented labour markets, some feminists may ascribe too much power and intentionality to trade unions in the area of recruitment.

Although overly deterministic accounts of managerial power have to be rejected, management in most organisations do hold and seek to maintain their prerogative particularly to recruit staff (Winstanley 1986: 3). Despite extending the analysis of early segmentation theory and the female-reserve-army perspective by focusing on resistance and on patriarchal practices, feminist accounts of the reproduction of segmented labour markets have tended to present a one-sided focus on the role of organised labour in the recruitment process. In failing to attend to managerial strategy and practices, they have treated deskilling and feminisation as constant managerial imperatives. Accordingly, the extent to which the reproduction of job segregation might be an unintended consequence of pursuing other objectives rather than a highly deliberate managerial strategy has been largely ignored by feminist studies. Against this background, we now turn to another body of sociological literature which, although less gender-sensitive, has directly explored managerial recruitment practices.

Chapter three

Controlling recruitment

Introduction

In this and the next chapter we examine several sociological studies which focus specifically on the recruitment process and on the problems of power, control and conflict within the sphere of management. A key and consistent finding of this literature is that informality not only continues to pervade selection practices, but is also the major mechanism in the reproduction of sex discrimination in recruitment. Before considering in the next chapter the degree to which formalisation may be able to eliminate unlawful discrimination, we will now examine how informality often characterises recruitment channels, criteria and procedures in ways that can reinforce gender inequality.[1]

Informality in the channels of recruitment

There is considerable research evidence to demonstrate that employers, particularly in the recession, are intensifying their use of informal recruitment channels (for example, Jenkins et al. 1983; Ford et al. 1984; Maguire 1984; Bresnen et al. 1985; Winch 1985; Ford et al. 1986; Wood 1986; Fevre 1989). All of these studies suggest that informal channels reinforce management's power to influence and control labour-market practices. The research findings concentrate on (predominantly male) manual and/or routine non-manual job vacancies, where it appears that employers are extending their flexibility and control over labour by filling vacancies primarily through internal labour markets (ILM), or work-of-mouth networks (i.e. extended internal labour markets (EILM)). These two primary informal channels will now be discussed in turn.

The ILM constitutes a firm-specific internal market-place that provides an insulated boundary within which the career paths and wages of employees are protected from competition with the external market.

Ports of entry are usually limited to specific grades at the lower levels of the organisation. ILMs are most likely to emerge in monopoly firms, which have relatively stable product markets and where labour-market competition for scarce skills exists. The effects of such internal markets is to promote (upward) mobility within organisations, while reducing mobility between organisations.

Althauser and Kalleberg (1981) (cited in Dale 1985) differentiate between firm internal labour markets and occupational internal labour markets. The former refers to those ILMs which offer stable, regulated jobs, but which have no promotion opportunities. The latter consists of internal markets that require specialised knowledge and skills and that provide extensive promotion opportunities. Dale (ibid.: 12) suggests that many women in the UK, particularly those working in the public sector, are employed in jobs which offer relative security and employment, but provide few career opportunities. By excluding women from promotion opportunities, the use of segmented internal labour markets is likely to reproduce the prevailing gender divisions within the workforce.[2]

The available research[3] suggests, however, that the reproduction of job segregation is but one condition and consequence of the routine use of segmented internal labour markets. Managerial control is sustained by these informal channels in a great many other ways. From their combined research projects in the manufacturing, retailing, service and public sectors, Jenkins et al. (1983) conclude that the ILM tends to be used by recruiters as a first option. They point to the following reasons for its extensive use. First, the ILM reduces training and external advertising costs. Second, it facilitates the evaluation of candidates since their job-performance record is readily accessible to management. Third, using the ILM enhances flexibility by enabling the redeployment of staff from overmanned to 'essential' sections, thereby reducing redundancy payments. Finally, it may well contribute to stable industrial relations by establishing a 'ring-fence' agreement to satisfy the demands of trade unions (see also Jenkins 1986: 147). This illustrates how employees can invest themselves subjectively in the use of internal labour markets where systems of reward are not only available, but are also perceived to be 'fair'.

Hence, the ILM comprises a complex set of rules and regulations regarding upward mobility which can be seen as part of a system of bureaucratic control (Edwards 1979) that legitimises both the exercise of managerial power and the meritocratic ideals that reflect and reinforce the hierarchical organisational structure. Accordingly, there are important ideological control benefits accruing to management, from the rise of the ILM and the bureaucratisation of the administration and regulation of individualised staff, who subscribe to the pursuit of personal 'success' and career. Indeed, managerial prerogative in selection and the use of the ILM is usually supported and rarely challenged by labour. Trade-union representatives and their members tend to collaborate with the liberal meritocratic principles of the ILM by subscribing to the view that employees should be given first consideration for any vacancies. The only area of dispute between management and labour that tends to occur within ILM practices (apart from unlawful discrimination) concerns the relative formality and openness of procedures. While management sometimes prefers to appoint through closed procedures (Jenkins 1986), trade unions seek to render these practices more formal, open and accountable by securing the internal advertising of vacancies and the competitive application for posts by employees.

A second source of recruits highlighted by sociological research (for example, Jenkins et al. 1983; Maguire 1984; 1988; Manwaring 1984; Grieco 1987; Dick and Morgan 1987), which is even more informal than the ILM, is that relying on the recommendations of present employees for the supply and evaluation of recruits. These authors demonstrate how, in a variety of concrete ways, employers (and employees) can reap control benefits within the labour process, by insulating themselves from 'open', external labour markets through grapevine or social-network recruiting.

First, employer's control of both the labour market and labour process can be enhanced by the incorporation of the work-force into the process of organisational discipline. On the one hand, management's willingness to allow employees to participate in the recruitment process by influencing the supply of candidates is usually treated as a reward for the latter's loyalty to the organisation. This practice is therefore often understood as a benevolent, paternalistic policy which constitutes a 'perk', particularly for long-standing workers whose relatives are thereby able to enter the company. On the other hand, by guaranteeing the future work performance of recruits, employees invest their organisational status and reputation in the recommendations that they make. Accordingly, they will be concerned to ensure that their friend or relative will comply with organisational requirements. Equally, the recommendee is likely to be grateful for sponsorship and would therefore not wish to jeopardise his or her relationship with their contact inside the organisation. In addition, this recruitment strategy can facilitate the transfer of informal relations from the locality into the work-place. Consequently, as Maguire (1988: 78) discovered, supervisors can draw on local and personal knowledge about the domestic circumstances of particular employees when seeking to motivate, control and discipline them.

Second, these informal channels tend to build up employee dependencies on the organisation, thus further reducing the likelihood of worker resistance. This is especially the case when companies are located in local labour markets in which they are the major employer. As Maguire (1984) demonstrates, in a context where 51 per cent of his survey sample had one or more relatives working in the company, employees were much more reluctant to resist by withdrawing their labour and losing two or even three wage packets from the same family. This community dependence reflects and reinforces a highly paternalistic form of managerial control (Maguire 1988: 74). The 'ethics of the family firm' (Jenkins et al. 1983: 265) therefore help to stabilise industrial relations.

Stability may also be enhanced by the way that company recruitment practices can be adapted to the culture and information structures of the local community. As Grieco and Whipp (1986) have argued, it is family networks in particular which come to play a crucial role in the EILM. This network facilitates labour-market closure by limiting information about employment opportunities to members of the family (Grieco 1987: 41). By transmitting labour-market advantage to members of the family and close community, other jobseekers are thereby effectively excluded. Similarly, Maguire (1988: 83) argues that informal recruitment channels in a Northern Ireland Telecommunications company facilitated the reproduction of a work-force that was overwhelmingly Protestant. The reinforcement of sectarian divisions was therefore advantageous, not only to Protestant jobseekers, but also to management since it avoided problems of sectarian conflict often found in Northern Ireland organisations where religious denominations are more equitably mixed. Hence, as in the use of the ILM, the incorporation of labour within the recruitment process through the use of word-of-mouth recommendations is likely to generate a level of stability which is advantageous to employees and management alike.

Third, a reliance on word-of-mouth networks helps to ensure that recruits either possess, or can quickly acquire, the 'tacit skills' (Manwaring 1984; Manwaring and Wood 1985) which, although often not formally acknowledged, are essential for productive efficiency. Because of their immersion in particular working communities, candidates can demonstrate a (potential) ability to learn specific tacit knowledges passed down through successive generations of workers.

Fourth, these selection channels reduce the cost of administration by restricting the number of applicants that might otherwise be attracted by the external advertising of unskilled and semi-skilled jobs. They also limit some of the risks involved in selection decision-making by providing greater information about candidates.

Finally, informal networks can become a criterion of selection as well as a channel of recruitment by assisting management in screening out 'trouble-makers', and by ensuring that an 'acceptable' type of employee is recruited, who is stable, reliable, responsible and flexible. As will be elaborated later, 'acceptability' often becomes synonymous in practice with the 'family man', who is 'self-motivated' by financial commitments and family dependants. Jenkins et al. conclude that in the context of a predominantly white or male work-force, informal recruitment channels are likely to be detrimental to both black or female jobseekers, respectively:

> It is obvious that some groups of jobseekers – women, young workers or black ethnic minorities – regarded by some recruiters as potentially 'unstable' or 'difficult' employees, may increasingly find themselves left out in the cold of a hostile buyers' labour market.
>
> (1983: 266)

Having said that, female-dominated social networks may also serve as crucial sources of information for women seeking to return to work (Chaney 1981).

Internal search and word-of-mouth recruitment processes are thus likely to reproduce the prevailing work-force profile. In the context of either a small number of black/female employees or a larger number confined to low-status jobs, such practices might thereby constitute indirect discrimination. Whether management's control of recruitment by these informal means, which draw on and seek to harness employee commitment and contacts, is intentionally or unintentionally concerned to exclude one sex and reinforce job segregation cannot be fully explored without a corresponding consideration of the selection criteria that characterise specific recruitment exercises.

Informality in selection criteria

In his study of racism and recruitment, Jenkins (1986) highlights how employers' extensive use of informal selection criteria may result in indirect discrimination. Although his arguments are concerned primarily with race discrimination, they are equally pertinent to the position of women in the labour market.

From his interview material with managers about general recruitment practices for manual and routine non-manual vacancies in forty organisations (retail, manufacture and public-sector), Jenkins distinguishes between selection criteria of 'suitability' and 'acceptability' (ibid.: 46). The former refers to the technical and functionally specific criteria of performance, defined primarily by job requirements and measured typically by technical and educational qualifications. The latter is functionally non-specific and relates to the question of control where the emphasis 'is upon the predictable and reliable person, who will not cause management any problems' (ibid.: 49–50). The evaluation and measurement of acceptability is clearly more difficult since it involves judging the character and potential of an individual to fit in with, and conform to, organisational requirements. Selectors therefore remain concerned to evaluate the motivation and personality of candidates as well as their objective skill levels. From his empirical material, Jenkins concludes that these highly informal and implicit criteria of acceptability are of vital importance for selectors whose primary interest in recruitment, he argues, is the control of the labour process.

Since the prediction of acceptability is much more uncertain than suitability, Jenkins suggests that it is here where the operation of unlawful discrimination is most likely to occur. Through the extensive use of these implicit and nebulous criteria of acceptability, such as 'manner and attitude', 'appearance', 'maturity', 'gut feeling' and 'personality', the cultural reproduction of white male hegemony is all but guaranteed. The other acceptability criteria highlighted by Jenkins are 'labour-market history', 'speech style', 'relevant experience', 'age and marital status', 'literacy' and 'ability to "fit in"'. When these criteria are used, race discrimination is likely to result, Jenkins contends, partly because the managerial concern with control may in itself unintentionally lead to the exclusion of ethnic minorities and partly because these requirements of acceptability are likely to interact in a largely tacit and taken-for-granted process, with the ethnic stereotypes that he records. These include (ibid.: 83) 'West Indians are lazy, happy-go-lucky or slow', 'Asians are clannish and don't mix', 'West Indians have a chip on their shoulder' and 'Asians are lazy, less willing.'

Drawing on Jenkins's (1986) study, Curran (1986) argues that gender, like race, is a key aspect of acceptability, particularly because in our society, it tends to be inextricably linked with personality. Her study of clerical and retail recruitment in the North-east of England examined 101 advertised vacancies. From her research interviews with selectors, she found that they tended to prioritise highly informal acceptability criteria that, in turn, required subjective evaluations which were very susceptible to both intentional and unintentional sex discrimination. The most common required attribute overall was that of 'personal qualities' which covered such intangibles as common sense, confidence and liveliness. Relevant experience and family and domestic circumstances were also revealed to be high priorities of selectors.

Curran's research discovered that almost half of employers expressed some preference about the sex of recruits. Of those interviewed, 14 per cent preferred a male applicant, while 33 per cent favoured a female. Gender preferences were most evident in: the retail sector; and in work-places which were non-unionised, had little recent experience of recruiting, were relatively small (i.e. less than 100 employees), had no personnel function and provided little or no training in recruitment procedures. Overall, 70 per cent of the gender preferences discovered by Curran were for women. These preferences were closely linked to job characteristics such as low pay, poor promotion prospects and female-dominated work-forces and supervisory grades. They were also usually based on employers' 'common-sense stereotypes' about male bread-winners and female homemakers. This was particularly the case where selectors attributed importance to the criteria of 'family commitments, married status and dependents'. Many of the 73 per cent of respondents, who did emphasise these criteria of acceptability, tended to see young children as 'a problem' (ibid.: 49) for working mothers.[4]

Probably because this research project focused primarily on jobs sex-typed for women, Curran (ibid.: 52) also observed that 'employers in the survey were concerned only about the family commitments of female applicants'. However, it is clear from other research (for example, Nichols and Beynon 1977: 98; Blackburn and Mann 1979: 105) that the male-bread-winner specification is a parallel selection device where jobs are sex-typed for men. So, for example, in the recruitment of manual workers, Jenkins (1986: 67) reveals how 'age and married status' were used as criteria of acceptability by recruiters in order to select stereotypical male bread-winners, whose stability, maturity and motivation was believed to be assured by their harmonious family and financial responsibilities. An Employment Officer in manufacturing illustrates this point:

> Preferably twenty four to twenty five, married...they're more stable, more likely to settle into shift work. I don't like young single lads for shift work. A married man with a wife and two kids and a mortgage around his neck is more likely to stick it.
>
> (ibid.)

Jenkins, like Curran, discovered that those managers, who were concerned about this criterion in relation to women applicants, saw young family dependants as a 'definite handicap' (ibid.: 68). This suggests that particularly (but not exclusively) in male sex-typed jobs, domestic responsibilities for men are viewed *positively* because they are believed to indicate stability and motivation, but *negatively* for women since they suggest divided loyalties between home and work. Resting on the assumption that domestic work is primarily women's responsibility, these gender stereotypes were seen to inform the criteria of recruitment acceptability. It is precisely because of such vague, impressionistic and non-job-related criteria of acceptability that conventional gender stereotypes continue to be so prevalent and influential in selection decision-making. As Jenkins argues, the highly implicit and ambiguous nature of these criteria shrouds candidate evaluation and decision-making with a 'degree of mystery' that 'allows racism (and sexism) the opportunity to flourish' (ibid.: 79).

The studies discussed in this chapter provide a valuable insight into the way that sex discrimination and job segregation can be reproduced through informal recruitment channels and selection criteria. However, they are less able to illuminate the operation of selection procedures, particularly the screening and interviewing of candidates. This is because they share in common with conventional liberal studies of sex discrimination in recruitment the methodological weakness of relying exclusively on *managerial accounts* about selection. Somewhat paradoxically for sociologically based studies, rarely do they *observe* selection practices as a means of illuminating or checking the validity of accounts.

This, of course, is less problematic when merely discussing organisational recruitment channels, and is almost inevitable on a short-term project (for example, Curran 1986). However, when, as in Jenkins's study, the relationship between selection criteria and recruiter stereotyping in selection practices is intimated, but is not demonstrated empirically, analytical problems begin to emerge. Although Jenkins's study is particularly valuable in emphasising the more subtle discriminatory implications of informality in the criteria and channels of recruitment, it omits to consider a potentially rich source of empirical material concerning formal and informal social practices – namely, the selection interview and the decision-making process.

Partially acknowledging his failure to observe the procedures of selection, Jenkins (1986: 73–4) turns to the psychological literature (for example, Arvey and Campion 1982) as a means of confirming the existence of unlawful discrimination in recruitment practices. He also concedes that his research focus on general rather than specific vacancies resulted in a much lower profile for gender issues than might otherwise have been the case. This precluded, for instance, an exploration of how selectors often regard women as inherently better at certain tasks than men, and vice versa.

By relying on managerial accounts of selection, and in omitting to explore formal and informal practices or specific vacancies, Jenkins' data confine him to a detailed examination of selectors' requirements. In making no attempt to observe specific selection exercises, he is also unable to provide empirical support for the assertion that his research is primarily concerned with social practices and that managers *act* upon the stereotypes and criteria of acceptability which he records. It is one thing to argue 'very strongly' that managers 'do act upon...the stereotypes of acceptability' (Jenkins 1986: 245); it is quite another to illustrate this empirically.[5]

Theoretically, Jenkins justifies his methodological concentration on managerial accounts by rejecting the dualism between thought and action, thus arguing that thinking has to be defined as an (albeit unobservable) practice. Treating managers' statements as a form of action is an attempt to deflect potential criticisms of the failure to observe practices directly. Yet it raises as many difficulties as it resolves. Most important is the sense in which assertion or accounts frequently involve a subjective rationalisation and legitimation of action rather than an accurate report of events. Consequently, there is no way of identifying *discrepancies* between respondents' accounts and their *practices*. To do so would require both the observation of selection practices, and a theorisation of human agency.[6]

Three other sociological studies which have gone beyond an empirical focus on managerial accounts of selection channels and criteria to observe and examine screening, interviewing and decision-making practices will now be considered. Although these are concerned primarily with class inequality, they help to illuminate how sex discrimination can be perpetuated in recruitment procedures. Their focus on selection practices also discloses some of the complexities of human agency that have been neglected in the studies so far examined.

Informality in the interview process

In contrast to the studies explored above, which concentrate on manual and routine clerical work in the private sector, the vacancies examined in following accounts involve the comparatively higher-status, public-sector positions respectively of secondary school headteachers (Morgan et al. 1983), graduate trainee administrators in a nationalised industry (Silverman and Jones 1973, 1976) and army officers (Salaman and Thompson 1978). The degree of access secured by these researchers enables them to provide rich and detailed qualitative material highlighting the way in which informal selection criteria of acceptability pervade interviews and decision-making.[7] Accordingly, these studies are able to overcome some of the methodological weaknesses discussed earlier. A recurrent theme running through much of the data is the inconsistent, contradictory and highly impressionistic character of interview and decision-making practices.

This is particularly well illustrated by Morgan et al.'s (1983) study of secondary-school headteacher selection. Funded by the Department of Education and Science, the researchers enjoyed a privileged access to the interview and decision-making process and were able to observe recruitment procedures in some detail throughout twenty-six local education authorities.

This was complemented by research interviews with education

63

officers in fifty-nine local education authorities (LEAs) and a questionnaire sent to the remaining forty-six. In addition, primarily for comparative purposes, an external questionnaire was administered of selection practices in public bodies such as the Civil Service, Police, National Health Service and other education services. This highly intensive study concluded that the routine selection procedures and processes discovered in the LEAs were completely inadequate to their task and recommended that they be made much more systematic, structured and formalised.

Morgan et al.'s examination of interviews and of selectors' evaluations of applicants exposed a serious inconsistency and irrelevance in relation to the criteria through which candidates were eliminated at the various stages of recruitment. In the absence of a specific and detailed job description, selectors' written observations indicated that applicants could be rejected on the basis of looking 'like a big teddy bear', having a 'broad Birmingham accent' and subscribing to particular political and religious affiliations (ibid.: 56). The all-pervasive tendency for interviews to focus on the personality and background of candidates to the exclusion of job-related characteristics reflected a selection process which the researchers described as arbitrary, haphazard and highly secretive. Their study revealed that candidates were often accepted and rejected on the basis of essentially whimsical and inconsistent criteria and inferential information. The procedures adopted appeared to prioritise social and interviewing skills at the expense of evaluating those attributes more indicative of future work performance.

At the final selection stage, there was no preparation of interviewers and neither were topic areas for the interview discussed or prepared in advance. This reflected the unarticulated but widely held assumption among selectors that the very existence of standardised criteria and practices precluded the need to discuss these matters further. According to Morgan et al., final interviews, on which selection decisions were exclusively based, were characterised by a curious combination of *ad-hoc* and ritualistic procedures, where the personal-acceptability qualities of candidates were of primary concern. Rarely were issues of perceived technical competence made explicit as the evaluation of candidates was conducted through 'the different coloured filters of selectors' perceptions' (ibid.: 90). The basis of the final selection choice was 'invariably a shaky one' in which 'conjecture, hypothesis and uncertainty ruled the day' (ibid.). One important condition and consequence of these practices was the persistence of conflict between the different vested interests represented on the selection board. Morgan et al. demonstrate the heterogeneity of recruiters by revealing the political struggle between headteachers, governors and advisers over the appointment of candidates.

The empirical material presented by Morgan et al. also illustrates the way in which selectors may project their own self-image and narrow experience on to their evaluation of candidates. It was found, for example, that selectors consistently evaluated positively those candidates who had been educated at the same school as themselves. Similarly, selectors' preconceptions about the nature of the head-teacher's role were shaped largely by personal experience in which stereotypical images were primarily influenced by their own school-days or through social acquaintance with headteachers. Hence, the self-identity and the personal experience of selectors played a crucial role in structuring their evaluation of interviewees. One consequence of this was that selectors were found to disagree amongst themselves about the necessary requirements associated with a successful headship.

The specific impact on female candidates of this informal, unsystem-atic and largely unaccountable set of selection practices was explored by Morgan et al. (1983: 66–78). Statistically, the percentage of female applicants and of women appointed as headteachers was equivalent (i.e. 11 per cent). Moreover, the authors noted how the arbitrary character of decision-making affected both male and female applicants. None the less, concern about women's ability to maintain discipline in mixed schools[8] was repeatedly expressed by recruiters, while the similar ability of men was never doubted. Women needed to have 'special qualities' because 'in most selectors' eyes appointing a woman involves greater risk than appointing a man' (ibid.: 74). The evidence suggested that, paradoxically, women could be rejected for being either too author-itarian ('a tough cookie') or too soft. The authors therefore argued that 'The differential treatment of women candidates, is, in our view, one of the strongest arguments in favour of validated selection exercises' (ibid.: 77). Where current procedures were dominated by 'non-explicit, non job-related' factors, women were found to be relatively disadvantaged, not least because many more models of male head-teachers were available to selectors as the basis for stereotypical reference in selection decision-making. As they elaborated, 'Only assessment on job-related criteria can equalise not only women's opportunities, but those of men with beards, quiet voices or the wrong accent' (ibid.: 77).

The researchers concluded that the dominant characteristic of the LEA procedures was that 'nothing be made explicit' (ibid.: 152). Candidates were selected in an arbitrary, amateur and often chaotic fashion, with selectors relying upon their intuition and feel in a way which allowed preconceived stereotypes to predominate. Procedures varied between different selectors, different selection boards and different elimination stages, with decisions dependent upon taken-for-granted but unspecified views of the jobs. Hence, selection was found to be 'primarily a gamble on familiar or unfamiliar horses' (ibid.: 153).

The research findings of the next two studies extend this analysis of informality in the interview and selection process by focusing again on the way in which selectors' evaluations and decision-making tend to be based primarily on vague, impressionistic and non-job-related criteria. They also point to the connection between selector agency and self image in highlighting how the interview process can be characterised by a self-fulfilling dynamic through which (class) inequality is reproduced.

The empirical material presented by Silverman and Jones (1973, 1976) examines the graduate recruitment of trainee administrators into a large public-sector bureaucracy.

Here, interviewers were found consistently to make their judgements early on and then spend the remainder of the session confirming their negative or positive original preconceptions. Questions would be asked of favoured candidates which intimated both the rules of the game and the required answer (for example, 'Do you suffer fools gladly, Mr Fortescue?').

In explaining the different degrees of success of three specific candidates, Silverman and Jones reveal that the interview process is analogous to a game in which the rules of acceptability favour those of a particular class background. They argue that interviews are important to selectors because they can test whether a candidate is likely to 'fit in' – that is, whether they are acceptable. Their research found that candidates from a public-school background were much more likely to be successful at the interview because they knew precisely what selectors were looking for and were therefore able to present an acceptable self (Goffman 1959). Unlike other candidates, they were able to demonstrate the social skills believed by selectors to be a prerequisite for administration work.

This study is particularly distinctive because it demonstrates how the presentation and manipulation of a socially acceptable self is a routine preoccupation in the practices not just of candidates, but also of recruiters. In exploring the way in which selectors seek to account for, rationalise and reread their decisions, the authors implicitly display how the former's evaluations and stereotyped decisions are often inextricably bound up with a concern to preserve personal dignity as competent judges. The latter's evaluations of candidates were often conditioned by, and came to reflect on, the kind of person the selector perceived themselves to be.

Silverman and Jones surmise that the rationality of selection accounts may well shift over time and space.[9] Yet recruiters in this study sought to protect the 'correctness' of their decisions through a complex series of *post-facto* rationalisations. For even when selection decisions were later proved to be wrong, recruiters were found to rewrite history by recalling earlier reservations or unavailable information about the individual. By so doing, any doubt about the rationality of a decision or the 'good sense of selectors' (1973: 104) was alleviated.

Salaman and Thompson (1978) report on the observation of a three-day selection programme for army officers. They reveal that, in spite of highly formalised and bureaucratic recruitment procedures, members of the army-officer selection board operated implicit and unacknowledged class-based norms and criteria in their evaluation of candidates. Salaman and Thompson discovered that a key informal criterion of acceptability was that candidates should have 'gentlemanly qualities' (ibid.: 284). These required a style of 'leadership' that was not the result of theory and training but of 'natural, essential, aristocratic superiority' (ibid.: 285). The authors display how this crucial informal criterion contributed to the disparity between the formalised objective recruitment system and actual practice, where selectors judged candidates 'so as to achieve a final decision that was in line with their shared preference, while all the time appearing as mere executors of the formal selection process' (ibid.: 239). Selectors were also found to favour boys who were 'like themselves' (ibid.: 292). Such informal and taken-for-granted criteria of selection based on social-class attributes closely parallel those deriving from conventional gender assumptions that we explore in subsequent empirical chapters. Moreover, these criteria are not easy to detect when they are hidden beneath formal procedures. Selection interviewers in this study drew on the formal recruitment scheme to justify their preference for those who displayed a familiarity with, and a commitment to, public-school culture. The study thereby highlights the way in which interviews may be self-reproducing in perpetuating class and sex inequality even where procedures are relatively systematic and standardised. Indeed, where judgements are shaped by informal criteria and are heavily circumscribed by selectors' evaluation of the extent to which candidates either contrast, compare or identify with their own experience and perception of themselves, they almost inevitably reproduce the prevailing employment profile.

On the basis of their findings, Salaman and Thompson question whether many 'scientific' and systematic selection techniques are in themselves a sufficient condition for the establishment of accountable and meritocratic decision-making. Despite the comparative rigour and systematicity of army-officer selection practices, informal practices persisted which resulted in the perpetuation of class-based inequalities. They conclude that the various levels of subjective interpretation which pervade the recruitment process render the execution of any formalised selection scheme an 'inherently problematic enterprise' (ibid.: 289). The arguments surrounding formalisation will be examined in more detail in the next chapter.

To summarise, these three studies of managerial agency in the interview process illustrate how selection procedures and decision-making can be characterised by vague, informal and impressionistic criteria which have the self-fulfilling effect of reproducing various forms of structured inequality. This is particularly so where criteria of acceptability are prioritised since, in evaluating such qualities, selectors are most likely to project their (limited and often prejudiced) experience and self image on to their judgements. In focusing upon managerial (and candidate) practices within the asymmetrical power structure of the interview, these final three studies begin to reveal the complex nature of power, consciousness and agency in recruitment procedures.

Conclusion

This chapter has discussed the available sociological research which focuses directly on the recruitment process. The evidence suggests that management's preoccupation with labour-process control crucially shapes the channels, criteria and procedures which are used in routine selection practices. A recurrent finding of this literature is that informality continues to be the preferred option of selectors. One possible consequence of these informal and often unaccountable practices is the intended and/or unwitting reproduction of direct and indirect race and sex discrimination and thereby the reinforcement of labour-market segregation.

Underlying this preference for informality is the concern of selectors to manage the contradictory nature of organisational control. As Chapter 1 outlined, managers' claim to exclusive control of the enterprise is contradicted by their continued dependence upon the willing agency, co-operation, or at least compliance, of employees. It is this concern with employee motivation and commitment which crucially shapes selectors' preference for internal search and word-of-mouth recruitment and their prioritisation of acceptability criteria in conducting interviews and making selection decisions. Implicit in these informal practices is the recognition that neither employees nor job candidates can be reduced simply to objects of control and evaluation.

In seeking to relax control over recruitment practices, management implicitly recognises the irreducible agency (and potential resistance) of workers. The strategy of drawing on employee recommendations is thereby based on the principle of sharing control in order to regain it (Flanders 1970). Equally, the high priority attributed to acceptability criteria, seemingly regardless of the status of the job and whether candidates are attracted through internal search, word of mouth or open advertising, reflects the way in which employee discretion and (relative) autonomy remain crucial factors to production in all labour processes.

Partly because of the contradictory nature of managerial control, the recruitment strategy of informality may itself have unintended and even self-defeating consequences. These could emerge in the relationships, first, between management and labour and, second, within the managerial function itself. The use of informal channels might be counter-productive, for example, in generating a form of inertia within the organisation since candidates with vastly different but useful skills, experience and orientation may be excluded. Equally, it could reinforce collective solidarity in the work-force (Manwaring 1984: 109) by enabling employees to 'circumvent managerial prerogatives' (ibid.) through forms of communal resistance. Finally, if recommended candidates are rejected by management, the employee sponsor (particularly if they are a relative) could perceive this as an indirect criticism of themselves. Consequently, this practice again might stimulate antagonism and labour resistance within the organisation.

Much of the foregoing evidence suggests that recruiters' concentration on vague, informal and impressionistic criteria of acceptability may produce selection decisions which are less than fully rational and coherent. As the work of Morgan et al. demonstrates in particular, the use of informal criteria in the matching of candidates to jobs is likely to be an inefficient process. That this is so is especially likely where recruiters project their own self image and personal experience on to the evaluation of candidates, thus generating a self-fulfilling dynamic through which inequality is often reproduced.

In addition, the use of informal channels, criteria and procedures of selection could be counter-productive since these practices might well constitute unlawful sex and race discrimination. This may lead, first, to suitable candidates being rejected on the grounds of sex and, second, to public complaints being made against companies that are then taken to tribunal or which lead to a Formal Investigation by the EOC. Hence, for economic reasons and in order to protect the public image of organisations, some managers are likely to see advantages in eradicating informality from their recruitment practices. However, as the following chapter will now discuss, attempts to render selection practices more systematic, accountable and formal might reinforce deep-seated divisions between and within managerial functions.

Chapter four

Formalising recruitment

Introduction

Having discussed in the previous chapter the implications for equal opportunities of informal recruitment practices, we now seek to review the arguments in favour of formalisation as a strategy for eliminating unlawful discrimination in employment. These liberal recommendations usually include not only the standardised and systematic implementation of recruitment practices, but also statistical monitoring, scientific testing and the training of employees in equal-opportunity principles. In what follows, an assessment is provided of the extent to which these prescriptions find managerial support in principle and/or are effective in practice. The overall theme of the chapter is to explore the socio-economic and political barriers to formalisation within organisations incorporating a particular emphasis upon the competing divisions between personnel and line management.

The case for formalisation

There are a variety of legal and organisational measures which can be introduced in order to overcome barriers to the establishment of equal opportunities in employment. Here we concentrate attention on the recommendations produced by Jenkins (1986) since, in contrast with many others, they are based on research findings. Jenkins is particularly concerned to highlight the problems facing any attempt to secure a tribunal ruling of indirect discrimination on the question of informal recruitment practices. At present this is unlikely to be successful because of the prevailing legal definition of 'justifiability' which provides employers with a ready escape from prosecution under the anti-discrimination legislation. First, there is little likelihood of word-of-mouth practices being accepted as a 'condition or requirement' at a tribunal (as stipulated by the 1975 SDA) because they would be considered to be simply a preferred channel of recruitment. Second, the legal definition of justifiability is extremely vague and consists of 'reasons which would be acceptable to right-thinking people as sound and tolerable'. (The Court of Appeal in Ojutiku v. MSC 1982.) This definition[1] tends to be a catch-all, upon which managers can draw easily in justifying their practices as non-discriminatory.

Accordingly, Jenkins advocates the tightening-up of justifiability to include the more stringent criteria of 'unavoidable necessity' (1986: 252) combined with a greater willingness on the part of the Courts and Tribunals to accept social-science-based evidence and, following Commission for Racial Equality (CRE) proposals, the creation of a specialist Discrimination Tribunal dealing exclusively with questions of equal opportunities. To complement these legal adjustments, Jenkins outlines certain changes to organisational employment policies and practices.

Arguing that the lack of accountability of recruitment decisions is 'a major precondition' (Jenkins ibid.: 245) for the perpetuation of race and sex discrimination, he advocates the formalisation of procedures such as: the establishment of a highly visible and comprehensive equal-opportunities policy applied to the specific needs of the organisation and able to secure the active participation of other managers; detailed and meticulous monitoring and record-keeping processes and the implementation of the formalised 'professional' model of selection advocated by personnel-management textbooks.[2] In addition, Jenkins (ibid.: 167) argues that the emphasis of selection criteria must primarily be suitability rather than acceptability, where 'a candidate's personal attributes should only be relevant inasmuch as they relate to the requirements of the job in question' and where decisions are subsequently meritocratic. Despite criticising Silverman and Jones (see footnote 9, previous chapter), Jenkins (ibid.: 243) draws on their work to confirm the importance of formalisation on two counts. First, it demonstrates that recruiters will orientate their decisions to formalised and *explicit* criteria, if they are available. Second, it illustrates how criteria of acceptability are almost guaranteed to result in ambiguity, uncertainty and confusion.[3]

Jenkins recognises that the relative managerial power, ideology and status of the personnel profession has a particularly crucial impact on selection practices and their potential to be formalised. Most textbooks (for example, Fraser 1966; Plumbley 1974; Rodger 1974; Thomason 1978; Finnegan 1983; Torrington and Chapman 1983; Torrington and Hall 1987) and other guidelines on selection emphasise that it is the professional responsibility of personnel managers to ensure that recruitment is well structured, systematic and formalised. Equally, another well-documented central element of the personnel function's professional role is to eradicate unlawful discrimination and to establish and implement equal-opportunity practices. The IPM's Equal Opportunities Code (1986: 2) emphasises that 'Personnel Managers have a special leading role in combating discrimination.' Advocates claim that these combined formalised practices, in which personnel managers play a central and influential role, are more efficient, consistent and accountable. Subscribing to the liberal meritocratic ideal of individualism, personnel-management textbooks usually advise systematic and bureaucratic procedures for the whole selection process.

Summarising this literature, Jenkins (1986: 159) identifies the following elements in the formal 'professional' approach to selection:

(1) Recruitment follows a logical and ordered sequence.
(2) Personal attributes are only treated as relevant in relation to the job requirements.
(3) Standards of 'best practice' facilitate the 'fair' and equal treatment of all candidates.
(4) The personnel profession are the guardians of 'best practice' in their adherence to formal and sound selection methods and in their ability to police the implementation of formal practices.

This professional model offers both a *technical* rationale for systematic recruitment practices, on the grounds that 'the right person will get the right job', and a *moral* rationale, since the procedures are expected to guarantee the 'fairness' of the process. Moreover, these bureaucratic procedures of formalisation are central to the personnel function's claim to technical expertise and professional management status and thus constitute part of its 'ideological armoury in its struggles for power and influence within the organisation' (Jenkins and Parker 1987: 63).

Jenkins notes a strong compatibility between the equal-opportunity interests of the CRE and EOC and personnel managers' commitment to the 'professional model of selection', for the welfare and technicist traditions in personnel work dovetail with the formalised meritocratic liberalism in which the EOC and CRE have their origins. This is partly why these equal-opportunity agencies have concentrated their promotional efforts on reinforcing the commitment of personnel specialists to formalisation. Yet despite this, informality continues to pervade much of the recruitment process. This, in turn, indicates that there might be significant barriers in the form of internal opposition and resistance to the formalisation of selection.

Barriers to formalisation

On the basis of his research, Jenkins questions the strategy of equal-opportunity agencies in seeking to promote change exclusively through influencing personnel practices since they may inadvertently be drawn into a public-relations exercise on behalf of personnel and/or corporations as a whole. In effect, through formalisation, the claim to equal opportunity can belie its substance. Not least this is because line, rather than personnel, managers tend to dominate recruitment practices generally and selection-decision-making processes in particular. Of the line manager's interviewed by Jenkins (1986: 238), 92 per cent asserted that they *should have* total responsibility for selection. Not only is it rare for organisations to operate formalised practices, he argues, but also the personnel function is largely marginal and seen as 'peripheral' to and an interference in business activities. He therefore suggests that it is 'naïve and unrealistic' to expect personnel managements to combat unlawful discrimination through formalising selection (Jenkins, ibid.: 89). The marginal role of personnel managers in recruitment is also confirmed by Curran's (1986) study in the North-East of England. She found that personnel managers usually had a 'neglible input' (ibid.: 26) into selection practices.

Jenkins concludes from his research that many personnel specialists in practice retain, at best, only a very weak commitment to the professional personnel model. Instead, he suggests, they are more likely to subscribe to a 'management model' which focuses on 'what actually happens' in recruitment in a routine, practical and 'operational' sense. This approach, which is primarily concerned to 'get the job done', is characterised by a preference for informality in recruitment practices and a generalised resistance to the 'red tape' of bureaucracy. The most important aspect of this managerial model, according to Jenkins and Parker (1987: 66), is a 'general opposition to monitoring and outside interference'.

Part of the reason for personnel specialists' predilection for this managerial model is that many are themselves ex-line managers who, as 'poachers turned gamekeepers' (Jenkins 1986: 211), have been appointed to personnel posts with primarily technical experience and thus have no allegiance to the professional personnel principles of systematic formalisation. Rather, they subscribe to the 'short-terminism' of line managers' preoccupation with control, production and profit. However, even where personnel managers do invest in, and seek to implement, a professional model, it is argued that this approach will often be undermined by the demands of the organisation (Jenkins and Parker 1987: 66).

Despite these problems, Jenkins remains heavily committed to formalisation as a means of promoting equal opportunity. Apart from the need for an additional 'political commitment' (1986: 253), he assumes that the liberal initiative of formalisation constitutes, at minimum, 'a powerful intervention against racism in employment' (ibid.: 253). Although he concedes that formalisation is not a 'panacea' (ibid.:

246–7), it is unclear from his analysis what else might be needed to eradicate unlawful discrimination.[4]

By contrast, Jewson and Mason (1984–5; 1986a, b) have questioned the exhortation to greater formality in selection, not only by Jenkins, but also by bodies such as the Confederation of British Industry, CRE, EOC and IPM. While Jewson and Mason concede that formalisation may reduce discrimination 'under certain circumstances' (1986b: 43), they reject the view that this *necessarily* guarantees fairness and efficiency, and indeed suggest that its consequence may be to 'entrench existing patterns of disadvantage' (1986b: 59). Their critique of these liberal prescriptions rests primarily upon an analysis of how formalisation is conditioned by organisational power and control in ways that facilitate resistance and the subversion of formal objectives.[5]

Jewson and Mason assert that formalised prescriptions are based upon a mistaken image of 'the' recruitment process. The ideal-typical unitary model of recruitment (Jenkins's 'professional model') will only ever be applicable (if at all) to the selection of certain high-status posts, such as academic, professional and upper-managerial occupations. It has to be accepted, they argue, that recruitment is essentially multivariate; it is shaped inevitably and crucially by the occupational nature of the vacancy as well as by the objectives of, and power balance between, employers and employees.

Drawing on an intensive case-study of recruitment practices,[6] Jewson and Mason highlight how various modes of selection may be operating simultaneously at different levels and in different sections of an organisation. They reveal how senior management's attempts to impose formalised procedures generated the unintended consequence of resistance from line managers at local level, who were concerned to preserve their autonomy. Jewson and Mason also display how senior management itself (including personnel managers) did not always adhere to these formalised practices when it seemed convenient not to do so. Indeed, even the Asian work-force began to see greater benefits in the old informal practices. Hence, the formalisation of rules constitutes at best only a structured guideline for selection practices. Extensive autonomy for selectors persists within these prescriptions. As Jewson and Mason write, 'Notwithstanding the appearance of solidity and permanence of formal rules, their shifting operation gives those who have control over their elucidation and application a good deal of room for manoeuvre' (ibid.: 56).

Perhaps of most importance for their critique of formalisation is the observation that on occasion it provides a means whereby managers can conceal their discriminatory practices. Jewson and Mason refer to this process, where 'the letter of the law is studiously obeyed but the outcome is not in keeping with its avowed intention', as 'circumvention by manipulation' (ibid.: 54). The danger of formalisation, then, is that managers seeking to discriminate informally and unlawfully may be furnished with a formal alibi which is very difficult to penetrate. More broadly, the authors (ibid.: 57) argue, that the 'individualistic' and meritocratic principles underlying formalisation often contribute to the perpetuation of disadvantage for both women and blacks because they reflect 'implicit assumptions about individual ambition, responsibility and autonomy' which are more deeply internalised within the white male population.

Jewson and Mason provide a critical analysis which demonstrates the dangers of formalisation and the intractable nature of informality in selection. They reject formalisation on the basis that because of prevailing power struggles within organisations, it is often subverted in practice or used to conceal and legitimise practices which are unlawful. This is certainly a valid critique of those who treat formalisation as a panacea for unlawful discrimination.

However, although it is clear that Jewson and Mason believe formalisation to be an insufficient condition for the elimination of unlawful discrimination in employment, it is by no means certain that they consider it to be even *necessary* to achieve this objective. Rather than seeking to eliminate informality, they advocate 'equality of access to...informal channels of recruitment' (1984–5: 129) (for example, leisure and informal business relationships). Yet this seems unrealistic not least because it would be far more difficult to impose such access in contrast with reducing its influence through greater formalisation.

From the standpoint of equal opportunities, the bureaucratic character of formalisation does provide the *possibility* of rendering practices more visible, accountable and systematic. This is the cornerstone of formalisation. Empirical evidence of its manipulation and subversion within organisations cannot become a justification for the wholesale rejection of the policy. And yet, while it is clear that the primary responsibility for implementing and maintaining formalised recruitment procedures is likely to remain with professional personnel managers, their role in recruitment is often found to be marginal and peripheral. Although the research findings which will be presented in Part II suggest that this attribution of marginality to the personnel profession is slightly exaggerated, it is important to recognise the difficulties under which the function often operates in organisations.

Power, knowledge and the personnel function

There is now a considerable literature documenting the marginal role of personnel managers within the organisation as a whole (for example, Braverman 1974; Watson 1977; Legge 1978, 1987; Tyson 1983, 1985;

Purcell 1985; Curran 1986; Hyman 1987). Tyson (1985) has suggested that three common 'models' characterise personnel management in the UK. These are the administrative/support; systems/reactive and business manager models.[7] The first is the most typical of all personnel roles and describes the basic and routine administrative practices conducted at local level on behalf of line managers. The second refers principally to those corporate personnel departments whose systems orientation concentrates on the creation, maintenance and monitoring of rules of work through agreed policies and procedures. The final and more recent model consists of those personnel managers who are primarily concerned to integrate their activities and objectives with top management's long-term strategic purpose. The personnel role is therefore interpreted as largely helping to achieve the company's business ends and is particularly likely to emerge where organisations are undergoing significant and frequent change. Tyson argues that changes to traditional industrial-relations patterns in the 1980s are leading to a polarisation between, and a concentration on, either the administrative-support model, on the one hand, and/or the business-manager model, on the other. In both cases, the personnel specialists' professional principles and role are compromised and marginalised, while the influence of the systems model, where the personnel function is most likely to be engaged in the construction and implementation of formalised selection practices, is reduced.

Legge (1978) has provided the most thorough account of the personnel function's (lack of) organisational power and authority. She argues that any managerial function's intraorganisational power 'derives from its ability to create dependency on the part of competing groups, for its services in controlling contingencies which the latter define as strategic to themselves and to the organisation as a whole' (ibid.: 36). She suggests that the control of these contingencies is determined by pre-existing ground rules that arise from dominant social values and ideologies. These values are expressed in terms of organisational success criteria used to measure a function's performance. Legge contends that in western society, the prevailing dominant values, which shape the definition of success, tend to be 'capitalist utilitarianism' (ibid.) measured almost exclusively in terms of financial criteria such as profit, return on capital, share prices and so on. As a consequence of these definitions, line managers tend to de-emphasise the significance of human resources and define effectiveness largely in terms of immediate financial results. An interrelated outcome of the ensuing preoccupation with costs and returns is that line managers tend to downgrade the personnel function as one which, in theory, should merely provide a service, but which, in practice, is often 'out of touch'.

In so far as organisational success is measured primarily in financial terms, the problem is one of demonstrating how personnel contributes to its general achievement. This is because in dealing with human resources and means or inputs rather than ends and outputs, the results of personnel work are often nebulous, diffuse and unquantifiable. Thus, for example, it is almost impossible to isolate and measure the specific contribution of the personnel function when its activities are fused with other functions and dispersed throughout the organisation. In addition, because other areas and divisions perform personnel functions, the work does not have the exclusivity that permits a claim to specialist expertise. Perhaps of greatest difficulty is the fact that most initiatives instigated by the personnel department have to rely for their successful implementation on the co-operation of other functions over whom it has no control. Accordingly, because it is difficult for personnel managers to demonstrate a direct and exclusive contribution to the achievement of organisational ends[8] their lack of authority and status is self-perpetuating. As Legge (ibid.: 67) puts it, personnel managers are caught in a vicious circle in which the following characteristics reinforce one another: a lack of authority – a denial of information and support – low levels of expertise and credibility – inability to demonstrate success – diminished authority and so on.

In a later paper, Legge (1987) argues that, historically, it is only when the industrial-relations aspects of personnel work have secured a high organisational profile that the power and status of the function has increased. An indicator of the perceived organisational importance of personnel, she argues, is the extent to which it has remained a gendered occupation. Legge demonstrates that since its origins in pre-First World War British factories (as 'welfare workers'), the occupation has been largely sex-typed for women. While this has reflected and reinforced the function's downgrading and marginality, the personnel department's higher profile has itself been the medium and outcome of not just the growing importance of industrial relations, but also the large-scale influx of men. In 1927, for example, 95 per cent of IPM members were women (Legge ibid.: 34), by 1950 they constituted less than half and by 1970 less than 20 per cent (ibid.: 42). As the contribution of the personnel function to the control of the labour process has been recognised, men have simultaneously entered the occupation with the consequence that women have been increasingly confined to junior personnel posts. Legge (ibid.: 47) cites Long (1984) in displaying how senior male managers often appreciate the value of a 'lady assistant' to deal with 'all the lady staff problems'. Similarly, Armstrong (1986: 39) describes how routine selection interviewing invariably continues to be attributed low status and to be the responsibility of junior female personnel managers.[9]

Hyman (1987) develops the argument that personnel managers' power is contingent upon the perceived importance of their contribution to controlling the labour process. He argues that generally, personnel specialists tend to act either as 'fire-fighters', used by production management only at moments of crisis, or as 'paper strategists' producing policy blueprints which bear little relation to operational reality. Hyman cites a recent large-scale survey of British industrial relations (Daniel and Millward 1983) which found that personnel managers were employed at only a minority of the establishments surveyed and that formal qualifications were a rarity among those practising personnel managers who were identified.

Yet despite the evidence of personnel management's weak organisational position,[10] Hyman (1987: 42) also insists that the function has played a role in facilitating the ability of capital to manage its contradictory relationship with labour. He argues that personnel management in Britain emerged out of employee 'welfare schemes' during the First World War. The provision of relatively inexpensive facilities (for example, canteens, sports clubs and so on) and 'fringe' benefits reflects a policy which pursues 'consent through contentment' (ibid.: 43). These welfare practices are designed to reinforce discipline by cultivating workers' dependence on the firm. Hence, employers may sometimes draw on personnel-management techniques in certain market conditions when seeking to resolve their contradictory requirements, which demand that workers are not only disposable and malleable, but also dependable and reliable (ibid.). This argument is also supported by Loveridge (1987: 179), who suggests that the development of personnel management has been a condition and consequence of the increasingly prevalent managerial policy of segmenting both the labour market and the labour force. Personnel specialists have been needed because of the increasing adoption of 'discriminative human resource planning and selective siting of new plants' (ibid.: 179).

Similarly, Hollway (1984a, 1985) has highlighted the historical compatibility between the production of specific psychological knowledges and the ideological requirements of the personnel function in the changing power relations and control strategies between management and labour. She exposes a mutually reciprocal relationship between psychological knowledge and attempts by personnel management to wield power. From the First World War onwards, personnel selectors have looked to psychologists for 'scientific' improvements in the efficiency of their techniques for evaluating people and jobs. These prescriptions are described by Hollway as 'technologies of the social' (1984a: 26), to which management is attracted, she argues, precisely because of the former's social-'science' legitimacy, which enhances the exercise of power, while also camouflaging it.

Hollway shows how psychologists have designed a variety of 'technologies' (that change according to the economic climate) intended to stratify, regulate, discipline and individualise employees so as to maximise productivity and profitability. In times of full employment, for example during the 1960s, the focus of psychological research shifted from selection and evaluation to training, development and the 'quality of working life'. This change directly mirrored the transformation in managerial approach from an 'autocratic' (direct control) to a more 'humanistic' (relative-autonomy) style as a result of increasing labour scarcity. The subsequent emphasis on 'developing relationships with subordinates' and on the need for managers to learn 'interpersonal' and 'social skills' thereby gained currency. The training courses of the IPM were particularly influenced by these recommendations for the effective management (and manipulation) of organisational relations. The primary intention of these technologies was to harness the agency and subjective commitment of employees by convincing them that they were in fact participating in a moral, honest and equal relationship.

Hollway's analysis therefore reveals the close relationship between changing personnel-management knowledges and actual managerial practices, which are crucially shaped by the prevailing economic and political conditions. Whilst Hollway has pointed to the *transitory* character of the knowledge base of personnel professionals, others have argued that it is not only superficial but also too generalised (Legge 1978; Armstrong 1986; Sisson 1989).

Legge suggests that standard personnel management textbooks present generalised prescriptions of 'best practice' which often rest on special-case models rendering them inappropriate to many organisational contexts. Equally, 'best practice' tends to neglect the organisational and political constraints that circumscribe any manager's ability to pursue a prescribed course of action. Legge therefore contends that the implementation of this body of knowledge, which is supposed to secure the distinctive expertise and legitimacy of the professional personnel function, is likely to be counter-productive. The irrelevance and/or inappropriateness of these generalised prescriptions generates a major credibility gap for personnel managers who seek to implement them. This inevitably reinforces the failure of personnel to advance its power, authority and status.

Sisson (1989) has recently summarised the problem facing personnel specialists as follows: 'Many personnel managers are caught in a mismatch between a pretentious abstract model of what they should be doing, and the reality of a relatively fragmented and routine set of activities which receive little recognition' (ibid.: 13). He insists that the universal prescriptions of personnel management textbooks ignore important differences that characterise the function and which emerge according to the nature, size, ownership, structure, strategy, marketplace and industrial-relations history of the specific organisation.

Against this background, it is hardly surprising that the use of psychological tests, usually sponsored by the personnel function, are treated with scepticism by many line managers. Whilst tests are often recommended by occupational psychologists, it would appear that managers are doubtful that these more formal and bureaucratic techniques offer the same degree of personal control as job interviews, particularly in relation to the assessment of acceptability criteria and candidate personality. Test designers have always claimed that the efficient use of selection tests will facilitate industrial harmony, overcome class antagonism and eradicate strikes (Evans and Waites 1981: 26). Yet in practice, 'scientific' tests themselves have been criticised for containing serious weaknesses. Hollway (1984a: 46), for example, argues that Cattell's widely used '16 PF' embodies 'essentialist' assumptions about the individual, because it assumes that personality can be objectified and rendered predictable. This ignores the multifaceted and shifting character of personality, which may change over time or in different social circumstances and relationships. Equally, Hollway argues that the 16 PF implicitly assumes white middle-class male values as its reference point. The tendency of psychological tests to incorporate sex-discriminatory elements has also been highlighted by Pearn, Kandola and Mottram (1987).

In sum, personnel managers often have difficulty in demonstrating their specific contribution to overall organisational success. As a result, recruitment practices in particular continue to be dominated by the 'managerial' model subscribed to by line management in which formalisation is rejected as unnecessary and less reliable than informal methods. It is also seen as more costly and time-consuming and likely to hinder managers' personal control of their function or department. In so far as it is not readily interpreted as functional for profits, formalisation is also viewed as damaging to their career interests.

Yet as the previous chapter described, in the absence of formalised procedures, managers' selection practices are often inconsistent, inefficient and potentially unlawful. This intramanagerial struggle is best understood as comprising two competing modes of managing the recruitment and labour process, namely 'personal' and 'bureaucratic' control (Edwards 1979). These modes of managerial control are not merely located in different historical periods in the transformation of the capitalist labour process, as Edwards suggests, for they remain simultaneously embedded, and in competition and conflict within contemporary organisations. These divisions within and between managerial functions reflect and reinforce the contradictory nature of managerial control as outlined in Chapter 1. Formalisation is therefore merely one alternative and competing mode of managerial control. Unlike personal control, formalisation is a 'top-down' form of discipline which provides senior management with the possibility of controlling some of the practices of subordinates. Its implementation will therefore tend to erode the influence of middle management and trade-union officials over the recruitment process.

Conclusion

The foregoing discussion has extended the argument of Chapter 5 to address the conflicts which may arise within the managerial structure itself over the continued use of informal practices and over attempts by the personnel function to render these procedures more formal, visible and accountable. Concerned to examine whether, and if so how, the formalisation of recruitment could be accomplished so as to overcome the detrimental consequences of informality for gender divisions, we concluded that formalisation is an important first step in increasing selector accountability by rendering practices more visible. However, given the routine operation of power and the conventional intra-managerial relations and occupational ideologies within organisations, which reflect and reinforce the subordination of professional personnel managers, there are also significant dangers associated with formalisation. In particular, it may simply become a more sophisticated means of reproducing and legitimising sex-discriminatory practices through formalised policies which are not so much implemented as subverted. Hence, the liberal prescription to formalise tends to neglect pre-existing power structures and the agency of both management and labour within the recruitment process. While the bureaucratic processes of formalisation may help to *structure* recruitment practices, they could never predetermine in a mechanical and uniform fashion the implem- entation of policy at local level.

Formalisation carries the promise of allocating the 'best' person for the job. However, this claim assumes that the future conduct and agency of job candidates can be rendered predictable. Yet the attempt to produce invariant scientific laws on which to base the formalised testing, interviewing and selecting of candidates and thereby to predict future human behaviour ignores the open, contingent, interpretative and changing character of social life and social relations. For as Mcintyre (1981) has argued, human affairs are characterised by irreducible sources of systematic unpredictability. He contends that it is impossible to predict, first, human creativity and innovation, second, the future agency of self (and therefore of 'other') with any certainty and, third, the possibility of specific contingencies in human affairs. Moreover, Mcintyre (ibid.: 92) argues that the 'indefinite reflexivity' of social life further reinforces the unpredictability of human action, which (as Hollway suggested earlier) is not conducted in a vacuum, but is always a medium and outcome of social relations. Hence, in order to predict another's actions, 'I must predict what you will predict about what I will predict about what you will predict...and so on' (ibid.). Accordingly, attempts to isolate individuals from their social relations and to evaluate them as predictable objects will always remain a highly precarious, problematic and contradictory business.

While formalisation can provide structured guidelines which might help to eliminate the most overt reliance on crude objectified stereotypes based on sex, race and class, more subtle forms of sex discrimination will require further measures. Suffice it to say here that the degree to which such policies are likely to be implemented will be determined by the nature of the power relations between, and the consciousness and agency of those engaged in, the recruitment process. We now turn in Part II of the book to an examination of the empirical research. By drawing on case-study data, we will not only examine the key issues of managerial control, job segregation and informal recruitment practices, but also explore what other measures in addition to formalisation might be necessary to eliminate sex discrimination in recruitment.

Part two

Empirical studies of sex discrimination in the recruitment process

Chapter five

Managing to recruit

Introduction

To date, the available literature on sex discrimination in the recruitment process has been criticised for its neglect of a combined analysis of power and agency. That perspective will now be elaborated and developed through an analysis of the research findings. This and the next chapter draw on data from all five sectors of the EOC research to illuminate how job segregation can be reproduced and rationalised in recruitment practices. In particular, we are concerned to disclose how managerial control, ideology and divisions can reinforce job segregation.

As the previous chapter outlined, personnel-management textbook models of formalised recruitment seek to prescribe and combine a concept of efficiency with that of social justice. These 'ideal' methods assume that the personnel department not only organises and controls recruitment procedures, but also shares the responsibility for candidate evaluation. In the conventional division of labour within the interview process, personnel managers judge candidates' behavioural/social skills in the first interview (acceptability criteria), while line managers evaluate their technical experience and potential in the second (suitability criteria). After intermanagerial dialogue, a 'professional and impartial consensus' on the merits of each candidate is expected to emerge. While in theory, line and personnel managers are assumed to share the responsibility for managing and controlling the recruitment process, in practice significant variations from this pattern were found to emerge in the research.

Case-studies are presented in this chapter which indicate that the contribution of personnel managers to routine recruitment practices is often marginal, despite the function's claims to professional competence and expertise in selection. What follows, however, is a more detailed exploration than has been presented heretofore of the typical ways in which personnel departments remain *distant* from recruitment practices and decision-making. In particular, it focuses on the importance that line managers attach to their functional autonomy. When refusing to accept the incursions of professional personnel managers, line managers often articulated a 'bread-winner ideology'[1] through which they justified claims to exclusive power over recruitment by emphasising their significant contribution to the success of the organisation as the producers of profit and wealth. This self-serving ideology reflects and reinforces line management's personal forms of control by drawing on patriarchal imagery both to insist on their prerogative over recruitment and to perpetuate the subordinate status of the personnel function.

Of the forty-five companies studied, only three[2] had no separate independent personnel department, either at corporate or local level. Yet despite this apparently pervasive presence, the study continually revealed the frequent failure of personnel managers to ensure implementation of formalised practices because they were either too *remote* at corporate level or confined to the *subordinate* service role at operational level. Accordingly, this chapter highlights the spatial and hierarchical *divisions* that were found to characterise relations between line and personnel managers in the recruitment process.

On the one hand, *corporate* personnel departments sometimes had the hierarchical power and influence, yet were too distant *geographically* from the operational level to have a direct impact on routine recruitment processes. This rendered them unable and/or unwilling to monitor closely the implementation of recruitment policy. On the other hand, *local* personnel officers were much closer to everyday practices but they tended to be excluded from selection decision-making. This was largely because they were frequently subordinate in *hierarchical status* to the line managers with whom they worked, thus leading them to avoid the 'responsibility' for final selection choices. How and why line managers resisted the incursions of corporate and local personnel specialists together with the consequences for formal and lawful recruitment practices is the focus of the following section.[3]

Resisting corporate personnel

The geographical separation between corporate personnel specialists and local line management was found to be a recurrent source of interfunctional conflict over selection practices. Typically, clashes resulted from head-office personnel's attempts to formalise and standardise selection procedures, so as to render line managers more accountable and their practices more consistent. These interventions were often perceived by line managers to be a direct challenge to their prerogative and autonomy. This dynamic is illustrated by the first case-study, which focuses on one highly profitable engineering maintenance branch of a computer manufacturer owned by a US multinational.

During the research, both the regional and branch managers launched into bitter and virulent attacks on what they called the 'anti-personnel' department at head office. To these line managers, steeped in 'practical engineering', the impersonal rules and 'theoretical' models on selection and staff appraisal issued from head office were both 'impractical' and 'insulting' to their present informal managerial practices. Their emphasis on a 'practical, personal and paternal' managerial style had been effective in resisting the incursions of

> young high-flying, ex-undergraduate personnel guys who come along with their theories that they've read in a textbook, but they haven't thought through. They're so wet behind the ears it's untrue and it shows in the way they conduct themselves.
>
> (branch manager)

The line managers prided themselves on their practical skills and experience. In their view, the introduction of formalised procedures would actually reduce managerial accountability because a manager could always claim that, regardless of the consequences, he merely followed the prescribed formal procedure, as the regional manager stated, 'that is a lovely way of walking out of responsibility'. Both managers insisted that they were already accountable through the company's financial control system and argued that in contrast to their own revenue, cost and profit targets, personnel managers had no system of accountability: 'what targets do personnel have?', the branch manager asked.

In defending this autonomy from corporate intervention, line managers drew attention to the successful record of the engineering function when contrasted with other areas (for example, sales, marketing and software). They claimed that engineering was the one function on which the rest of the organisation was dependent. Arguing that customer services was the 'best organised, most efficient, and cost effective division in the company', they saw no need for change in their formal practices, as they insisted, 'We don't abide by the rules. We live flexibly, but we're fair.' Yet, while recruitment practices were certainly flexible, the evidence suggested that they were far from fair, especially in relation to gender. This was because of the way in which criteria which prioritised acceptability qualities were often founded upon taken-for-granted gender stereotypes.

At the time of the research, these managers were seeking to recruit customer service engineers. This role was important because the company included a contractual maintenance guarantee that any mainframe or micro-terminal breakdown would be repaired or replaced within the hour. The branch manager's ideal recruit was a male bread-winner:

> It's obvious to us the sort of guy you want. He is under thirty-five, has a hefty mortgage, children and is good at his job. They're the ones who worry more. It's a terrible thing to say but it's true.

In the Northern region, two primary sources of candidates were used. The preferred channel was the 'grooming' of seventeen- to twenty-year-old school-leaver apprentices. The three-year trainee scheme covered the full range of company products as well as basic electronics. The second source of recruits was to advertise in the Press. In February 1985, the branch required three engineers quickly because of business expansion. As no trainees were available, the company advertised in the local paper. According to the branch manager, this 'guarantees a local man'. His primary selection criteria emphasised acceptability qualities: 'We're looking for people who care about the company. In this business now, the need for a genius gets less and less. What we need is a guy who's keen and will get on with the job.'

Not surprisingly given the managers' preference for men with dependants and financial commitments, with the exception of secretarial staff, the branch was completely male-dominated. All nineteen maintenance staff and seventy-eight participants on the four-year-old training scheme had been men. In the past, girls had applied to become trainees but the branch manager had always rejected them, because:

> It would be very difficult for a woman. I mean they have to be on call twenty-four hours a day. It's very difficult to send a woman out at night...with all the other restrictions. The language is a bit choice in here at times too. So it doesn't break my heart when none apply!

Any doubts concerning the sex bias in his recruiting practices were readily rationalised by the reference to physical aspects of the production process. As he put it, 'I'm not sure that a woman could do it. I think there would be real problems...asking a girl to carry some of this heavy kit.' So fundamental were his gendered assumptions that despite a high turnover of male trainees, which made recruitment a common occurrence and a serious difficulty, female candidates continued to be rejected.

In terms of our focus on sex discrimination three principal conclusions may be drawn from this case-study. First, it reveals potential organisational inefficiencies that would appear to derive from the perpetuation of labour scarcity. Second, it illustrates how line mangers will tend to resist any 'interference' from corporate personnel managers who might seek to challenge the former's personal and paternal mode of control. Finally, it demonstrates the way in which these practices and perspectives are sustained through the adherence of line managers to a 'bread-winner ideology' which insists that they are the independent, creative source of the company's well-being, upon whom all other employees are ultimately financially dependent. This ideology tends to undermine personnel managers as dependent and unproductive. When downgraded in this way, personnel managers can often be dismissed as a welfaristic soft option, whose role is best confined to administration.

Case-studies in the life-assurance industry also found extensive evidence of recruitment practices based on a bread-winner ideology. Again this was related to the status, power and autonomy of branch managers in their dealings with head-office personnel management. An example of this comparative power was evident in one of the companies where research took place when the head-office personnel department sought unsuccessfully to challenge the jealously guarded autonomy of local branch managers by introducing selection tests for the sales-force. The 'personal-profile analysis' was designed to quantify and évaluate the following key factors for sales work: dominance, influence, suitability and compliance (DISC). Basically, this attempt to formalise recruitment, introduced in order to reduce the turnover of the self-employed sales associates (around 60 per cent per annum), was met by open hostility from branch managers who saw such procedural changes as implicit criticism of their selection skills.

One manager, for example, preferred to rely on his own 'tried and tested' check-list on which he graded interviewees. This consisted of the following factors:

(1) first impressions
(2) could I work with *him*?
(3) education
(4) stable work record
(5) acceptability, e.g. experience, manners
(6) leisure activities
(7) what can *he* offer us?
(8) potential
(9) motivation
(10) does *he* want to sell, or is *he* just looking for a job?

Candidates were given a grade out of ten on each of these criteria and only those who secured a total above fifty would secure further consideration. This particular manager suggested that by contrast to his own well-tried approach to recruitment, the use of psychological tests would be no more effective than applying the principles of astrology to selection. In a similarly cynical vein, another manager remarked, 'the people who sell these tests, I'd give them a job selling insurance!' The potential reliability of such tests was easily weakened by this managerial opposition expressed as it was in an indifferent attitude to administering procedures imposed from head office. Indeed, the imposition of corporate procedures upon local practices could be self-defeating since it can generate a polarised antagonism between branch and regional managers. While the former preferred to use their own judgement based on past experience, the latter were more convinced about the reliability of psychological testing. Major conflicts tended to arise, especially when candidates supported by the branch manager were ultimately rejected by regional management because of poor test scores.

Within the life-assurance industry as a whole, it is common for branch managers to enjoy extensive autonomy over selection, appraisal and promotion. An ability to 'select winners' particularly for the salesforce, was a key factor in establishing personal prestige and future career prospects within the company. Several managers boasted about their disregard for the formal recruitment procedures recommended by head office. Thus, for example, the informal word-of-mouth recommendations of personal contacts within the industry were by far the preferred and most trusted recruitment channel by selectors in insurance. Similarly, branch managers often claimed to ignore the formal recruitment guidelines distributed by head office. They preferred to select on the basis of 'experience', 'personal judgement' and 'gut feeling'. As one put it, 'I just fly by the seat of my pants when it comes to recruitment.' In practice, however, the likely outcome of branch managers' aversion to tests, and their preference for informal sources and criteria, was the evaluation of candidates against a taken-for-granted, stereotyped ideal recruit who was white, male, married (with a wife, children and mortgage) and aged between thirty and forty: in short a 'bread-winner' image of the selectors' view of themselves and their branch. Such candidates were considered a relatively 'safe bet' because they brought with them their 'motivation to work'. The further away candidates moved from this ideal, the more likely they were to be rejected.

The failure of the corporate personnel function to impose formal recruitment practices in insurance is a clear example of its subordinate relationship to branch sales which perceives itself as the organisational bread-winner. In almost all cases examined, attempts by corporate personnel departments to formalise practices tended to generate branch line managerial resistance. At one major insurance company, it is common for head-office personnel managers to rationalise away their recurrent inability to secure the compliance of line managers to national agreements with trade unions by claiming that 'we pay our managers to manage'.[4] Personnel thereby implicitly accept the ideology promulgated by line management.

Similarly, at another insurance company, the way in which corporate personnel ignored the sex-discriminatory practices of line managers is illustrated by the following statement from one senior personnel manager. Although beginning in a highly 'progressive' tone, he finally concedes the impotence of personnel in relation to branch-manager autonomy:

> I can honestly say that if women have the right drive and ambition, there really shouldn't be anything to stop them. I'd be the first to say if I thought there was any sort of discrimination...of course we have individuals who are prejudiced against women or colour, but we can't do anything about that.

A more senior colleague elaborated the passive policy of head office on this issue:

> There are quite patently one or two of the bigger branches...where I think the manager isn't quite so keen on training female sales inspectors. But I wouldn't be looking to press because if the manager's not committed I don't feel it's the right environment for a young lady to succeed.

This paternalistic claim to 'protect' females from an antagonistic manager fails to conceal the underlying weakness of the head-office personnel department to challenge the resistance of line managers. Because of the 'bread-winner' contribution to company revenue of sales occupations, corporate personnel departments have considerable difficulty in establishing procedures that might eradicate the informal and unlawful practices of the branches and especially the larger ones.

Our research in the banking industry disclosed a parallel set of practices and personnel problems. Again, branch management asserted its independence and autonomy from corporate personnel in ways that allowed sex-discriminatory practices to prevail. At one bank, for example, the manager of the largest branch was known to be dismissive of what he called 'this sex-equality business'. Expressing his belief that young women were not motivated enough to develop a career, he stated:

> You find that you don't get the commitment from the girls. In their heart, they know it's not a career. They only want to get on for the money because they want to get married. The first year of the exams they sail through. But as soon as it gets sticky, they haven't got the motivation. It isn't really a career you see.

When asked if it was always the young men who secured career progression, he replied: 'Yes, because that's life isn't it? The woman has got to produce the baby. You can have your fun, but they have to produce the baby. There will never be any equality.' Despite contradicting the bank's formal equal-opportunity policy, these gendered assumptions were built into the manager's routine personnel practices. This was illustrated by his insistence that newly recruited women trainee clerks go on a rota for the filing and registration department to 'do a bit of leg work for the two old dears' who worked there. While quite clearly impeding the progress of female staff, this task was simply bypassed in the case of male clerical training. Ignoring an informal challenge by the branch training officer to include males on the rota, the manager rationalised his sex discrimination as follows:

(1) 'A lot of lads would feel demeaned, because they would be working with some part-time, and mostly elderly ladies.'
(2) 'The very experienced lady in charge feels as though she has better control over the girls; the lads tend to ridicule the job and everything that goes with it.'
(3) 'So my claim is I've got the best people to do the job and I've got away with it so far! The thing is it's a very mundane job.'
(4) 'Someone's got to do the job for God's sake! and she'll do it one month in four, for perhaps the first twelve months....I've done boring jobs you know, we've all done them.'
(5) 'On the cheque-book section, the lads do a lot of humping of big parcels and I have said to the girls "you wouldn't want to lift that parcel and carry it downstairs would you?" and they've said "No". "Well you want equality...!" It's a bit mean really, but it's there and it has to be said sometimes.'

These gendered assumptions influenced this manager's approach to work allocation. Thus, for example, when one female trainee complained about the unfairness of this sex-typed task, the manager simply 'had a few words with her'. While resistance on the part of the boys was enough to alleviate them of this 'demeaning' task, her opposition was interpreted as 'arrogance' since it contradicted the branch manager's sexist assumptions about women's 'natural passivity': 'If they're expressing views about what they want and don't want to do, it begins to turn you off a little bit.'

However, because the woman did not register a formal complaint, the manager continued to afford different treatment to males and females, as he explained:

I have a system that works. I have to concede that the law says I'm discriminating, but I'm insisting that I'm putting the right people there to do the job. I've got away with it so far, but it keeps raising its ugly head.

Even though the system only 'worked' for men, the personnel department preferred not to insist on change but to wait until this manager retired in four years' time. Passively accepting the situation, one of the assistant personnel managers claimed, 'With the exception of one or two older managers, the bank encourages everyone to "get on" regardless of sex.' In effect, the personnel department had relinquished responsibility for ensuring that equal opportunities were implemented in practice not least because it felt powerless to assert its authority over and above branch management. In the end, it fell back on the 'progress' of evolution to remove 'outdated' anomalies.

Although reflecting a diverse range of industries, each of these case-studies illustrates how the corporate personnel function can be too remote from everyday selection practices to secure their formalisation. Head-office personnel managers were often unable – sometimes even unwilling to try – to challenge the control and autonomy over recruitment that line (branch) managers sustained in particular through their appeal to a bread-winner ideology of strategic self-importance. This bread-winner conception of 'organisational provider' reflected and reinforced the imagery of the conventional, domestic division of labour. Equally, these assumptions sometimes reflected selectors' preference for recruits who were themselves male family bread-winners. The research evidence suggests that despite having the necessary hierarchical power and authority, some centralised personnel specialists failed to police and monitor the implementation of formal and lawful recruitment practices at the local level. We further explore these problems by examining the typical relationship between line and personnel managers at the operational level.

Controlling line managers

At local level, the technical experience, knowledge and proximity to production of line managers contributed significantly to the development of a bread-winner ideology through which their complete autonomy and control in relation to recruitment and selection decisions could be sustained and justified. As we have seen, the power of corporate personnel management to influence recruitment practices can be extremely limited. But what of local personnel specialists? Surely, they would be less remote and therefore more capable of influencing recruitment practices precisely where they took place. The research findings suggest that this was not the case – local personnel managers often preferred to relinquish responsibility for decision-making, thus leaving themselves marginal to the recruitment process. This is illustrated in the following two case-studies.

One of the most extreme examples of the marginality of local personnel to the recruitment process was found at the head office of a major multinational electronics company. Here, only three personnel managers were employed and they were not only completely excluded from interviewing but were also limited to organising the job advertisement and to selecting interviewers from the list of suitable line managers. Part of the explanation for the small-scale and marginal role of the personnel department could be attributed to the heavy engineering bias of the company culture.

The company had come to rely upon highly priced contract labour because permanent staff could not be found. At the time of the research, there were 160 vacancies in design, development, marketing and manufacture. In the previous eighteen months, 500 people had been recruited. As a result of a boom in product demand the pressure to recruit was intense so that around twenty to thirty candidates were interviewed every week. Yet the absence of personnel managers from selection created major tensions and contradictions in the recruitment process.

On the one hand, line managers complained that too much of their time was taken up with interviewing – a task for which they were not employed. Consequently, they had to be cajoled and sometimes even begged to conduct interviews. This shortage resulted in scientists and engineers interviewing candidates whose technical skills were completely different from their own. The mismatch of interviewer and candidates meant that line managers had, as one pointed out, 'to shoot in the dark. How can I assess candidates for other fields of work?' So what were intended in theory to be evaluations of technical competence in practice turned out to be no more than behavioural interviews which, paradoxically, the personnel department might well have been better equipped to perform.

On the other hand, personnel officers complained that line managers often let them down. On one day alone, for example, two serious procedural breakdowns occurred. One candidate who was ten minutes late was left waiting at reception for over an hour because his interviewer had gone for lunch. No one else was available to conduct the interview. Another interview had to be extended artificially by over twenty-five minutes because the second manager had failed to arrive. Given the severe shortage of skilled labour and the massive product demand, it was at the least surprising that the company persevered with such inefficient and to some extent chaotic selection practices. In addition, however, and particularly because they were difficult to monitor, these recruitment practices also tended to facilitate sex discrimination.

Along with other women employees and female job applicants, the assistant personnel manager had frequently been at the receiving end of extensive sex prejudice on the part of line managers. The work-force composition revealed a marked level of sex segregation. Out of a head-office labour force of 1,092, the managers and craftsmen were all men, as were, 90 per cent of the scientists/technologists, 94 per cent of both technicians/engineers and of draughtsmen and 95 per cent of supervisors. Women comprised 69 per cent of clerks, secretaries and typists.

Sex discrimination was readily discerned on conducting four interviews with line managers, who were all heavily involved in recruitment. Each of these managers stated that the pressure of work due to the time penalty clauses built into contracts was not conducive to employing women. Stress and even 'burn-out' was a severe problem on site as understaffed teams worked ten to twelve hours a day to meet deadlines. It was implied that women 'couldn't cope' and that domestic responsibilities would limit their capacity to do overtime. One manager confirmed that he always asked the 'ladies' at interview whether they considered themselves 'a career person, or are other considerations still there?' 'Other considerations' made it 'doubtful that they would stay' or that they would be 'flexible enough to be away from home'. Geographical mobility was another important working practice, to which line managers referred when seeking to justify sex-discriminatory recruitment practices. Mobility was a routine aspect of the work because of the need to install systems on site. Each manager confirmed that this question was covered in detail at interview, particularly with female candidates. The selectors' doubts about women were compounded by the possible requirement for international mobility.

During the research, a project manager interviewed a female candidate for a programmer/analyst vacancy. The assistant personnel manager was aware that he 'grinds the women into the ground. Then in his three-page report he goes to great lengths to say how totally unsuitable they are!' About this woman he wrote: 'She is a very liberated independent lady. Not at all the type who would walk two paces behind her husband. I personally would not like her working with me.' While he had earlier criticised women for not being mobile because of their subordinate domestic role, he now recommended the rejection of a woman, paradoxically, because she was too independent.

Thus, in spite of labour shortages and selection inefficiencies at this major hi-tech company, professional personnel managers continued to make only an administrative contribution to recruitment. Not only, therefore, was the recruitment process very inefficient, it also tended to facilitate the reproduction of sex-discriminatory practices. Although the female assistant personnel manager was committed to establishing formalised and meritocratic practices, she was unable to monitor recruitment because she was excluded from it. Moreover, her concerns about sex-discriminatory practices received little support from the two senior male personnel managers.[5] Of the three personnel managers, only the female assistant had any professional IPM training in formal personnel practices while her two male seniors had been appointed directly from the technical areas. This case-study demonstrates the way in which divisions within the personnel function can reinforce its organisational marginalisation and hinder attempts to establish formalised and systematic recruitment practices.[6]

In a number of respects, our final case-study in this chapter provides a summary and perhaps the clearest example of the tensions that can emerge at the operational level between personnel and line managers over selection and decision-making generally and with regard to equal opportunities in particular. It also displays the analytical importance of line managers' bread-winner ideology and the tendency of personnel managers to deny responsibility for recruitment decision-making. Like the previous case, it involves a female assistant personnel manager who is committed to equal opportunities, but who receives little support on this issue from her immediate male superior. The extensive research access provided by this company enabled the observation of all job interviews so that the empirical analysis presented here is able to reveal some of the more subtle tensions and conflicts between personnel and line managers.

At the time of the research the catering division of a major food processor was suffering a rapid decline in its three traditional bulk-purchasing product markets, which comprised: wholesalers, industrial canteens and institutions (for example, prisons, schools, hospitals). As a separate operating unit, pressures on the catering division to improve profitability were growing. Moreover, the marketing department of this division had a particularly high turnover rate of management trainees. In an attempt to introduce continuity and stability at assistant manager level, a new post of 'Assistant Advertising and Promotional Services Manager' (APSM) was created and advertised. We now follow through sequentially the selection process in regard to this post.

Selection criteria

According to the internal advertisement, the ideal recruit would have a clean driving licence, preferably A levels or degree, a minimum age of twenty-five and at least two years' experience in marketing, advertising or sales. The marketing manager outlined an additional requirement: 'the key factor is stability. I don't want somebody who wants to be chairman in five years.'

This manager and his assistant prided themselves on their 'structured and sophisticated' approach to recruitment and management generally. For them, being 'professional' meant taking a detached, rational and impersonal stance on all decision-making. They believed in a 'hard-nosed approach to business' which encompassed a concern with 'objective choices', 'economic constraints' and 'practical realities.' Yet despite their 'professional' commitment to formalised, meritocratic practices, both line managers were antagonistic to the appointment of women.

The senior manager interpreted his informal intention to appoint men as an integral part of his 'realistic professional' approach to 'managing personnel'. He considered the employment of women to be incompatible with his main priority which was the commercial success of the division measured in terms of profit and production. The poor economic results of the catering division had hardened the manager's resolve to reject all women applicants, as he outlined in the following statement:

> Through all my twenty years with [the multinational] I have always been open-minded about women. But I've had more problems with them, either getting married, getting pregnant whether they're married or not, and leaving, or if they're married their husbands move and they go with them. So there are four basic problems that make the turnover faster that I can do nothing about. Now obviously it is technically illegal to discriminate but I am basically saying this time I want a man, a male.

For his assistant, this was 'simply a matter of being practical',

> It's something we've thought about for a long time and it's not for anti-feminist reasons. But just because, a woman, if we're looking for long-term stability, she can get engaged, married, have a baby and you know .... off.

When it was suggested to him that the last three female resignations in his department were all due to frustrated career ambitions and not for domestic reasons, the assistant replied that even when women remained in employment they were still unstable, because they were too 'aggressive':

> Women tend to feel that they have to really prove themselves in front of men. There are a lot of middle-aged men in our business and you've got to get on with them. The worst thing that can happen in marketing is that this young twenty-two-year-old girl comes in and tells the sales manager 'This is what's going to happen.' Over the years men generally have been very much more successful, more stable, and we're looking for stability.

The line managers' *informal* ideal recruit was a young male bread-winner with children and financial commitments, as the assistant manager elaborated: 'This does tend to make people far more stable.

97

They can't just flit around, move house and so on.' The formal requirement of stability was thus underpinned by an informal preference for a male bread-winner.

However, in research interviews, the assistant personnel manager was highly critical of the line managers' thinking. First, she argued, 'It's a load of crap, this whole issue of stability. Men are much more likely to clear off and go for promotion. They're certainly not likely to stop any longer.' Second, she dismissed the dual requirements of stability and ambition as logically incompatible and contradictory. Third, she criticised the general indecision, confusion and prejudice of line management, pointing out how it conflicted with their claim to adopt a 'professional' approach to selection.

Given the company's public commitment to equal opportunity, it might have been expected that the assistant personnel manager would have formally confronted the line managers about either their inconsistent selection criteria or the legal and public-relations implications of their discriminatory intentions. Instead, she maintained an advisory/service approach to her dealings with the managers by relinquishing responsibility for the selection decision:

> It's up to them who they choose. I don't want to push for someone who they clearly don't want because if something goes wrong they might want me to carry the can. It's their responsibility. I'm just there to offer advice and question them about any decision that seems wrong.

She sought to preserve the 'professional' integrity of the recruitment process and her own part in it by limiting her role to one in which she would be responsible for the procedure, but not for the actual selection decisions made.

The marketing managers also sought to sustain their credibility as 'professional' managers. Indeed, they claimed a formal 'professional consensus' and 'special rapport' with the personnel manager, as the assistant line manager elaborated: 'It's rare for Lyn [personnel manager] and I to disagree. Crikey, there's something wrong if we do. We're both professionals so we shouldn't be disagreeing to any large extent.' Aware of Lyn's commitment to equal opportunities and concerned to seek her formal approval of their selection decisions, the line managers had to establish the meritocratic and professional credibility of their practices, particularly when rejecting female candidates. Accordingly, they adopted a division of labour in which the senior manager retained an 'open-minded', 'highly reasonable line' while his assistant, who was not known for outspoken prejudice, promoted the appointment of male candidates. This was intimated by the assistant manager: 'We have had some bad experiences with females. Lyn knows this. We've been very honest with her. But she's hoping I'm rather different from the marketing manager [laughs]...I'm not!' The following account of recruitment practices outlines how the line managers were able to achieve their objectives.

Internal applicants

The internal advertisement attracted applications from two women and one man. The most obvious choice was a woman who had worked in the catering advisory section of the marketing department for over two years and had a Higher National Diploma (HND) in catering management. Yet she, like the others, was rejected by the marketing manager:

> My girl here is a super girl. *She could probably do the job.* But she's courting strong, liable to get married in twelve months and 'tatty bye', where's my continuity?....I have to face up to reality and so yes, I am being completely biased in saying this time I want a man. (emphasis added)

It became obvious to this candidate during the interview that the managers were just 'going through the motions', not least because they asked several 'personal' questions such as,

- Would she be working in the long term?
- Would she stay at home or be moving in with her boy-friend?
- Would she have children if she did move in?

The line managers were able to reject this candidate because of the absence of the personnel manager and the acquiescence of the female candidate.

In November 1983, the company advertised in the local press. At this point another female trainee product manager resigned and it was decided to recruit a replacement from the influx of applications for the APSM post. Although the vacant product manager's job was evaluated at one grade higher than the APSM, the personnel specification was essentially the same. The application forms were screened by the two line managers who then presented a list of preselected candidates to the assistant personnel manager. This was broken down as set out in Table 5.1. The personnel manager approved the rejection of five women and only questioned the preselection of one male applicant who had resigned his previous job without first securing another post. Her doubts were informed by the line managers' insistence that they wanted a stable recruit. Far from being rejected, however, David L. had already been earmarked as a favourite candidate by the assistant marketing manager: 'Oh I did a bit of research on that one. I know the family and he's a good lad. Yes we should see him.' This intervention illustrated the way in which personal contacts were able to influence the manager's decision-making in the case of male applicants.

Table 5.1 The screening process

	Male	Female	Total
Applicants	36	7	43
First interview	9	2	11

First interviews

The eleven candidates were initially seen by the assistant personnel manager, and then by the assistant marketing manager. A brief examination of the job interviews with the two female candidates reveals the adverse treatment afforded the women by the line manager.

Gill K.

27 years	1977–80	Insurance clerk
single	1980–3	Production assistant
10 O levels	1983	PA advertising agency
3 A levels		

Prior to the candidate's arrival, the manager emphasised that this was merely a 'courtesy interview' because she worked for the company's advertising agency: 'Of course she might be OK but I doubt it.' His immediate post-interview evaluation illustrated his patriarchal preconceptions: 'Lovely, lovely, lovely! She was a right dolly bird wasn't she?' His doubts had been confirmed on meeting the candidate at the lift where he instantly evaluated her appearance, making sex-stereotyped prejudgements about her work history and personality:

> The way she dressed, the way she was made up. You could tell almost immediately she's just been a glorified assistant. That sort of job doesn't demand a great deal of detailed knowledge. A nice pleasant girl but I recognised the type of person she was which is why I didn't pursue some of the more detailed questions. She was a typical sort of dolly bird, the type you get in an advertising agency.[7]

This prejudgement resulted in by far the shortest interview, which the manager dominated on his own admission: 'Did you notice how I just didn't ask her so many questions as I did the other two? (men). No, I'd already decided.' The manager spent the majority of the interview talking about the company, himself and his career. His heightened sensitivity to the opposite sex of the candidate was further exemplified by the post-interview repartee between the two marketing managers:

Manager: 'Well from the rear she looked very attractive.'
Assistant: 'She weren't bad from the front either! (laughs). I fully understand her domestic arrangements now. [She had a personal relationship with the advertising manager.] Very good choice, I mean for that partic- ular function.'

But the assistant marketing managers' formal 'meritocratic' rationale for her rejection emphasised the problems of a hostile product market- place. As he stated to the assistant personnel manager, 'It's a fairly harsh business world with some pretty keen buyers. How would she face up with one of our staff managers?'

For purposes of recall, the personnel manager had marked each candidate out of ten, and had graded Gill K. as nine; the joint top mark. Her written comments were as follows:

Very neat, smartly dressed and made up. Very pleasant, confident, used to PA type work. Would be a fairly solid type who'd run the job for a while, rather than be looking elsewhere, which is what we're trying to reconcile, isn't it?

Janet H.

24 years	1981–3	Marketing assistant
single	1983	Information officer
7 O levels		
4 A levels		
BA English		

Although the line manager had previously emphasised the need to be able to work in a 'harsh business world', he now sought to reject Janet H. as 'too pushy'. Unable to dismiss her as either unambitious or unqualified, he drew on the opposite stereotype,

I am worried about her getting on with people in our business. I am always very suspicious of people who bring attaché cases full of their work and then try to push it down your throat. I don't like people overselling themselves.

Yet by contrast, the personnel manager considered Janet H. to be the best candidate: 'Lively, outgoing, very creative and capable. Everything about her was very professional.' At one research interview, the personnel manager again expressed her frustration about this sharp contrast in views:

> It's so difficult to work out what they want. One minute they want someone who is bright, lively and full of potential and initiative and the next they say 'we don't want a high flyer'. How the hell do you strike a balance?

She clearly identifies here the inconsistent demands of the line managers whose requirements would seem to vary depending on the sex of the applicant.

The short-listing meeting

At this meeting the personnel manager argued strongly that by bringing her work Janet H. 'showed initiative' and that 'she didn't push it at me'. Yet in her concern to support Janet H. without generating too much conflict with her line managers, the personnel manager accepted the rejection of Gill K. even though the latter's qualifications were better than all three short-listed males. Thus, the inclusion of by far the most qualified candidate and most impressive interviewee was secured only by sacrificing the second most qualified candidate.

Other inconsistencies in the decision-making process also emerged. Steve C. was included despite neither interviewer remembering much about him. It was felt that he had perhaps not received equal treatment because he was the first candidate. The marketing manager did not interpret Ron S.'s frustration at being 'held back' in his previous jobs as 'too pushy' nor as an indication of an unstable work commitment. Instead, his identification with male candidates led him to 'sympathise' and 'share his frustration'. Equally, the poor educational performance and unstable work history of the third male interviewee, David L., was disregarded. The lenient treatment offered to David L. reflected the existence of informal contacts between him and the manager. In contrast, Gill K. was only afforded a 'courtesy interview' despite strong recommendation from the advertising manager. The line manager openly expressed his gendered preference: 'I admit it was coloured by our views about employing females...but as you saw I ended up agreeing to see Janet H. again.'

Final interviews

Final interviews were scheduled to be conducted exclusively by the line managers. However, at this stage Janet H. withdrew. Her place was taken by a late applicant (Sue H.) whose qualifications also appeared to make her ideal for the job. She alone saw the personnel manager first. The interview and appraisal of each candidate (in the order they were seen) will now be summarised.

(1) Steve C.

26 years	1975–7	Sales assistant
married	1979–81	Audio-visual technician
5 O levels	1981–3	Relief sales representative
3 A levels		Sales representative

He did not impress at final interview. The interviewers worried that 'he could readily give in in an argument', and the marketing manager concluded, 'I'd like to see someone with a little more spark, more aggression, with a rounded personality.'

(2) David L.

25 years	HND Business Studies	
married	1980–2	Product manager
5 O levels	1983	Branch manager
1 A level		

This interview was by far the longest, lasting one and a quarter hours. The managers' attention focused on David L.'s application form, where he had stated that he wanted to be successful 'without displays of aggression towards other people'. The manager was concerned that this implied a morally based refusal to be assertive and aggressive. Only after intensive questioning was he accepted:

Marketing Manager:	I think I'm prepared to give him the benefit of the doubt because of the occasion and the nerves. In terms of appearance, presence, background, ability to do a sound job, he was the better candidate. He'd be OK with the right direction and training.'
Assistant Manager:	'There's the basis of something pretty sound there.'
Marketing Manager:	'And remember we're not looking for someone who is going to be Chairman in five years' time.... The first time that he hesitates to be critical in the right way, I'll

be down on him like a ton of bricks. Our training will concentrate on this issue.'

In justifying and reinforcing their decision, they also emphasised the strength of his handshake and his 'real enthusiasm, drive and natural ebullience'. Despite David L.'s past job instability, the assistant manager stated, 'He hinted at the first interview that he was after a bit of stability now that he's got a family.'

(3) Sue H.

25 years	BA Business Studies
single	1980–2 Export sales
12 O levels	administrator controller
3 A levels	1982 Advertising controller
OND Business Studies	

It was agreed by all three managers that Sue H. had performed well at her interviews, that she was the best-qualified candidate and had the most relevant work experience, 'obviously intelligent', 'a hard worker' and 'not at all nervous without being overconfident' (marketing manager). Yet the line managers argued that she lacked ambition and seemed 'scared stiff' of the product-manager job when it was proposed to her.

This was a highly exaggerated interpretation since she had merely stated a preference for the APSM. Indeed, it was unlikely that someone who was on the dole would reject a job that was so close to his or her own experience. This candidate in a research interview later confirmed that she would have taken the product-manager job if it had been offered.

(4) Ron S.

21 years	1979–82	Advertising clerical officer
married	1983	Telephone sales supervisor
5 O levels		
ONC Business Studies		

This interview lasted less than twenty minutes. The candidate was immediately favoured by the marketing manager as 'a very likeable, live character who had no hang-ups or complexes. An uncomplicated individual. You didn't have to dig or probe, it was all there laid out in front of you.'

The final decision

After the interviews, the two managers concluded immediately that David L. would be selected as the product manager, whilst Ron S. was an ideal APSM. This decision ignored the doubts about the former's history of employment instability and about his personality. It also disregarded the latter's age and qualifications, both of which were well under the minimum required.

However, as the recruitment exercise progressed, such inconsistencies were eradicated by redefining the key selection criteria. In effect, it became clear that the central criterion of selection was the informal and sex-discriminatory one of male bread-winner. In meeting this criterion, the perceived weaknesses of the two selected candidates had to be redefined and de-emphasised in order that line management could justify their decision on more formal grounds.

At the final decision-making meeting, the assistant line manager led the discussion and began by considering the final candidate Ron S. While all agreed that he was 'very likeable' the personnel manager concentrated on his 'intellectual limitation'. The assistant manager acknowledged that he was 'more mechanical than creative', but asserted that this was 'not crucial, as he would be operating under the strict control of us both'. This argument contrasted with his earlier reasons for rejecting Gill K.: 'She would be a very good administrator doing what she was told, but she is not creative and able to use her own initiative.' The strength of the line managers' united support for Ron S. provided the basis for the rejection of Sue H. whom the personnel manager was supporting, instead of Ron S., for the APSM.[8]

Other factors influenced this recruitment exercise not the least of which was the personnel manager's own career ambitions. Her failure to insist on the strict application of meritocratic principles reflected her concern to avoid being seen or labelled as 'unreasonable', a 'trouble-maker', or a 'loony feminist' within the paternal, informal culture of the managerial structure. The seniority of the marketing manager was particularly important since his remarks to other managers could well impact on her career prospects.[9] As a result, she chose to deny responsibility for the appointment decisions, as the dialogue during the last minutes of the meeting illustrates:

Marketing Manager: 'If you said "try the girl in the APSM", I honestly don't think Ron has the intellectual ability to do the product-manager job. So the slight edge comes down to Ron for the APSM and its just a pity the girl showed horror at the product manager's job.'

The personnel manager expressed her surprise that Sue H. had 'shown horror' because during her interview with this candidate, 'She said that marketing generally was where she wanted to work, not particularly advertising and promotion.' However, her intervention was couched in advisory terms and consequently was simply ignored by the line manager.

Marketing manager:	'Well it seems to be coming down to David and Ron, doesn't it?'
Assistant Manager:	'Well that's where you and I agreed first time, Lyn.'
Personnel Manager:	'I would be fairly torn between Ron and the girl. She is more intelligent, whilst he is more settled.'
Marketing Manager:	'Are you unhappy with Ron, Lyn?'
Personnel Manager:	'Oh no. They're very different. I liked him.'
Marketing Manager:	'Yes, so forthright. He'll do this place a power of good.'

This dialogue reveals how the line managers were able to draw Lyn into a 'consensus decision'. The personnel manager found herself forced to approve a selection decision with which she disagreed, as she outlined immediately afterwards:

> Do you see now how they just can't make decisions? I thought Sue H. was the best candidate for the APSM. She was much better intellectually than Ron S. but they didn't seem to know what they wanted: someone with 'get up and go' or someone who was stable.

Lyn's failure to resist these inconsistent practices was conditioned by her junior status as assistant personnel manager, her narrow advisory definition of the role of personnel and her primary commitment to establishing a managerial career. And yet, the evidence demonstrates that Sue H. had been judged on different and contradictory criteria from the two successful candidates. It is indeed difficult to see how a female would have had to perform in order to be appointed, without extensive and much stronger support from the personnel manager. Throughout the recruitment exercise, the line managers were able to apply selection criteria in wholly inconsistent ways to males and females. On the one hand, qualities of male attributes that were incompatible with the requirement for stability and ambition were either ignored or discounted, since it was argued that training would resolve the problem. On the other hand, attributes of women which fitted the personnel specification were either disregarded or even interpreted negatively. The very criteria used to justify the appointment of men became the reasons for the rejection of women. Indeed, if the candidates are placed on a sliding scale based on educational qualifications, the two successful candidates are shown to be at the bottom of the list, as is illustrated in Table 5.2.

Table 5.2 The candidates' highest qualifications

Candidate	Highest qualification
Sue H.	BA
Janet H.	BA
Gill K.	3 A levels (10 O levels)
Steve C.	3 A levels
David L.	1 A level/HND
Ron S.	5 O levels/ONC

The line managers were successful in excluding female candidates while simultaneously drawing upon formalised recruitment procedures and securing the personnel manager's approval, thus providing an alibi should their sex-discriminatory strategies be exposed. Having completed an exercise in 'circumvention by manipulation' (Jewson and Mason 1986b), line management were able to produce *post-facto* rationalisations in order to legitimise practices that were guided primarily by a sex-discriminatory decision made prior to the recruitment process.

To summarise, the evidence reveals that even though the assistant personnel manager was committed to efficient and meritocratic practices and was heavily involved in the selection exercise, and although the company was a declared 'equal-opportunity employer', her resistance to the informal sex-discriminatory practices of the senior marketing managers was only half-hearted. And yet, the personnel manager was aware of their intention to discriminate and of a major contradiction in the personnel specification, which required someone who was not only stable, but also ambitious. She denied responsibility for selection decision-making by providing only an advisory recruitment service. In consequence, the line managers were able to hold firm to their 'professional' and 'personal' opinion that only male bread-winners were stable, ambitious and worthy of training. To sustain this view in the complex process of candidate evaluation, they provided context-specific rationalisations which were applied in wholly inconsistent ways to men and women.

Indeed, regardless of what the candidates said or did, the line managers retained their gendered preconception that women employees were inherently unstable, while male bread-winners were stable and reliable. When the evidence contradicted this belief, the managers then switched to a concern with candidate ambition. Their success in realising objectives that contradicted the law on sex discrimination, official company policy and the formal views of the personnel manager demonstrated the degree of control exercised by the line managers over the recruitment process.

Conclusion

Each of these case-studies has reaffirmed the view presented in Part I of the book that management cannot be treated as a homogeneous, monolithic and omniscient force. They illustrate how management is characterised by heterogeneity, defensiveness and fragmentation, the politics of which can often militate against the achievement of equal opportunity. Attempts by corporate and local personnel to implement formal, accountable and lawful recruitment practices often failed because of these managerial divisions. In particular, line management resisted the intervention of personnel, resulting in the latter's marginalisation in precisely those areas – that is, recruitment – where it might have expected to be most influential. *Age* and *gender* differentials also reinforced the marginal and subordinate status of personnel managers. This was particularly so at the local level where recruitment was often perceived to be a mundane task, the responsibility for which could be allotted to assistant and junior personnel staff. While line managers tended to be older with extensive knowledge of the production process and its management, local personnel specialists involved in routine recruitment were usually younger and/or women who found it difficult to challenge the authority of experienced male line managers.

Finally, an interrelated dimension dividing personnel and line managers concerned their distinctive *control strategy and ideology.* Personnel tended to subscribe to a bureaucratic mode of control involving recruitment practices that were formal, consistent, meritocratic and accountable. By contrast, line management insisted on their autonomy and independence to select staff in their own informal way. This personal control strategy was usually strengthened by line managers' attachment to a self-sustaining occupational ideology in which they were elevated as the bread-winners and as the organisational 'providers' of production and profit. As the self-appointed organisational bread-winners, line managers typically dismissed formalisation as a bureaucratic encumbrance impeding their ability to recruit and manage production effectively. Formal procedures were seen as unnecessary, time-consuming and costly.

This bread-winner ideology could be seen as both a condition and consequence of the recruitment practices of line managers, who continually resisted the incursions and violated the formal demands of personnel specialists based at corporate or local level. Not surprisingly, there was a considerable overlap between the articulation of a bread-winner ideology and the use of informal and patriarchal selection criteria that enabled line managers to recruit in their own likeness, i.e. male bread-winners.

In practice, personnel managers often failed to take responsibility for the organisation and control of the recruitment process and, as a result, collaborated by default in the reproduction of sex discrimination. Although this failure was largely an effect of line management's demand for autonomy, it was also the outcome of internal divisions *within* the personnel specialism itself. These divisions operated along the same axes: gender, age, ideology and status. Very frequently, young women junior personnel managers could not rely on the support of their superiors when challenging the sex-discriminatory practices of line managers.

As the last case-study outlined, personnel managers may limit their own opportunities to challenge line management because of an overriding concern to secure personal and professional credibility, identity and career within the managerial structure. Just like the line managers who secured a personal and organisational sense of significance in the bread-winner ideology, personnel managers in the case-studies prioritised the protection of their identity and credibility within the organisation over and above any struggle to assert the authority of their function. Yet the paradox of this conformity and compliance was their continued marginalisation and subordination to line managers and the consequent perpetuation of both inefficient and sex-discriminatory recruitment practices. This recurrent concern to secure personal identity and its relevance for an analysis of power, control, compliance and resistance within management–worker relations is an important focus of subsequent chapters. However, we now turn to an examination of the ways in which personnel managers rationalise their collaboration in the reproduction of sex discrimination in recruitment.

Chapter six

Rationalising discrimination

Introduction

The previous chapter presented empirical evidence illustrating how personnel managers have neither the power nor the commitment to ensure that line managers' recruitment practices are formal and meritocratic. By contrast with these findings, which tend to corroborate certain earlier studies of personnel management (discussed in Chapter 4), the evidence presented below suggests that the foregoing literature exaggerates personnel specialists' marginality within the recruitment process. For in several of the case-studies researched, personnel managers, particularly at operational level, enjoyed extensive autonomy to control recruitment practices. The research also suggests that despite the professional responsibility of personnel managers to ensure equal opportunities, their practices were not always exemplary with regard to establishing visible, accountable and lawful practices. Both male and female personnel managers, in junior and more senior positions, sometimes contributed to the taken-for-granted reproduction of both highly informal selection criteria, channels and procedures and sex-discriminatory practices.

This chapter seeks to highlight three key research findings: first, the relative autonomy of some personnel managers in specific recruitment exercises; second, the practices they adopted which contributed to the reproduction of job segregation; and third, the way in which such unlawful practices were understood and explained by personnel specialists who formally embraced a professional and legal responsibility to ensure equal opportunities. Following the work of Silverman and Jones, which highlighted the routine concern of interviewers to establish the 'good sense' of selection decisions through *post-facto* rationalisations, this chapter explores the particular ways in which practising personnel managers rationalised their contribution to the reproduction of sex-discriminatory selection practices. Hence, whilst the previous chapter examined the bread-winner ideology of line managers, the following discussion explores the contrary ideological position of personnel managers who were concerned to 'explain away' sex discrimination.

Four primary and consistent rationalisations for sex discrimination reoccur in the data. On the one hand, personnel managers tended to *deny any responsibility* for sex discrimination by blaming the women themselves, 'society' generally or by emphasising how such unlawful practices were merely an unintended consequence of seeking to control the labour process and to stabilise production. On the other hand, personnel managers were only prepared to *accept some responsibility* for the reproduction of gender divisions where they could insist that their practices contained socially beneficial consequences. In both cases, these rationalisations tended to be used to deny that the practices described amounted to sex discrimination. Invariably, these rationalisations reflected and reinforced assumptions and practices which took for granted that the patriarchal division of labour at home and in employment was 'inevitable', 'normal' and 'natural'. The *agency* of personnel managers in the recruitment process and the ways in which they *reproduced* and *rationalised* informal and sex-discriminatory recruitment practices will now be illustrated by the empirical findings which are presented through the three subdivisions of recruitment channels, criteria and procedures.

Recruitment channels

Particularly in those case-studies where employers were seeking to fill manual vacancies, some personnel managers were found to exercise significant power over the recruitment process. Two examples from the hi-tech sector illustrate how the use of word-of-mouth recommendations enabled personnel managers to reinforce job segregation in their manual work-forces. The first company was a leading manufacturer of computers. Of the 2,000 workers on site, 640 were hourly paid. According to the female assistant personnel manager, the hourly paid labour force consisted of 'skilled men and semi-skilled ladies'. While the 290 men undertook four-year apprenticeships to become millers, platers, electricians, turners and fitters, the 350 women worked as assemblers, labourers, cleaners, storekeepers and in the canteen.

As the largest and most significant employer in the centre of a densely populated council-housing estate, the company received many speculative enquiries which were retained for up to two years on a waiting-list. Thus, there was no shortage of potential recruits. Even if applicants took a job elsewhere, they could still be interested in a vacancy at the company because of the proximity of the factory to many homes. Applications from friends and relatives of present employees were also encouraged because of management's concern to maintain the stability of the old paternal family firm. Indeed, it was a specific policy of the personnel department that the recommendees of employees were guaranteed an interview and would be preferred when candidates were otherwise of equal merit.

This consistent supply of informal applications provided the assistant personnel manager with extensive autonomy and discretion, which she used to maintain work-force segregation. She was responsible for the appointment of the semi-skilled female work-force, for which her primary selection requirement was that recruits must 'fit in'. Gender played a key part in her evaluation of this informal acceptability criterion. The personnel manager had been convinced that female recruits would be most compatible with the semi-skilled work-force by a recently failed attempt to integrate four young men, all of whom had been recruited through recommendation. Soon after appointment, however, each had resigned because they 'felt uncomfortable working in a female environment' (personnel manager). This recent episode was drawn on by the personnel manager to justify her acceptance of the inevitability of segregation: 'Men won't stay. That's because the work's sort of labelled as semi-skilled female.' Her view exemplified how (female) personnel managers may seek to deflect responsibility for sex-discriminatory practices on to the work-force themselves by emphasising the significance in selection of gender compatibility.

Similar patterns of job segregation characterised the employment profile of the shop-floor work-force at a company which manufactured integrated electronic circuits and transistor products. Of the 120 skilled workers on the shop-floor, only two were women, but of the 1,000 semi-skilled, only 250 were men. That so many semi-skilled men were employed was the result of a management/union agreement (the unions being the AUEW, EEPTU, GMWU) that the night shift would remain exclusively male. There were less than forty men on semi-skilled day shifts. In contrast, the five to nine evening shift consisted *exclusively* of women (over 200). These gender divisions were reflected in, and reinforced by, the channelling of male and female applicants into separate reception areas and waiting-lists as well as the maintenance of segregated personnel records. These practices were widely taken for granted and historically ingrained. For the male personnel manager, segregating the applicants by sex was merely 'a convenient way of dividing the customers up'.

The female domination of the 'twilight shift' was also maintained through the use of a waiting-list. According to the male personnel manager, the majority of recommendees and casual callers seeking evening employment were women: 'It's very popular with ladies who can come out when their husband has arrived home. That's always the longer queue. It's not because there's any sex discrimination, but basically that's where the demand is.' By focusing on the supply of labour, this manager implied that the sex segregation of jobs was the complete responsibility of the work-force itself. He thereby failed to acknowledge how company-selection practices structure and reinforce pregiven sex-segregated patterns in the labour market and domestic labour process.

While word-of-mouth practices increase management's ability to control the labour market, the selection methods adopted at one case-study company within the mail-order industry demonstrate a particularly extreme example of power and autonomy in the hands of personnel. At one of the two major mail-order companies researched, traditional selection practices for warehouse manual labour had been 'far from discerning' according to the senior head-office personnel manager. Because selection was geared to short-run seasonal market changes, speed was the primary consideration of recruiters who 'did not look closely at who was brought it. If they'd got two arms, two legs, could fit in, and do what we are asking, we'd have them.' He described this indiscriminate selection of massive numbers of temporary female pickers and packers as the 'Chinese army approach to selection'.

Picking and packing are the two central functions in the warehouse and for which a large proportion of permanent and temporary 'direct' labour is employed. *Picking* involves the selection of items required by individual agents from the many thousands offered in the catalogue, while *packing* is concerned to ensure that goods are securely and correctly parcelled and sent to the appropriate agent.

At one particular warehouse, or mill as they were known locally, new recruitment practices had been introduced that extended management's discretion by linking employees' previous work performance with future re-engagement. Since this warehouse specialised in the storing, issuing and distribution of children's toys, a 'Christmas rush' was an annual occurrence. Massive numbers of temporary workers were thereby needed each year to meet this seasonal demand. The vast majority of these temps were women, recruited primarily as pickers or packers. In the four months up to December 1983, for example, over 350 temps were hired, of whom 95 per cent were women. This was against a background of male unemployment in the region running at 18 per cent during this period.

The sex-typing of the work-force was, in part, a consequence of the recruitment methods adopted. Until 1982, previous experience of working at the warehouse guaranteed future re-employment for temps. Since then, however, by extending the amount of information about employees' performance history and by involving the line management and the Jobcentre in preselection, the personnel manager had secured much greater control over the labour market.

113

At the completion of each period of work, all temporary staff were now evaluated by their department managers. Those whose previous performance was judged to be unsatisfactory had been sifted out and placed on the 'do-not-re-employ list'. By adhering closely to the assessments of departmental managers, the personnel manager created what she defined as a 'people bank', comprising those employees whose 'satisfactory performance' ensured their re-employment. So rather than rely on the word-of-mouth recommendations of the work-force, as in the previous examples, this recruitment process was informed by the more detached assessments of line managers based on the actual work performance of temporary employees.[1] These lists of temporary and available ex-employees were held not only in the personnel department, but also at the Jobcentre. On being informed of vacancies at the warehouse, and provided with an updated 'blacklist', the Jobcentre would ring experienced temporary staff and arrange for their attendance at the warehouse as required.

Figure 6:1 The mail-order people bank

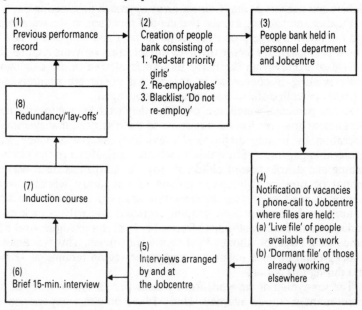

Thus, in terms of time and money, this collaboration with the Jobcentre was extremely inexpensive for the company. In effect, the personnel manager had created a tightly controlled 'reserve army' of tried and trusted temporary labour that could readily be called upon at speed and at little expense for short periods of re-employment. Those who were called first were always the 'red-star girls', whose work performance had been rated 'excellent'. Within this reservoir of available labour, therefore, was an elite 'platoon' of highly rated female staff, who were the first to be called and most used temporary workers (see Figure 6:1).

The reliance on this extremely closed system of recruitment was facilitated by the temporary and part-time nature of the vacancies, the seasonal product-market fluctuations and the relative autonomy of the personnel manager over selection and within the mill generally.[2] The personnel manager considered these practices to be more formal and efficient than previous methods and also to be more meritocratic since only those who had performed satisfactorily would be reappointed. Yet her claim of meritocracy could only be sustained if the gender consequences of these practices were ignored.

That this more systematic and standardised recruitment process was intended to ensure a female labour supply is illustrated by the following two cases where the Jobcentre was bypassed because recruits were needed at short notice. The following dialogue displays how, on such occasions, management was concerned to maintain a single-sex work-force, by drawing on its people bank reserves:

Assistant: 'Do you want pickers or packers?'
Manager: 'Could you mix them, half and half if possible? To start tomorrow night.'
Assistant: 'You don't want no men do you?'
Manager: 'No, just ladies.'

The manager explained the reason for this: 'We're choosing from our "red-star list". They are all good girls and we want to give them a chance of earning more money, plus they've got more experience.'

The second example not only displays the deep-seated nature of job sex-typing, but also confirms that the people bank did exclude some unemployed men, who would otherwise have taken picking and packing jobs. The case concerns the chance appointment of a man for packing. Despite being on the waiting-list, he only heard of the vacancies by accident. The personnel department wished to contact a 'red-star girl', who had left his number to ring because she had no telephone. By answering, he was able to insist on an interview. Desperate for any job as a stepping-stone to permanent status, he was willing to work on the packing line with sixty-one women.

Within two days of his appointment, the man was transferred to the loading bay, where heavy parcels are lifted on and off the lorries. Although he was 'pleased' to be moved, this was not due to a request by him, but rather was the decision of the female packing supervisor. She explained, 'I know I shouldn't treat anyone differently, but he just didn't look right on the packing line. I think this is a woman's job really.' Working on the loading bay, the man was quickly promoted from the status of 'packer' to 'general labourer', which entitled him to an extra £4 per week. While women were called 'warehouse assistants', men were known as 'general labourers'. Yet two of the loading-bay workers were women, whose reputation for lifting heavy loads was well known. They, however, had not been upgraded. According to the (female) line and personnel manager, this was because general-worker status required total employee flexibility to undertake tasks, some of which were specifically defined as 'fella's jobs', such as fork-lift truck driving and heavy-load lifting. The case reveals how men could be paid a higher rate for heavy lifting, even when they were not engaged in such tasks, yet women were denied the extra pay even when they did lift heavy loads. This was not treated as unfair by anyone, least of all the two women managers whose attitudes to gender sustained the practices.[3]

In addition to ensuring a female-dominated supply of labour, the people bank also benefited management by increasing its control over the labour market and labour process. First, it facilitated informal collusion between the two main mail-order companies in the town. Drawing on their increasingly detailed employee records, the personnel departments were able to warn each other of 'difficult staff'. This was usually done informally via the telephone, as the personnel manager explained: 'We can say things about ex-employees that we wouldn't dare put down on paper.' Hence, this informal means of communicating recommendations facilitated management's control over the labour market.

Second, the control over present employees was also reinforced by the people bank, as the personnel manager confirmed: 'It puts the fear of God in them. Now they know that the manager can say "we don't want so and so back", standards should improve.' The increasingly coercive character of warehouse employment impacted on all workers. The restructured recruitment process increased competition for stable jobs, both within the ranks of temps, and between aspiring temporary and permanent staff. The latter were aware of how they might easily be replaced by experienced and highly rated 'red-star' temps who aspired to permanent status. In addition to the use of the people bank, the agreement with the union to consider temporary staff first for permanent vacancies exacerbated this informal work-force competition.

The impact of the people-bank mechanism on management's control of production was illustrated at a thirty-minute induction talk to forty recruits (39 women, one male teenager) for the evening shift. A coercive message of possible sanctions and work-place regulations formed the core of the session. Married women with children in particular were warned of the company's hard line should they be absent because of domestic commitments. The personnel manager highlighted the importance of reliable time-keeping and attendance: 'If anyone falls sick or is off for any length of time, let me apologise in advance for terminating you. We're very busy at the mill and we do need the actual bodies in.'

During the short interview prior to induction, the personnel manager had spent a great deal of time questioning women with children as to their child care arrangements with neighbours and family.[4] Thus, despite recruiting from a tightly controlled labour market predominantly of married women with dependants, the management was unprepared to make any concessions to their specific needs. The personnel manager's reason for deliberately seeking to appoint only women as temps will be discussed in the following section, which concentrates on the sort of discriminatory selection criteria prioritised by personnel managers in the research project.

Selection criteria

Despite considerable evidence to the contrary, the female personnel manager in the mail-order case-study above insisted that she had no specific preference for men or women candidates. She viewed recruitment as a neutral practice, which merely reflected conventional gender divisions and assumptions, as the following statement illustrates: 'You don't find men on the packing line and you don't find ladies wanting to unload the lorries. Recruitment is about putting the right person in the right job.' She preferred to explain this job sex-typing as a consequence of the sex-segregated supply of female labour, which, so she claimed, management was powerless to influence:

The work-force tend to set the discrimination, not us. They discriminate against themselves. The women'll say, 'Oh I know it's £4 per week less than on the loading bay, but I'll have a packing job.' Whilst the men say, 'I don't want to stand on the packing line when I can get £4 more unloading the vans.' That's a man's job, you see. It's the public that set it, not us. We're quite prepared to have men on the packing line and ladies unloading the wagons if that's what they want. It's the staff who hold back.

In emphasising the voluntary choices of male and female employees, this manager denied any managerial responsibility and blamed the work-force for the reproduction of job segregation.

She also insisted that the reliance on female temporary labour was merely a *consequence* of management's main concern which was to protect production. A key priority of the personnel manager was to ensure that recruits 'fitted into' the ongoing culture of the shop-floor. Candidates' technical level of skill was considered less important than acceptability qualities such as reliable time-keeping and attendance, conscientiousness and co-operativeness. Concerned to maintain a stable and dependable work-force in the interests of continued production, the personnel manager at the warehouse was very reluctant to challenge the long-standing traditional gender segregation of the work-force. She believed that men 'just wouldn't feel comfortable working with a load of women'. Where selectors prioritise gender compatibility, job segregation often becomes a commonsensically plausible rationalisation for its own reproduction. Blaming the victim and protecting production are rationalisations which attribute the responsibility for discrimination exclusively to the work-force.

Admittedly, there is an element of truth in the claims that the 'work-force set the discrimination' by stereotyping itself within pregiven patriarchal working-class cultures[5] and that management must give first priority to maintaining a stable work-force and an organised labour process. Yet in denying responsibility, this personnel manager ignored how managerial power, practices and vested interests were heavily implicated in the reproduction of job segregation. Managerial recruitment practices did not merely reflect pre-existing gender divisions in paid and unpaid work, they also *reinforced* them. The way in which the people-bank mechanism structured the labour supply has already been discussed. Even prior to recruitment, however, a predominantly female labour supply was all but guaranteed by management's definition of these picking and packing vacancies as temporary and part-time. This was conceded by the personnel manager: 'Men just won't stick it. They're after permanent jobs.' Equally, in respect of part-time work she agreed: 'It makes sense. A man supporting a family can't do it on a part-time basis because they'd get more on the dole. A lot of part-timers are working for pin money.' Full-time pickers and packers received £76.29, while part-timers were paid £44. Work-force segregation was therefore built into job definitions that were constructed prior to the recruitment process. These gender divisions were then compounded by the people-bank recruitment mechanism.

In addition to the way in which managerial practices were implicated in the reproduction of job segregation, there were extensive vested interests for management in the use of temporary female labour. First, their lack of legal protection extended managerial flexibility. As 'peripheral' workers, these temporary employees could be disposed of when no longer needed since they were not covered by unfair-dismissal legislation. Women were recruited because of their divided responsibilities between home and work, which meant that they could be treated first and foremost as wives and mothers, easily laid off, replaced and/or re-engaged. Like the women who toiled in these same warehouses when they were cotton mills a century earlier, employees worked in unskilled, low-paid jobs that offered no security. In the middle of December 1983, for example, 346 women were dismissed with one day's notice as work began to slacken immediately before Christmas. The personnel manager explained that many of those who performed well would be re-employed in January, but it was cheaper to recruit again, rather than retain excess staff over Christmas. She was also well aware that the length of service of temporary staff did not entitle them to redundancy pay, maternity leave, sick-pay, holidays and pensions provision.

Apart from being cheap and highly flexible, the employment of women temporary workers was also advantageous to management because, according to the personnel manager, they were less of a security risk than men. Thousands of pounds worth of goods may be housed in the warehouse at any one time. Consequently, those men who were recruited to fill the new jobs requiring heavy lifting were all scrutinised for past criminal records, in order to ensure that a (male) crime ring within the staff did not emerge. As the personnel manager explained quite openly,

> In my experience it's much more likely to be the blokes who steal. So we always phone the police for all the men without fail, to ask if they've got a record. We could get done for this on the Rehabilitation Act, so publicly we say, 'Yes we do have ex-cons and are willing to take them', but in fact we definitely don't. If they've got a record, that's it straightaway.'

By predominantly employing women, the personnel manager believed that the company was minimising its potential losses resulting from work-place theft.

The personnel manager at another warehouse within the company considered that a female labour force also increased productivity, as he stated:

> Women are always better at producing in mundane jobs. They can work and talk at the same time, but men'll stop when they're talking about sport. If Ford's employed women, not men, they'd get a lot better productivity.

Rather than seek to blame the work-force for the existence of an all-female evening shift at the warehouse, this male manager preferred to highlight the *benefits* accruing to these women from management's practices. He argued that the twilight shift was a 'bargain of mutual convenience' because of the following benefits available to the temporary and part-time workers.

First, the company would 'see them right in the future' by providing more temporary labour in return for working at short notice. Second, since many of the women were wives and mothers, their family domestic commitments could then be organised around the part-time work at the warehouse. Third, the job, which did not demand a full-time or permanent commitment, would provide a valuable additional income in periods of increased spending, such as Christmas: 'It's useful for a bit of pin money to pay off some outstanding bills. But they wouldn't want to work full-time.' Fourth, according to the manager, in addition to these economic benefits, the women enjoyed the social advantages of 'meeting new people with similar interests and problems as them. It's an outlet to come and talk to their mates. It gets them out of the house after they've sorted the family's tea out.'[6] Finally, he suggested that temporary work was 'ideal' for women, because they also 'choose' to be disposable: 'some tend to get sick of it after a bit and start asking when they're to be laid off.' By emphasising the mutually reciprocal and voluntary nature of part-time jobs, the manager ignored the way in which this warehouse work was predefined as low paid, temporary, part-time, 'dead-end' and highly insecure. He also disregarded the advantages to the company in extending production throughout a highly unsocial working period. His rationalisations thereby drew on the unintended consequences of the company's practices to conceal the original motive behind these recruitment procedures.

To summarise, personnel managers' explanations for sex-discriminatory practices in the mail-order industry, which benefit or blame the victim or protect production, are based on a highly selective and partial account of these labour-market practices. In particular, such one-dimensional rationalisations, which concentrate exclusively upon supply-side factors, ignore the way in which the people-bank mechanism shaped a female labour reserve that was cheap, flexible and easily disposable. Hence, this case-study illustrates the extensive power that the personnel department *can* enjoy over the labour market and labour process and how women temporary workers can be used as a reserve army of labour.[7]

In certain sectors, personnel managers were found to declare a definite preference for men. In such instances they often tended to emphasise how the employment of women was incompatible with the production process. The vacancies examined in the following three case-studies all involved manual jobs and in each example the male personnel manager was an ex-line manager who consequently had received little training in personnel.

At a company specialising in the manufacture of office machinery, the personnel manager openly expressed a determination to preserve an all-male sales-force in the Northern region. His ideal recruit would have substantial financial responsibility because they're more likely to take the job seriously. We're looking for guys with energy who can cope with the pressures of sales work and keep reaching targets. That's why we don't employ women because of their attrition rate. Women can't take the pressure of sales. We've had four or five in the past, but their attrition rate is high, so we don't bother now.

Despite an equally high male attrition rate and regardless of the successful record of one saleswoman in another region, this personnel manager was sceptical about women's performance because they 'can't take the pressure of sales'. When obliged to interview a woman, he always 'gives them a harder time than men', as he outlined:

We come down heavier on women because we've got to see if they can take it. Most of them can't. They go out of here in tears. But it's part of the job and women have got to be able to take it.

Although his intention was to simulate market conditions, it is debatable whether such experiences of aggression and intimidation were a routine 'part of the sales job'. Rather, his intimidatory interviewing style merely reflected a preconceived scepticism about female candidates, which clearly embodied self-fulfilling consequences. In expanding the sales team from forty-two to seventy-five, the manager interviewed a number of women, but appointed none of them. Yet this 'world leader' in hi-tech office machinery was a declared 'equal-opportunity employer'.

Similar negative preconceptions about women in sales positions were expressed by a male personnel manager at a food-processing company. This company also claimed to be an 'equal-opportunity employer'. In the retail division there were seventy-three sales reps, only one of whom was a female. The division's personnel manager was an ex-salesman who recruited the field-force. He expressed a deep-seated prejudice against women applicants: 'You can publish all the legislation you like, to say that men and women are equal. They are not, they never will be, God forbid they should ever be. Emotionally they are not equal.' He considered that women were 'biologically inappropriate' for saleswork: 'Women turn over quicker. I don't know why. The emotional problems of dealing with a sales job is a bit of a burden for some of them.'

At yet another declared equal-opportunity employer, this time in the retail sector, a male corporate personnel manager conceded:

We've got a reputation in this field that I think is not totally deserved. For example in chain-store management, if I'm honest, I'd have to say we discriminate. It took us until 1982 to appoint our first female store manager. We do discriminate, I know I shouldn't say that, but we do.

Although this manager was a frequent attender of equal-opportunity training seminars, his willingness to acknowledge sex-discriminatory practices merely reflected an underlying prejudice against women. Indeed, he defended line managers' discriminatory practices on the basis of the company's history of high female turnover, which he viewed not as the outcome of employment polices, but of 'biological inevitability'. He remained cautious about the employment of three female managers, whom he viewed as 'test cases': 'They seem very good, so long as they don't go and get themselves in the family way or push off. That would kill it.' Believing that 'women are going to get married and have children, whatever the extreme feminists want them to do', his concern with equal opportunity focused almost exclusively on race:

I'm slightly ambivalent about male/female discrimination in a way that I'm not about black/white discrimination. I think there are no circumstances where you should discriminate against a black man....I think...I feel...that women are different to men. Men can't bear children and women are more likely to drop out for biological reasons. So in the trainee store scheme there's a bit of prejudice. In a situation where there's no women, this dies hard. It's still seen to be a handicap to be a woman in chain-stores.

This view is indicative of how male personnel managers, in particular, may focus on a perceived incompatibility between economic production and biological reproduction in justifying their selection preference for men.

In each of the three above cases, women were prejudged as unstable and uncommitted employees and thereby blamed for the discrimination that was perpetrated against them. The implication of these rationalisations for equal opportunities was that sex discrimination would only be eliminated when women could convince selectors that they were willing to subordinate any interest in child-rearing to the pursuit of a career – in short, to act as 'honorary men'.

The examples in this section have illustrated how the bread-winner/homemaker dichotomy often remains influential in personnel manager's informal selection criteria, either in the preference for women (for example, temporary and part-time work) or for men (for example, sales, supervisory, managerial positions). Depending on the nature of the vacancy, men or women were often considered by personnel managers to be more stable, reliable, motivated and compatible. Yet the adherence to these gendered selection criteria of acceptability was often rationalised by these managers as simply inevitable, natural and normal. The way in which such assumptions can inform selection procedures will now be discussed.

Selection procedures

These next three case-studies concentrate on the actual practices of personnel managers in specific recruitment exercises. In each case the personnel managers concerned were women. The first example examines a personnel manager's input into the screening of application forms. It is drawn from a major hi-tech firm and of all the case-studies completed in this research this is the only example of a personnel manager overruling a line manager on a selection decision.

The company was undergoing a changing sales philosophy from a 'hardware to a systems-driven approach' offering 'total solutions' for customers' business needs. Traditionally, maintenance of large mainframe systems had been carried out by the 600 all-male engineers throughout the country, who tended to be 'machine-orientated not people-orientated' (line manager). However, during 1983 and 1984 'customer-service representatives' (CSR) had been recruited to provide a rapid maintenance of the company's personal computers and word processors. If the machines could not be repaired in twenty minutes they would be replaced and taken back to the workshop to be mended. Thus, 'productivity' and 'service' were the key components of the job. The objective, according to the line manager responsible, was to achieve a '95 per cent first-time fix' and for each CSR to conduct eight calls per day. The posts were to be filled by younger, less-skilled and therefore less-costly employees than the mainframe engineers.

Shortly before Christmas 1984, the Northern region advertised four job vacancies to expand its complement of six (all male) field-service reps. The personnel specification outlined in a local evening paper advertisement was as set out in Figure 6.2.

Figure 6.2 Job advertisement

18–24 years old
A levels preferred
'presentable appearance, helpful personality, able to work independently'
'able to demonstrate a practical interest in things' and 'a keen logical analytical mind to solve simple problems quickly'.

Offering a salary of around £6,000 plus benefits and a fully equipped vehicle, the company received around 350 telephone applicants. The 336 returned application forms were screened *only by the personnel manager* on the criteria of: proximity to work-place, age, educational background and hobbies. In order to sift the applications down to twelve candidates, who would be interviewed by the young (female) personnel manager and the older (male) customer-service manager separately, the former scrutinised 'leisure and other interests' for indications of 'an interest in things technical and an interest in people'.

As a result of this screening process, all the female applications were rejected. The personnel manager openly conceded that in her 'personal opinion' women did not have the appropriate attributes for the job. Although constituting over 20 per cent of the applicants,

> Women tended to write down that they enjoyed reading and flower arranging and gave no evidence in school subjects that they were interested in things practical, such as dressmaking... something that shows that they can read instructions and interpret them and some sort of indication of dexterity.

Although the failure to display dexterity skills was given as one reason for excluding female candidates, more fundamental was the personnel manager's preconception that the job holder ought to be male since 'Women have sociable interests, not technical interests, and as such will want socially acceptable jobs and computers is not one of them.'

She also believed that women could not be flexible enough for the routine working practices which required CSR staff to start work on a different day each week. The flexibility involved in working an 'offset week' was partly necessary because machines used in retail outlets were likely to break down at peak times, such as at weekends. However, as a key selection criterion flexibility contributed to the screening out of women.[8]

The personnel manager's automatic rejection of all the female candidates was criticised by the older line manager, who was responsible for the final decision. He argued,

> Oh there were lots of women who applied. I've told Liz she's going to have to sort herself out. In future I want to interview at least two females at a time. She's wrong to see that as a filter. There's no reason why girls can't do this job successfully, because it's not technical skills that we're looking for.

The division of labour between personnel and line management in this recruitment process resulted in a fundamental breakdown of communication. While the personnel manager screened and interviewed the candidates primarily on indications of *technical* ability, the line manager conducted the second interview and made selection choices, on the basis of *behavioural* qualities. As he emphasised,

We're not looking for technical ability. The kit is all there, so all we're asking people to do is to know how to apply what is already there. More than anything I'm looking for people who come across as the type who can get on with people. They have to sort out what people's needs are.

The customer service manager was confident that, with these qualities, the three-week training programme, which covers both product technology and 'people handling', would provide recruits of either sex with all the knowledge they would need to perform the new job.

The second case-study in this section illustrates how female candidates can also be labelled and prejudged by women personnel managers at the interview process. The example focuses on three junior-clerk vacancies in the banking sector. Pre-selection was a relatively simple task, since the bank maintained a waiting-list of spec-ulative applications sent largely by school-leavers. From the list, four males and one female were chosen for interview. According to the assistant personnel manager, this sex imbalance was designed to redress the tendency in the first six months of 1984 to recruit women. The short-listed female was the sixteen-year-old sister of another junior personnel manager. While this candidate had yet to sit her nine O levels and four CSEs, the males were older and already held the following qualifications:

Age	Qualifications
17	Eight O levels plus banking experience
$17^{1}/_{2}$	Six O levels
18	Seven O levels, four A levels
19	Nine O levels, studying for three A levels

Selecting the males primarily on the basis of qualifications, the assistant personnel manager was looking for people with management potential who had a 'certain amount of confidence' and could 'organise thoughts under pressure'. Prior to the interview, she admitted quite openly to a maternal 'soft spot for lads' and argued that, generally, although girls were more mature and confident at eighteen, they were not 'as well dressed', 'slouch in the chair' and 'don't care what other people think of them'. She believed that girls tended to be over-confident, which was 'a pain in the backside. They cause you more trouble because they are so independent of thought.'[9]

By contrast, her maternalistic soft spot was displayed in a willingness to interpret the boys' greater nervousness, particularly during the five short tests that were administered, as a positive sign of how much they wanted the job.

In the event, with one candidate failing to appear and another vacancy arising in the branch, all four applicants were appointed after interviews with the personnel and branch administration manager.

The personnel manager's scepticism about women candidates was revealed in the job interview by her emphasis on the need for commitment and flexibility on the part of female, but not male applicants. As she stated to the former interviewee,

> Once you've reached grade four, you've got to be prepared to move. There are career opportunities but as I have said it depends on your own commitment and how far you see yourself going. You have to apply for promotion and you have to work very hard for it as well.

After the interviews, the personnel manager concluded, 'So we've got two future branch managers and one work-horse. The girl's a good work-horse, nothing more.' Yet her qualifications were potentially as good as, if not better than, all the male candidates, while her selection test scores were higher than two of the others. The personnel manager remained sceptical of this candidate's expressed determination to pass professional banking exams and to build a career:

> The girls tend to cop out after stage one. It's an unhappy fact...they meet the love of their life. But the boys are looking for a career. They are going to support a wife and family. They know that is the only way for them. The girls are coming for a job, very few are coming for a career.

Given her taken-for-granted understanding of women as homemakers and men as bread-winners, it is hardly surprising that the personnel manager was unwilling to challenge the branch manager's practice of placing female clerks on a filing rota (see previous chapter).

Similar inconsistencies in the evaluation of male and female interviewees by a female personnel manager were discovered in the next study. At the head office of a food manufacturer, where an internal vacancy existed for a sales-statistic controller, the female personnel manager was seeking to appoint a 'number cruncher', who would ideally be over thirty and capable of independent and speedy work. Even before the exercise began, she had automatically assumed that the recruit would be a female 'The job is quite tedious actually. It requires typing lots of bits of information into a word processor. I find that women are inherently better suited to doing repetitive, boring jobs like this one.' Four men and three women applied to the internal advertisement. The women and two of the men were lower-graded clerks, while the other two males worked on the shop-floor. These manual workers were two of many who were scheduled for redeployment as advanced technology was being introduced into the factory. With their futures uncertain, both men were attracted to the security of an office job. One in particular was optimistic about his chances, because he had been a bookmaker's clerk and therefore had experience of numerical work.

Yet despite their commitment to the job, the two shop-floor workers were evaluated as the poorest interviewees by the personnel manager. Her first explanation for this was that both were a 'bit dull'. However, when pressed, it became clear that she had rejected them because they were men, who 'wouldn't really fit in working with an oldish lady and a secretary'. Here again, the criterion of compatibility is shown to have a gendered dimension. The personnel manager expressed a concern that the men's shop-floor experience of union affairs was likely to make them 'disruptive'.

Her preconceptions about both these male candidates and her preference for a female recruit were illustrated in the way that she interpreted the result of the selection tests. These were designed to examine basic numerical skills and were intended to 'alleviate the natural prejudices that one may have in appraising the numerical ability of the shop-floor workers' (personnel manager). The results of the tests were as set out in Figure 6.3. Because these results were incompatible with the personnel manager's predefined choice of candidate, they were completely disregarded. She ignored the fact that all the men were the best performers, with the two shop-floor workers outstanding. The higher-scoring women were also rejected and the job was offered to the *lowest-scoring candidate*.

Figure 6.3 Selection test results

Female clerks	Raw score	Standardised score
1	15	60
2	10	42
3	12	48
Male clerks		
1	17	66
2	18	70
Male shop-floor workers		
1	19	72
2	22	82

The personnel manager tried to justify the decision by claiming that 'The tests are only a guide. I was worried when she actually took it because she was absolutely petrified. She was physically shaking and anxious and worried about how to fill the boxes. She just didn't settle down.' Every attempt was made to explain away the successful candidate's poor performance, yet no similar sympathetic treatment was afforded the four men, in spite of their test results:

> We had to ask ourselves 'Well what do we know about Sheila?' Common sense had to prevail. When you get an obviously wrong result like Sheila's, you've got to look for an explanation. I mean she's doing numerate work all day on a calculator. I was worried at the time that she was terribly nervous throughout. The ones she did, she got them right, it's just that she was working at an incredibly slow pace.

Finally, the personnel manager offered a moral rationalisation for the appointment of this candidate. This also indicated that the other two women, who were younger, were rejected because they might leave to have children,

> She is a spinster and her character is one of quiet confidence. She works very hard and is reliable. She is happy doing a responsible clerical job (i.e. senior sales ledger clerk). She has worked here for twenty years and has never applied for another job. She has been a steady influence on her department for twelve years. There seems to be no financial incentive involved as the salary at her present job is comparable to that of the sales-statistic clerk. This is the only job she's wanted so we shouldn't begrudge her the move. Plus *she won't want to move* on in a couple of years. (emphasis added)

This candidate was considered particularly appropriate for a 'non-career' job because her maturity suggested that she would be stable.[10] Rather than acknowledge the sex-discriminatory nature of this selection decision, the personnel manager treated these practices and rationalisations as a way of ensuring that the successful candidate received the treatment that she 'deserved'. Here again, the selection of a female is rationalised in terms of the *benefits* accruing to the woman. Yet behind these rationalisations, the personnel manager's preconceptions about the preferred sex of the jobholder had a much greater influence on her decisions than did the formalised interviewing and testing of these internal candidates.

So far, the case-studies in this chapter have illustrated that where personnel manages enjoy extensive autonomy in the screening, interviewing and decision-making process, they may also reproduce sex-discriminatory practices. Indeed, personnel managers were some-times even more discriminatory on the basis of sex than the line management whom they supported. Despite equal-opportunity personnel training and the fact that personnel managers were predominantly women, there was a strong tendency to take for granted the stereotyped assumption of men as bread-winners and women as home-makers. However, by contrast, our final case-study provides some evidence that the autonomy of personnel management, particularly if it is at the corporate level, *can* help to reduce sex discrimination in selection.

Focusing upon the internal labour market of a major bank, it shows how potentially unlawful promotion practices were successfully challenged by the combined resistance of the victim of discrimination and the corporate personnel department. The decentralised structure of the banking industry has traditionally afforded local and regional managers with extensive autonomy through which they have tended to operate a paternalistic policy towards staff (Egan 1982; Heritage 1983). This paternalistic strategy is reflected in the persistence of closed promotion procedures as a central characteristic of the ILM in the banking industry. These procedures, in turn, are highly informal and unaccountable. Accordingly, they can facilitate sex-discriminatory practices, as the following case-study illustrates.

In the spring of 1983, a new grade-three post was created at a branch where four grade-two women were employed. However, these women were overlooked. The vacancy was filled by a male grade-three from another branch. He was replaced in his old job by a male grade-two from the same branch. Because these jobs were not advertised, the women knew neither whether they had been considered, nor what the selection criteria had been. In addition, no announcement of the successful candidate was made until the change-over took place, rendering a reversal or even an investigation of the decision extremely unlikely.

Nevertheless, one of the women asked the regional personnel manager, who had conducted the exercise, whether she had been considered for either of these two vacancies. Despite the fact that in her appraisal she had been recommended for promotion, the manager stated that she had not been considered for the following three reasons:

(1) The branch manager's appraisal was not considered to be a 'cast-iron reference'.
(2) A present grade-three had to be transferred because the post needed 'someone with experience'.
(3) The other vacant grade-three post required someone with experience of that particular office routine.

In her view, these explanations were unsatisfactory because:

(1) all four grade-two women already carried out most of the tasks contained in the new grade-three vacancy;

(2) there appeared to be a contradiction between needing someone
     with experience of grade-three work to justify the transfer from
     outside, yet requiring someone with experience of the routine of
     that specific office for the subsequent internal appointment;
(3) the by-passed candidate knew the person who had been promoted
     internally from grade two to three. She was able to provide
     reasons why she was the better candidate because he had:
     (a) joined the bank after her;
     (b) been on fewer training courses;
     (c) not gained as much experience of deputising at higher
         levels;
     (d) not had a specific recommendation for grade-three on his
         last appraisal;
     (e) never attempted the banking exams.

Despite these arguments, the male regional personnel manager
reinforced his reputation for holding prejudiced views by remaining
firm in his decision. However, the complainant was a union representative at national level, and consequently she was able to contact a
corporate personnel manager who had special responsibility for equal
opportunities. Agreeing that the complainant had suffered 'a very raw
deal', and given the reputation of the regional personnel manager, the
corporate manager decided to intervene by exercising her seniority at
local level. Overturning the regional manager's decision, the corporate
personnel manager was able to ensure that the bank's formal equal-
opportunity policy, about which the organisation had received a great
deal of favourable publicity, was implemented in practice. Accordingly,
the complainant received an upgrading, because, as she put it:

> the management were afraid to go to Court and have to produce all
> this evidence about how the promotion system works. They did
> not want to be seen as a nineteenth-century Victorian employer, so
> they backed down. Promotion is totally dependent upon the
> manager's values and attitudes. No one dares to argue with him.
> He can literally do whatever he can get away with.

In the absence of her involvement in the union, it is unlikely that this
woman could or would have challenged the decision. However, her
experience of national-level negotiations provided a channel through
which to communicate her grievance to a manager with the necessary
seniority and, indeed, responsibility to resist the regional personnel
manager.[11]

Although somewhat unique in terms of the overall findings of the
research, this case-study demonstrates that personnel managers, at least

at corporate level, can and sometimes do exercise power so as to overturn sex-discriminatory practices and decisions. This is particularly likely where resistance is initiated by employees and/or trade unionists.

Conclusion

Whilst the previous chapter indicated that personnel managers are frequently marginalised by line management, the case-studies presented here have displayed that this is not always the case. However, they have also shown that where personnel specialists do enjoy some discretion and autonomy they may adhere to the managerial model of informal recruitment practices rather than adopt a professional and systematic approach to selection. At the same time, some male and female personnel managers were found to contradict the professional principles of their occupation by discriminating on the grounds of sex equally or sometimes more than their line-management counterparts. Accordingly, the empirical material also highlights the ways in which personnel managers sought to rationalise this inconsistency between professional policy and personal practice.

Both the present and the previous chapter have examined research data which exhibit at least four common and recurrent rationalisations for sex discrimination. Based primarily on one-dimensional accounts of the supply of labour, these rationalisations conceal, ignore or neglect the intentions, practices, power and vested interests of management which contribute to the reproduction of sex discrimination in recruitment. The following brief summary illustrates how each rationalisation was also designed to justify and preserve the sexual and organisational status quo.

Blaming the victim

First, managers were found to deny their responsibility for sex-discriminatory practices, while simultaneously exaggerating the choice and power of jobseekers. By emphasising supply-side factors, recruiters tended to slip into 'blaming the victim', which Ryan (1976: xiii) defines as 'justifying inequality by finding defects in the victims of inequality'. This refers to the process of 'stigmatisation' (Lee and Loveridge 1987), where characteristics are attributed to women that then become the justification for their segregated and disadvantaged position. As the case-studies illustrated, when managers required male bread-winners, it was often argued that women were 'their own worst enemy' because they were: too emotional; likely to leave for marriage or children; unreliable workers (particularly if they had children); lacked ambition, confidence, toughness and assertiveness; were not geographically mobile; were inflexible because they could not work nights or weekends and were not prepared to study in the evening and sit professional examinations. Equally, when managers wished to recruit temporary or less ambitious staff they looked to appoint female homemakers since it was believed that these workers would accept highly routinised and controlled jobs which offered only poor pay and conditions.

Blaming society

Another way in which managers denied responsibility for their own practices and economic vested interests was by claiming to be the victims of 'tradition', 'history', 'culture', 'society', 'customers', 'other workers', 'clients/intermediaries' and other managers. Blaming other social groups for the exclusion of one sex from particular jobs was invariably interrelated with the concern of selectors to appoint candidates who are seen to 'fit in' with the organisation. Against the social conditioning and values of the wider society, recruiters claimed to be powerless to intervene. Such ideological deflections of responsibility again severely under-emphasised the power of managerial practices and their perceived vested interests in the reproduction of job segregation.

Protecting production

A combined preoccupation with production and profit leads managers to seek control of the labour process and this reflects and reinforces the third ideological justification for the reproduction of job segregation. Accordingly, a recurrent explanation by personnel managers for the perpetuation of practices which have sex-discriminatory effects was that change could be destabilising for production and control. Production and management control imperatives could, therefore, be powerful and plausible justifications for continuing the exclusion of one sex from certain jobs, not least because it relieves management of responsibility for sex discrimination. As was seen in Chapter 5, the rationalisation of protecting production was an important dimension of the bread-winner ideology and has its academic counterpart in human-capital theory, which was discussed in Chapter 1 (see also Crompton and Jones 1984: 144, 147).[12]

Benefiting the victim

Only when emphasising the socially beneficial consequences of their practices were recruiters prepared to accept any responsibility for the reproduction of sex-discriminatory recruitment practices. The ideological content of benefiting the victim was usually reflected in managers' power-blind insistence on the mutuality of interests and in the tendency to draw on the unintended consequences of practices in ways that concealed or mystified their original motive. Such rationalisations were found to be interrelated with claims to be equal-opportunity employers. Thus, for example, the mail-order company discussed earlier publicly claimed to be an 'equal-opportunity employer' on the grounds that it recruited many women. This pronouncement neglected both the unlawful nature of such practices and the sort of jobs and the quality of work experience with which these female recruits were provided.

In sum, each of these four rationalisations enabled employers to deny that the foregoing recruitment practices were in fact sex discriminatory. By insisting that they were either the *victims* of conventional and historically ingrained social and gender divisions or the *protectors* of production and (female) applicants, managers could ignore, deny responsibility or conceal the way in which their recruitment practices reinforced job segregation. All of these practices have the effect of 'normalising' and 'naturalising' (Connell 1987) such sex-discriminatory practices.

Within the ranks of personnel management, the pressure to rationalise and de-emphasise the significance of discriminatory practices is particularly acute because of their public and professional commitment to establishing equal opportunities.[13] Female personnel managers might be expected to be especially concerned to combat sex discrimination, and yet, many of the managers wholeheartedly believed their ideological rationalisations for sex discrimination[14] and were also convinced of the efficiency of informal recruitment methods. Part of the reason why so many personnel specialists, of both sexes, perpetuate discriminatory assumptions and practices, we contend, is that these four rationalisations retain a certain plausibility for many of the perpetrators and victims of sex discrimination. The plausibility of these rationalisations is the result of their being grounded in *partial or half-truths* rather than outright myths. Whilst highly selective and exaggerated, these accounts are based on the social and material realities of production and reproduction.

Thus, for example, the ideology of managerial prerogative over production and recruitment (protecting production) is a distorted and exaggerated representation of the need for some form of control over the material and social relations of production. The familial ideology of the male bread-winner and female homemaker are similarly related to the conventional social organisation of domesticity and of the underlying material realities of biological reproduction and difference. It is precisely because of the 'common-sense' plausibility that gender and managerial ideologies are routinely taken for granted and reproduced through the rationalisations and practices of personnel and line managers. Although distorted, exaggerated and highly selective, these ideologies and practices have a partial truth in material and social realities.

Whilst some feminist theories prioritise gender ideology (for example, Barrett 1980), others focus on material and biological realities (for example, Brenner and Ramas 1984) in explaining the persistence of women's subordination. Few, however, seek to specify the relationship between the two.[15] An exception is Cockburn (1983: 212–13), who writes: 'Ideologies are grounded in material conditions and practices and have material effects . . . . It is the very interaction between material circumstance and ideological forces that makes any system so powerful and enduring.' However, the four rationalisations discussed above demonstrate that the interaction between material circumstance and ideological force is a highly partial one, which, although plausible, is also precarious and fragile. For example, management's claim that they do not create gender divisions since these are the product of wider social and historical forces (blaming the victim and society) retains a certain plausibility. However, the underlying denial of responsibility is exposed and fundamentally challenged by the argument that managerial practices might not *create*, but they certainly *reinforce*, gender divisions. Hence, because of their partial and selective nature, these rationalisations are highly precarious and can therefore be undermined.

The research suggests that the plausibility of these partial truths persists, despite their selectivity and precariousness, because they are not fully questioned and critically appraised. This, in turn, is due partly to management's organisational power, which tends to limit and curtail dialogue, debate and questioning such that the foregoing rationalisations are considered to be adequate explanations for discriminatory recruitment practices. It is also the result, however, of individual managers' preoccupation with preserving a stable and solid social identity.

The concern of personnel managers to secure managerial credibility and identity in the eyes of other senior managers within the organisation was found to be a crucial factor which reflected and reinforced their reproduction and rationalisation of job segregation. Research evidence presented in this and the previous chapter confirms that in their concern to be regarded as efficient and effective selectors for the organisation, personnel managers might avoid any challenge to the status quo of job segregation. They thereby elevated their organisational identity over their professional identity. In seeking to embellish self-image through the development of personal career advancement and departmental credibility, personnel managers not only failed to resist line-manager sex discrimination (Chapter 5) but also reproduced and rationalised informal and sex-discriminatory practices (Chapter 6). And yet, their prioritisation of the short-term protection of both production and profit to the neglect of professional principles of formalised and lawful recruitment practices appeared to be self-defeating since compliance merely reinforced their personal and functional subordination within the organisation.

So far, the empirical analysis has drawn on data from all five sectors of the EOC research project to demonstrate that for an understanding of the reproduction of job segregation, it is important to explore managerial *practices* and *ideologies* in the recruitment process as well as the *divisions* which fragment the function. In particular, this and the previous chapter have concentrated on the assumptions and practices of personnel managers in recruitment and in their relations with other managerial functions. The focus so far has been on external selection practices. In the next two chapters, however, we concentrate more specifically on selection practices in one industry. This enables us to examine the ways in which internal as well as external recruitment practices can contribute to the reproduction of job segregation.

Chapter seven

Males for sales

Introduction

In this and the next chapter we present a detailed focus on the insurance industry which facilitates the examination of internal as well as external recruitment practices. This analysis seeks to highlight some of the more subtle selection processes involved in the reproduction of job segregation. First, we examine external recruitment practices for the insurance sales-force. Here, the ideology of the organisational breadwinner is again shown to be embedded in labour-market and recruitment practices in ways that can reproduce sex discrimination. Chapter 8 then explores the recruitment of clerical workers and, in particular, highlights the processes by which women come to be allocated and restricted to 'jobs' rather than 'careers'.

In examining the recruitment of salespeople it is important to recognise that life assurance is a commodity that customers rarely actively seek. Hence, it tends to be a product which is sold rather than bought (Collinson and Knights 1986). Strictly speaking, a life-assurance policy is only a contract promising to pay a fixed sum of money to the dependants of the insured on death. Accordingly, it has to be attractively packaged and sold in a highly personal way if large-scale consumption is to be ensured. Moreover, since the underwriting of a life policy is an administrative act that can only take place once a sale has been made, conventional manufacturing divisions are turned on their head in insurance. Here, production and sales become one and the same activity. It is for these reasons that the life-assurance industry is especially orientated towards sales and marketing and why sales, in particular, is considered one of the most important functions within the industry.

Job segregation pervades the insurance industry. Life assurance in particular has come to be characterised by a sex-segregated labour process in which men are employed as inspectors (i.e. salespeople) working externally in 'the field' while women occupy most of the downgraded clerical positions and are restricted to internal office work.

Historically, the twentieth-century influx of women into insurance coincided with the growth of branch networks as companies expanded to take advantage of the national potential for the marketing of insurance through direct sales promotion (Supple 1970). It is these predominantly male sales personnel who have now usurped the status, salary and career prospects once held by the nineteenth-century male office insurance clerk.

Despite the work involving predominantly mental rather than manual skills, a certain 'masculine mystique' abounds in the selling of life assurance that is more usually associated with the heavy physical world of shop-floor production (Willis 1977; Collinson 1988b). Conventionally, the task of selling is described ideologically in terms of a heroic drama in which 'intrepid' and autonomous males stride out into the financial world and against all the odds return with new business. Male sales inspectors have little difficulty in promoting an aura of grandeur about their presence and an almost mystical perception of their skills, especially by contrast with the internal office staff of women clerks, whose work is assumed to be dependent, supportive and secondary.

This chapter concentrates on two distinct ways of selling life assurance.[1] It will be argued that the nature of these respective product markets and selling processes significantly shapes the ways in which insurance companies recruit their sales staff (see Figure 7.1). Indeed, recruitment tends to be merely an extension of the selling process. These selection practices in turn have a significant impact on the nature and extent of sex discrimination in the labour market. The first and longer-established approach involves the selling of policies through *intermediaries or agents* such as insurance brokers, bank, building-society and estate-agency managers, solicitors and accountants. Selling is conducted through 'gentlemanly' informal networks. Inspectors have secure employment contracts with salary and incentive schemes that encourage the provision of a 'professional service' to intermediaries, the great majority of whom are men. The latter receive a substantial commission and reciprocal business from the insurance inspectors and are therefore highly motivated to encourage their clients to purchase life and pensions policies.

However, these intermediaries are likely to have agencies with a number of insurance companies, who are therefore in competition with one another for the agent's patronage. Precisely because of the highly competitive and uncertain nature of this product market-place, a second approach, where policies are sold *direct* to the public, has become increasingly prevalent in insurance. Since a more aggressive and indeed predatory orientation is required here, employees are self-employed and have to rely on commission only. On the basis of research at twenty insurance companies,[2] the following discussion outlines the distinctive recruitment practices that were found in each of these two sectors of the industry. Furthermore, the consequences of these recruitment practices for the reproduction of job segregation will also be examined.

Figure 7.1 Marketing sales techniques in life assurance

	Intermediary	Direct
Product markets	*'Soft' selling through agencies.* Inspectors are engaged in 'gentlemanly' relationships often in more relaxed leisure settings where the intention is to secure the long-term loyalty of professional 'clients' through 'developing a rapport'.	*Highly aggressive* sales techniques by 'financial consultants' or 'associates'. 'Middle men' are dispensed with and selling is focused directly on the 'prospect'.
Labour markets	*High status and secure employment contracts.* Salary plus: commission; company car; entertainment expenses; non-contributory superannuation fund; private pensions plan (concessionary rates for dependants); concessionary mortgage rates; permanent health insurance.	*Insecure contracts.* Self-employed and commission only. Free holidays for the most successful. Termination of contracts for those who do not 'produce'.
Managerial strategy	*Paternalistic,* encouraging dependence, ethical behaviour, middle-class conformity and the establishment of long-term mutually instrumental relations.	*Economistic* demand for independence, autonomy, drive, entrepreneurship and the desire to make a lot of money fast.

The company bread-winners

Sales staff, working through intermediaries in particular, enjoy high organisational status and prestige. This is a reflection of their perceived importance as the 'providers' of business for the company. Yet the professional-bread-winner ideology of agency-based insurance selling, which emphasises the need for competitiveness and self-assertiveness, often contrasts with actual working practices, since inspectors' primary objective is to develop long-term 'business relationships' with agents, thereby encouraging them to sell the company product. Rather than aggression and competitiveness, the nurturing of these mutually instrumental relations in fact requires a high degree of interpersonal social skills.

The 'soft sell' and comparatively low profile of sales inspectors parallels the way that intermediaries in turn seek to act in the professional capacity of advising, rather than selling to, clients. This product market is particularly lucrative and cost-effective since it provides a steady source of business that requires little servicing. Apart from developing a diverse range of competitive products, it is a common and taken-for-granted assumption of selectors in this sector that the most effective means of retaining the steady supply of business from intermediaries is through a personal, informal and 'gentlemanly' sales approach. As the following analysis will demonstrate, such assumptions have clear implications for the preferred gender of sales recruits. The typical recruitment process found to operate in the case of these 'company bread-winners' in the indirect selling market will now be outlined. Following the practice of earlier chapters, recruitment is subdivided into its constituent parts of channels, criteria and procedures.

Recruitment channels

The research found that informal recruitment sources were widely preferred and used in the indirect market. Either inspectors would be drawn from an internal labour market of trainees or be recommended by professional, financial and legal contacts in business-community networks. Only as a last resort, when companies were severely short-staffed, would they advertise through recruitment agencies or in the trade and local press. The word-of-mouth recruitment of experienced sales inspectors was consistently the most preferred and successful channel according to selectors. Yet these professional networks were invariably male-dominated and were thereby likely to exclude women applicants.

The Lancashire branch manager of company 4, who had recruited all twenty-four sales and clerical staff by word of mouth, acknowledged this possibility:

> Yes, that's very true, women could be excluded. But I find word of mouth to be the most successful form of recruitment because then you find somebody who has experience. You get the best candidate by recommendation. I talk with plenty of insurance brokers in my job. And they might ask, or know that I was looking for a good inspector. They may say 'I know a chap working for ABC company who I also know is unsettled but he's jolly good.' So he's been well recommended.

In the ten years of his managership of the branch he had

always been able to recruit good staff without having to advertise.

It's far better to let it be known that we have a vacancy. There are always people wanting to work for us. So once I've informed the work-force, they let it be known in the business that there's a vacancy.

While all the sales-force at the branch consisted of men, all the clerical staff were women. During research at the city branch of company 4, three men were appointed to the sales-force through informal sources in the business community.

At company 5, this channel was highly valued because recommendations were based on intermediaries' first-hand experience of inspectors, as the branch manager confirmed: 'Our best line of recruits undoubtedly comes from personal recommendations so I want all my salesmen to be saying to their brokers, "Who is the best inspector after me who calls on you?"' Thus, the informal grapevine from which experienced inspectors could be drawn was constituted largely of existing salespeople who had contact with their counterparts in other companies and intermediaries whose recommendations and judgements were highly valued. Such incestuous channels of recruitment, in an industry where women are largely tied to subordinate jobs, all but guarantees that insurance sales remains a male preserve.

Selectors' preference to draw on the EILM was also an outcome of internal training practices in which job segregation was a key consideration. As the regional manager at company 4 disclosed, with the increase in the number of female office staff 'over the past ten years', the number of trainee inspectors had also declined:

This is something we've missed enormously, to say to lads, 'Wouldn't you like to be an inspector?' At head office it happens because there's a lot of fellas there, but in the branches we've got girls who haven't wanted to become inspectors, even if we'd been prepared to appoint them. Because the branches are now being built up again, many of the managers are trying to get the odd lad on the inside to bring him along. Because remarkably few women want to be an inspector.

Accordingly, recommendations from the EILM were generally the most favoured recruitment channel. This informal practice could be deemed to constitute indirect sex discrimination since fewer women are likely to be able to comply with its requirements. Such a tribunal ruling would have major implications since word-of-mouth recommendation is a traditional and widespread selection channel in the insurance industry. Nevertheless, as the Sex Discrimination Act is presently constituted and interpreted, managers', claims that there are 'sound reasons' for this recruitment method are likely to be more influential with tribunals. Accordingly, the justifiability of these channels will usually be accepted.

Word-of-mouth networks substantially increase selectors' power over external labour markets. Their primary purpose in the insurance industry, however, is not the exclusion of female applicants,[3] but rather the reduction of risk in selection decision-making. These informal networks of established social relations provide selectors with information about candidates' past work performance which would otherwise be unavailable, thus enabling a more informed selection decision to be made. The use of these informal channels therefore reflects recruiters' concern to minimise not simply cost, but also risk in decision-making. Having said that, there is always a degree of risk involved in attempts to predict future human behaviour, particularly where selection is for the comparatively autonomous occupation of insurance sales. Indeed, were it not for the use of word-of-mouth channels, the element of risk would be even higher because of the priority often placed by selectors on vague and implicit criteria of acceptability.

Selection criteria

Typically, insurance sales selectors were concerned to recruit candidates who would be able to 'develop a rapport' with insurance intermediaries. At company 5, the branch manager evaluated candidates' social skills through his key requirements of 'commitment', 'creativity', 'character', 'communication skills', 'trustworthiness' and a 'professional approach'. These acceptability criteria were inevitably highly informal, interpretative and subjective. Subsequently, the manager selected on the basis of 'gut feeling' and willingly drew on non-work criteria in his evaluation of candidates as he outlined in the following statement,

> The man must have a conventional attitude and a tremendous level of commitment. He can be secretary to the young Labour, Liberal or Conservative Party. He could be on the committee of his local football club. All right so it's leisure, but it's still commitment.

Although such an emphasis on the evaluation of candidate personality is vague and impressionistic, the manager was quite categorical in his belief that only men were appropriate for sales work. All seventeen inspectors were male. He required recruits to have 'gentlemanly qualities' which, for him, were essentially male attributes. They were also perceived to be class- or status-specific qualities, as he outlined when contrasting the different approaches of agency and direct selling:

> It's a different way of life, two sides of the coin. Direct salesmen stand alone. It can be interesting for the better-class ones. But the poorer ones only reach the lower strata so their minds are not stretched very much.
>
> Now if you look at our men, all their colleagues have a grammar-school education, some are graduates. So they have real peers who they are happy with. They also meet professional people, from accountants to tax planners to investment brokers. Enormously interesting. So they don't earn the same money, but money isn't everything is it? They get a good salary, a secure future and if they want to get into management they're more likely to in an agency-based company than in direct selling. It's a way of life, direct selling, which is alien to many people.

This selection criterion therefore includes a 'gentlemanly' disdain of, and distancing from, the purely entrepreneurial and economic aspects of modern business. Agency companies seek to recruit men who will conduct business in a dignified manner through the 'impartial' channels of their intermediary contacts.

Moreover, this manager consistently took for granted that sales recruits would be male, as the following statement indicates:

> The whole strength of our business is the capability of our man to project the company's image to our market-place. So we need high-quality guys who are very capable of producing volume business using the strengths of the company's reputation and their own personal ability. To succeed, they have to be recommended as a good class of guy who knows what he is doing.

These gender-specific assumptions[4] reflect the image of 'gentlemanly' dependability and conservative professionalism that characterises the product market-place of indirect selling, where 'excesses of demeanour and dress are quite unacceptable'. By restricting the selection of candidates to one sex, the recruiter believed that he could reduce the level of risk involved in the use of vague acceptability criteria as predictors of future performance. In this case sex was therefore an important selection criterion.

The branch manager's explicit refusal to appoint saleswomen was articulated in the following statement:

> It may sound sexist but I don't want women because it's not feasible for twenty-two year old girls to be sent up the tower blocks of Hulme[5] at nine o'clock at night. We only have females for the jobs that females do better than males, which are typing, secretarial and part-time. Women don't make inspectors, they're not successful in the long term.

Whilst this statement begins by recognising the legitimacy of the issue of equal opportunities (i.e. 'it may sound sexist'), it then collapses into a rationalisation for sex discrimination, which reflects the paternalistic practices common to selling in the male-dominated indirect market. Yet the concern to protect women from 'dangers' in the product market was contradicted by research interviews with inspectors at this branch who stated unequivocally that they were *never* required at any time of the day or night to enter the two blocks of Hulme. Similar paternalistic rationalisations for sex discrimination emerged in other agency-based insurance companies.

The requirement for inspectors to build 'personal' relationships and a rapport with clients was also claimed by some selectors to be a potentially hazardous aspect of the work for women. A branch manager at company 4 articulated this rationalisation:

> If it's a girl who's selling and she says to the client, 'I'll take you to lunch', he'll obviously read more into it than that. If the broker's wife knew about it, she'd be a bit worried. And again, selling insurance often involves night calls. Now how does a lady cope with that if she calls on a man's house at night? You see life for women is more difficult, they have problems in selling which are not of our making . . ., that males do not come across.

In addition to such 'problems' in the product market, another manager at company 4 believed that the recruitment of women would have negative implications for the members of the sales-force:

> Of course you have to see it from the wife's perspective. A lot of inspectors sell at night; obviously this could upset the 'wife'. I had to ask one inspector if his wife would mind about him doing night calls with our female inspector. No, I doubt if we'll be having any more women.

This manager had promoted one female from the clerical grades to a sales-inspector vacancy because of the massive expansion in business and the shortage of available recruits. Despite these pressures and the women's extensive experience in insurance, the manager acknowledged that his wife was 'amazed because I'm a male-chauvinist pig. She said, "But you don't have female inspectors".' Although he conceded that the woman had been very successful in her new role, the manager thought it highly unlikely that more women would be recruited into the sales function 'unless I really needed inspectors'.

Many selectors argued that it was 'unfair' to subject women to the dangers inherent in the informal practices of intermediary-based insurance sales. Accordingly, the exclusion of women was justified by using highly moral, ethical and protective rationalisations which sought to emphasise the apparent dangers of dealing with customers and clients in the product market. The branch manager at company 3, for example, prioritised the need for candidates to display the masculine competitive characteristics of 'independence', 'drive', 'initiative', 'integrity', 'ambition' and 'self-reliance'. In his view, women could not meet these requirements and were therefore unable to fit into the male world of gentlemanly selling because of the prejudices of insurance intermediaries:

> Women aren't taken seriously in the insurance world. It can be a soul-destroying job. Inspectors have to advise our professional clients, who recommend insurance and pensions to their clients and we want them to recommend us. Yes, it can be a soul-destroying job. And women are either not 'hard bitten' enough to ride off insults, or those that can are pretty unpleasant people.

Like the indirect selling process itself, the reasons for the automatic exclusion of women tended to be gentlemanly and paternal. Selectors' gendered assumptions, which sex-typed the role of 'business provider', also presupposed that the introduction of female inspectors would endanger both the women themselves and the commercial viability of the organisation. In the intermediary market, it was assumed that 'class', gender and educational background were crucial factors contributing to effective selling within a product market consisting predominantly of middle-class men. The very 'plausibility' of these ideological rationalisations reflects their grounding in partial truths, rather than outright myths about the male-dominated and potentially hostile nature of the product market.

Selection procedures

The high degree of informality in the use of selection channels and criteria was supplemented in several insurance companies by the use of job interviews conducted in the pub. Selectors claimed that this informal procedure simulated business meetings with intermediaries and facilitated the evaluation of the social skills and potential business contacts of candidates. It also provided an opportunity to discuss leisure and hobbies in a more relaxed atmosphere. As a recent recruit at company 5 explained,

> The idea is to see how you shape up informally, in a social situation, to see how you handle yourself over a couple of drinks and an informal chat. If you can operate on a sporting level and have a good chat . . . that's the sort of thing they're looking for.

This recruit's early experience of selling suggests that sport also provided a strong informal basis from which to 'develop a rapport', as it had in recent dealings with a building-society manager: 'It's a case of establishing contact. We're getting on already. He's a cricket fan like myself so that helped straight away.'

The importance of sport as an integral part of selling was reconfirmed by another recent recruit:

The biggest thing is the sport actually. I play cricket and football. There's a broker in town, who I've played football with for years so I now do business with him. At our sports club it's all solicitors and accountants, all the sorts of contacts you need . . . you see it's a lot easier to 'do things' on a Saturday, after the match, over a few pints in an informal situation.

Clearly, this preference for those already participating in the leisure networks of middle-class male professionals will tend to exclude women. At company 4, a male clerk was recommended for promotion into the sales-force after the regional manager had played cricket with him in a company-sponsored match. This sporting contact was enough to convince the regional manager of the lad's potential: 'He impressed me. His personality shone through.'

By contrast, the sporting achievements and contacts of female applicants may be evaluated in a highly negative and detrimental fashion, as the following case suggests. It concerns a female candidate who managed to break into the male-dominated informal channels of intermediary sales recruitment. Working for another insurance company, she was recommended by a sales inspector at the Lancashire branch of company 4. According to the branch manager she 'sailed through' a first interview with him because she was highly qualified with a degree; a thesis on insurance; pass certificates in all the professional examinations; and three years' practical experience in financial services. Her final interview was with the branch manager and his regional superior. Previously, the latter had claimed that he took an enlightened view of women in insurance: 'Oh, we're not the least bit averse to taking on women. We've got one here and one in Lincoln. With a couple of daughters myself, I'd be the first person to promote the interests of girls in commerce.'

However, despite these assurances, the interview, which he dominated, was largely devoted to the problems confronting salespeople generally, and women in particular, and was conducted in an entirely negative and hostile atmosphere.

Of the work itself, it was said:
-   Sales is not as glamorous as you might think as a member of the inside clerical staff.
-   You must be mobile – how do you feel about that?
-   You will have to start as a trainee, on a one-year contract, during which time either side can decide against it. Does that worry you at all?
-   If you're not succeeding, you will have to leave because of the cost of training.
-   The job is very demanding and highly competitive. The pressures of commission are very great.
-   In this business, people can be very hard and rude. You've got to be very resilient to take the rebuffs. How do you feel about this?
-   Our product is more competitive than ever because of the opportunities available; you have to realise that if you fail it's your own fault.
-   We expect results particularly after the first two years. Does that worry you at all?

Of female inspectors generally, it was said:
-   We do recruit women, but none have been stable and all of them have been dominated by their husbands and their careers.
-   Would you be able to cope with 'improper advances' from clients when you go to see them in the evening? You could be unprotected in a man's home, how would you cope?
-   In the past, our managers have had to protect female inspectors from, for example, building-society managers 'whose minds were not on business'.
-   Repeat: would this worry you?

And questions of a more personal nature were also asked:
-   I haven't seen you smile yet, do you find it difficult to smile?
-   Are you engaged or do you have a boy-friend?
-   Have you ever had to overcome adversity in your life?
-   Would losing your house worry you? I noticed you coloured up when you mentioned the loss of your house. You're obviously a sensitive person. [The implication here was that, if she were not successful, she would lose her cheap mortgage with the company and might therefore be unable to finance the cost of her house.]

From this breakdown of the main elements of the interview process, it is clear that the regional manager exaggerated the negative aspects of insurance sales work. Of the twenty central issues covered in the interview, fifteen concentrated on problems that *could* conceivably confront sales people. Apart from enquiring whether wives would accept their evening work, this manager's interviews with two (successful) male candidates on the same day did not emphasise such difficulties. The manager had disclosed at an earlier research interview that when interviewing female candidates, he *always* asked about the problem of doing night-work and the concomitant 'dangers' of male clients making 'untoward approaches', because a 'lot of them don't think about it as a possibility'. Far from 'promoting the interests of girls in commerce', such questions by the regional manager displayed a highly protective and negative orientation to female candidates that contradicted his earlier 'enlightened' statements.

This candidate was rejected immediately after she left the room. Despite being highly suitable on technical criteria, she was rejected on the basis of her gender and personality. According to the regional manager, 'she had a tendency to colour up', which indicated that 'she had not got the personality for the job'. In addition, they agreed that without a 'steady boy-friend, she had not had enough experience of men'. The branch manager stated sarcastically, 'Well, looking at the size of her, she'd be able to give them a belt if they tried anything.' Finally, her achievement as an All-England Crown Green Bowling champion was also viewed negatively. It was dismissed by the selectors as indicative of 'a very narrow existence. She's found something she can excel in and stuck to that.' This contrasted with the view of these selectors and many others in the insurance sector, when evaluating male candidates, that involvement in sport was a definite advantage.

At a research interview later, the interviewee demonstrated an awareness of the gender-specific treatment which she had received:

> I was surprised at a few of the questions. How would you deal with a personal assault in somebody's house? Are you going to settle down? Are you thinking of getting married? I can't imagine any man being asked if he'd got a girl-friend. What difference does it make? I got the impression it wasn't really a female they were looking for. They made you feel that it was so difficult to achieve anything, to succeed at all. It didn't sound too secure the way they were talking about it.

Yet while she believed that the managers' interview practices had been informed by a negative orientation to women, this candidate had no intention of taking a formal claim of unlawful discrimination. The experience of the interview had merely confirmed to her that she would not wish to work for company 4.[6]

Her response demonstrates how unlikely it is that external candidates will challenge sex-discriminatory practices but will rather tend to seek employment elsewhere. This is because they have little 'inside' knowledge of the organisation, of the selectors and of the specific recruitment process on which to form a judgement that sex discrimination has definitely taken place. Equally, as individuals outside the organisation, they do not have the potential collective support of a trade union to establish the legitimacy of their grievance. Accordingly, they are likely to respond in an 'individualised' (Sennett and Cobb 1977: 203) and self-protective way by separating and distancing (Goffman 1959) themselves from their rejection and from their unlawful treatment.

The final three examples of selection procedures from the indirect market illustrate that the sex-typing of intermediary sales jobs is so deep-seated that unlawful discrimination can also emerge in the more formal setting of job advertisements. First, an advertised vacancy for a trainee inspector at a local branch office of company 1, that appeared on 1 August 1985, quite blatantly contravened the SDA. The assumption of the need for a male trainee was so deeply rooted that the advertisement stated 'ideally the applicant would be in his early twenties' (see Figure 7.2).

Figure 7.2 Job advertisement

> ...have a vacancy for
>
> **GENERAL INSPECTOR TRAINEE**
> **Excellent training – sound career prospects**
>
> Continued growth of our organisation in the South West has resulted in a vacancy for someone to General Inspector status.
>
> Ideally the applicant would be in his early twenties and ambitious with several years' experience in the insurance industry. Progress in the Insurance Institute examination is essential and applicants already qualified would have a distinct advantage.
>
> Salary during training will be in the range £7,000–£8,500, depending upon experience. Upon completion of the training programme the successful applicant can expect a salary and the outstanding fringe benefits normally associated with a leading insurance company.
>
> Please apply enclosing a detailed CV to:...

This advertisement was brought to the attention of the company's corporate personnel department by the chairman of the union's equal-opportunities subcommittee who had been informed of the advertised statement by union representatives at local level. Corporate personnel subsequently communicated with the branch manager concerned to ensure that this practice was stopped immediately. The taken-for-granted nature of this unlawful practice reflected and reinforced the field-force profile of company 1, as shown in Table 7.1.

Table 7.1 Fieldforce profile

	Males	Females	Total
grade 15	32		32
14	44	1	45
13	37		37
12	40		40
11	98		98
10	131	3	134
9	25	1	26
	407	5	412

This profile included all five field-force occupations of: motor engineer and fire surveyor; and inspectors for claims, life assurance and general insurance. Only one of the five women worked in the sales function and she was a grade-nine.

Second, at company 3, a vacancy for a trainee sales inspector was advertised in the Jobcentre, rather than in the local evening paper. This meant that candidates had to apply through the Jobcentre. The manager believed that this process would stop applications from 'cranks' and would provide him with greater control over the sex of the applicants:

> If we advertised in the paper we'd have to think carefully about how to define the job to cut out 'the rubbish'. I thought two A levels would have blocked out a lot because they're not necessary for the job. But they seem to hand qualifications out as a matter of course these days .... Yes, we'd have to think very carefully about how to frame the advert .... Then there's this rubbish about sex you've got to watch out for.

When asked to elaborate on this final point, he continued:

> Well, say there's twenty thousand inspectors in the country, 99 per cent are males, 1 per cent are females, of which $\frac{1}{2}$ per cent are

failures, $1/2$ per cent are successful. Females tend not to last very long and we want people to stay forty years. So weeding out the females is a bit of a problem. Especially with the Jobcentre. Anyway, as it turned out three people they sent did not turn up for the interview and they were all girls. [laughs]

In the event, all seventeen interviewees for this vacancy were rejected despite the manager judging the only female candidate as 'presentable', 'well-spoken' and 'ideal . . . if she had been male'.

The final example from the intermediary sector also illustrates how female interviewees can be rejected despite being acknowledged as otherwise 'ideal'. With no trainees ready to become inspectors and word-of-mouth channels exhausted, company 5 advertised in the local paper because of a pressing and unexpected shortage of experienced salespeople. As a result, the assistant manager received seven telephoned replies, one of which came from a woman presently working for less money and fringe benefits in a rival company. Although prior to the interview, he felt that the discussion would be 'just going through the motions', he was in fact extremely impressed by her:

Despite the gender I'm keen. She is one of the most ideal, she is potentially one of the best recruits that we could have had . . .but I might be wasting my time because it could be kiboshed from on high.

In other words, he doubted whether his regional manager would accede to the recruitment of a female, no matter how competent. By the time he saw her again his enthusiasm had diminished:

She was very good but there's only one problem, we don't employ women. She has a perfect profile, right age, engaging personality, not only that she was a very good looker . . . . Yes, she's absolutely ideal, just the wrong sex so we're not interested . . . . Yes, she was a bit upset that I didn't show more enthusiasm, but we don't employ women.

Thus, even though these companies were all suffering severe shortages of sales inspectors, recruiters refused to appoint well qualified and experienced women applicants. The foregoing case histories illustrate the routine way in which women were excluded from indirect selling. Such practices were facilitated by the widespread use of informal channels, criteria and procedures of recruitment. Similarly, the rationalisations that were typically offered to justify the exclusion of women tended to be highly paternal, protective and gentlemanly.

The family bread-winner

In recent years the selling of life assurance *direct* to the public has emerged as a separate sector of the industry. Companies adopting this approach have replaced the soft sell, conservative professionalism and gentlemanly conduct of the agency-based organisation with more aggressive marketing and hard selling techniques. In their selection, training and motivation of new employees, direct-sales companies were found to emphasise the values of economic individualism, independence, personal success and the entrepreneurial spirit. This sales philosophy also informed the diversity of their recruitment sources, the informality of their selection criteria and the opportunism of their selection procedures. Each of these subdivisions of the direct-sales recruitment process will now be considered in turn.

Recruitment channels

Recruitment for direct sales drew on a great variety of selection channels. This reflected the fact that recruits were not required to have worked in insurance, although experience of selling any product was an advantage. The following list displays the extensive and informal recruitment channels that were discovered in this sector:

- *Blind job advertising* in local and national press, followed up by telephone interviewing where the company did not reveal its identity.
- *Purchasing 'names'* off the Professional and Executive Register and approaching them directly.
- *'Poaching'* successful direct-sales staff from other competing organisations with the offer of greater rewards.
- *'Cold calling'* where enquiries were made in businesses, shops and so on whether 'they have any representative calling on them who is bigger than his job?'
- *Local-radio* advertising.
- Advertising in *Armed Forces Resettlement Centres*.
- Securing names and addresses of ex-employers *made redundant*, particularly in company closures.
- *Agency appointment register*.
- Recruitment drives through *staff contacts*. At company 1 associates received £100 if their 'referrals' remained for at least three months.
- *Word-of-mouth recommendations* from the public.

In sum, recruitment channels in direct sales tended to include any social encounters which contained the possibility of finding or securing a recommendation of a direct-sales recruit. If this proved to be impossible, the individual under scrutiny could instead be sold a life-assurance or pensions policy. Given the predatory nature of direct selling and recruiting, the distinction between labour and product markets was in practice often found to be blurred.

Selection criteria

The particular employment status and payment system of the direct sales-force conditioned the selection criteria for recruits. Known as 'sales associates' or 'financial consultants', they were essentially self-employed and paid purely on a commission basis. Accordingly, they did not enjoy the same level of job security as inspectors in the agency market. Selectors invariably believed that only family bread-winners, who would have the added 'motivation' of dependants and mortgage responsibilities, would be successful in identifying 'prospects' and persuading them to buy the company's products. Selection criteria reflected the primary concern of direct-sales recruiters who prioritised the protection and extension of selling and production. Accordingly, a common attribute of all recruits in this market was their 'need' and 'motivation' to earn a high income. It was believed that only under such financial pressures would sales associates retain the necessary calculating orientation towards social relations in which everyone is treated as a potential recruit, 'prospect' or source of other sales 'leads'.

Branch managers in direct sales were concerned to find 'successful people', who were stable family bread-winners motivated by high incomes and aged between twenty-five and forty. This bread-winner specification tended to preclude young single people of both sexes and married women. A branch manager at company 13 summarised the widespread doubts about young, single people in the context of commission-only payment systems: 'They're going down the pub and are out courting in the evenings at that age. They've not got the same pressures on them as married men.' The most explicit refusal to recruit single people came from the branch manager at company 12:

> The life-insurance industry has a terrible record for single people. They fail miserably. With respect, most single people are bone idle. There's no big mortgage, no wife, no children, no school fees. I am generalising but a single man would have to be very special for me to hire him.

He also automatically rejected candidates who were unemployed. Implicit in the above statements was the view that recruits would be male.

This was equally true of the bread-winner specification, as it was outlined by a branch manager at company 14: 'I want someone who wants to better himself, who wants and needs to earn a lot of money. He needs to be motivated and will stay with us until he retires.' At company 12, a female interviewee was rejected precisely because her secure domestic life meant that she could not comply with the conventional bread-winner specification, as the selector explained: 'She didn't have that drive. She had plenty of money, husband successful, a Mercedes, but was a bit of scatter-brain. She had two kids at home and only worked because she was frustrated as a housewife.' The domestic life of candidates was therefore deemed to be of central importance in shaping aggressive salesmanship, as this selector elaborated: 'If there is a sound financial position, if the husband has a high income, women will probably lack the motivation to do the job as well as we would expect.' In explaining why there were only four saleswomen in the organisation's twenty-one branches, the head-office training manager at company 13 explained that they were only really successful in specialised 'female markets',[7] where they could operate a 'different, more personal approach'. However, he doubted whether the number of women would increase since he believed they were not ruthless enough: 'They're never very good at closing sales.'

These gendered assumptions were reflected in the work-force profiles of direct sales companies. At company 12, for example, of the 320 'sales underwriters' in the organisation's twenty-eight branches, only five were women. At the particular branch where research took place, there were twenty-seven male underwriters and one female. At company 13, there were twenty-seven salespeople in the three branches of the Northern region, all of whom were men. Throughout the country there were only four saleswomen out of 145. The branch office of company 14 employed only one female in a field-force of forty-six associates. Company 11, however, constituted a minor exception to this pattern, in that the Northern region employed nine women out of seventy-nine salespeople. Interestingly, all these saleswomen were divorcees, which is indicative of the selection criteria prevalent in direct sales. Indeed, some evidence was found that women who were family bread-winners could convince selectors of their need for money. The regional manager at company 11 outlined this limited willingness:

> The profile of women seems to be: in their thirties, single or divorced, and if they're in their thirties, the kids are more or less self-sufficient anyway . . . . We do pay close attention to outside influences in the case of women.

A similar view was expressed by the regional manager at company 13:

> You normally find that a woman who comes to you is divorced, so she's a different type of animal. She's obviously got some commitment to a young child so she needs to work. Without that type of commitment a woman is no good. If she's got a husband who's earning, there's not the same incentive.

During the research, the manager appointed a female divorcee in the Midlands region, but this decision only emerged after a rigorous interview in which he had tried to break the candidate down, but without success. Accordingly, he was satisfied that she possessed the necessary bread-winner qualities: 'There's no problem there. She was a strong character, single minded and very determined ... But whether she'll stay in the long term, I don't know.'

Thus, on the one hand, the self-employed bread-winner specification of direct sales reinforced widespread stereotyping of female applicants. On the other hand, precisely because they were self-employed, women associates were not considered by direct-sales recruiters to be quite the financial 'risk' that they were in the intermediary selling.[8] Yet selectors' willingness to appoint women was only maintained in so far as female candidates were able to display qualities which are traditionally the preserve of men. As the following section demonstrates, women were often rejected at various stages of a recruitment process that was itself diverse, interdeterminate and sometimes concealed.

Selection procedures

In contrast with agency-based companies, where job advertising for salespeople was a rarity, direct-selling organisations tended to conduct a 'trawl' of the local labour market on a regular basis. Indeed, the entrepreneurial culture of direct selling was found to produce a whole variety of aggressive and opportunistic selection procedures, some of which had a particularly negative impact on women applicants. Thus, for example, blind advertising in the local press was a constant feature of company 14's bi-monthly 'recruitment drives'. The advertisement set out in Figure 7.3 was always used.

This advertisement failed to outline the vacancy or the name of the company. Neither did a 'W. Loman' work there. The predatory mentality of direct selling was again evidenced by the recruitment manager's preference for this approach to advertising, which facilitated management's control: 'it's better because you can interview them over the phone that much easier if you know what the job is and they don't. That's how it should be.'

Figure 7.3 Job advertisement

**THREE PEOPLE
REQUIRED FOR AN**

established insurance-investment
group. Applicants should be
presentable with a reasonable
standard of education and be
capable after comprehensive
training of assuming a management
position. For personal interview
Tel: W. Loman (till 7.00 pm)

According to this recruiter, the advertisement attracted 'a lot' of female enquiries, yet he was rarely willing to invite them for interview because he was deeply sceptical about their potential:

> Most women couldn't argue the case with a man. Unless they are really very good on the phone, very confident and sound competent, I'll not interview them. I rejected five on the phone last night. Women in this industry tend to work in the office, they haven't got the bottle to go outside on commission only.[9]

He admitted to 'making it more difficult for women on the phone' and asking 'quite personal questions'. The manager's gendered preconceptions were reflected in the company's selection patterns, which were highly male-dominated:

1983	*Male*	*Female*
1 June–31 August	31	4
1 September–31 December	94	11

At company 15, advertisements were regularly used that failed to specify the industry in which the vacancies were situated (Figure 7.4). The manager who placed this advertisement believed that women's domestic responsibilities were incompatible with his bread-winner requirements, as he elaborated:

> If the husband doesn't come first, he should do. Therefore the job takes second place. And if they have a family, the job takes third place. I'm not saying that's wrong, it's just a statement of fact. The difference with a man is it's his first commitment to provide for all the family.

Figure 7.4 Job advertisement

```
┌─────────────────────────────────────────┐
│          SUCCESSFUL PEOPLE                │
│       Start a New Career in 1984          │
│     We are looking for Successful People  │
│            in the Manchester area         │
│     We require TWO TRAINEES to join our Training │
│   Programme and train to become one of the SUCCESSFUL │
│            PEOPLE IN OUR INDUSTRY         │
│     ■ Earning in excess of £10,000 per annum │
│     ■ Have two months' holiday a year     │
│     ■ Drive the very best cars            │
│     ■ Enjoy the good life                 │
│     ■ We are looking for                  │
│          THE SUCCESSFUL PERSON            │
│   If you believe you are or could be THE SUCCESSFUL │
│   PERSON, WE WANT TO TALK TO YOU. EVEN IF YOU │
│   HAVE NOT BEEN IN SELLING YOU COULD BE OUR │
│               KIND OF PERSON              │
│     To assist you with building your own future │
│    with us, we will pay you during your training │
│     Do you have the following criteria:   │
│             Aged 25 to 50 ?               │
│        Have an established pattern ?       │
│        Earn at least £7,000 per annum ?    │
│                Telephone                  │
└─────────────────────────────────────────┘
```

This view informed his suspicion about women's expressed commitment on the telephone:

> I take it with a pinch of salt. Most of the women say they want a challenge and all the rest of it, but then you find they've got five kids. You know it can't be there and that they're just after the pin-money to fit in around the husband and the kids.

Like word-of-mouth channels, blind advertising and anonymous telephone interviewing were found to be shrouded in a veil of secrecy and unaccountability that extended managerial power and facilitated the perpetuation of sex-discriminatory practices.

The preconception that candidates would be male bread-winners also permeated the recruitment documents that were usually distributed to applicants prior to, or during, the interview process in direct sales. Potential recruits were 'sold' the benefits of working for the company as if the organisation were itself an insurance policy. Glossy hardback booklets were provided full of colour photographs seeking to undermine negative images of insurance and offering the promise of exotic rewards. Their appeal was specifically to male candidates whose production levels could entitle them to membership of 'career clubs'. These documents promised company-sponsored holidays to Cannes, Marbella and Barbados, where bikini-clad women, sport, sun and entertainment awaited the successful sales associate. Success was contingent upon competition with other salespeople and was measured by a set of exclusive 'club'-status gradings, each of which was associated with differentially valued rewards (for example, ties, personalised sales aids, international conferences, free holidays and so on). To this end, a performance ladder was maintained on the branch noticeboard and monthly magazines announced the national and regional 'Man of the Month'.

A substantial part of the direct-sales selection procedure focused on the financial stability of the applicant. Typically, application forms asked detailed questions concerning the financial responsibilities of applicants. These forms were constructed specifically for married men with dependants and financial commitments (see Figure 7.5). The perceived importance of candidates' financial situation was also confirmed by the regional manager at company 13: 'We always look deeply into your personal financial situation, find out what your commitments are – family, mortgage etc., to see if you need the money.' In addition, this manager's interview check-list, which he followed very closely, assumed a male bread-winner interviewee throughout, as the following examples illustrate:

– 'What are his ambitions for the future?'
– 'Does his wife share his ambitions and will she accept evening work?'
– 'Has he been married more than once?'

The person profile for selected sales staff (Figure 7.6) used at company 16 again illustrated the importance for selectors of age, domestic stability and financial commitments. Clearly a male bread-winner is most likely to achieve a high score against this check-list.

It was standard practice at company 13 that in order to pursue these issues further, an interview would always be conducted at the candidate's home to 'meet the wife'. The reason for this was explained by the Lancashire branch manager:

Marriage is very important for this job. You need stability. You need a cat to go home to kick! You need a guy who's got commitments, with a need to better himself, and who's not too well heeled when he starts.

At company 12 a 'wife interview' was also conducted, this time on the firm's premises. Because 'marital stability' was a key aspect of selection here, it was preferred that the man's wife did not work outside the home. Commission-based payments and self-employed status presupposed a 'needy and greedy' orientation to work, as the training officer elaborated: 'If someone is comfortable, has a working wife, they're not hungry to earn.'

Figure 7.5 Application form from company 16

FINANCIAL POSITION

ASSETS		LIABILITIES	
House	£	Outstanding mortgage	£
Contents	£	Bank overdraft	£
Car	£	Hire purchase outstanding	£
Bank	£	Second mortgage or other loans	£
Approx. cash value of Life Ass.	£	Any other debts	£
Any other assets	£		
TOTAL ASSETS	£		
Wife's income	£ p.a.	TOTAL LIABILITIES	£
Private income or service pension	£ p.a.		

MONTHLY COMMITMENTS

Mortgage repayments or rent	£	Minimum monthly draw required £			
Rates	£	Life Assurance in force			
Heating, lighting etc.	£	Company	Amount of cover	Additional benefits	When effected
Normal housekeeping	£				
School fees	£				
Travelling expenses, etc.	£				
Assurance premium	£				
Any other dependants	£				
Repayments on loans	£	Total Life cover			
Any other commitments	£				
TOTAL minimum monthly commitments	£				

Have you ever been bankrupt, or insolvent, or have you compounded with your creditors ? If so, give name and address of trustee who acted for you:

_____

_____

I hereby declare that the foregoing information is correct, without any reservation whatever.

DATE _____   *SIGNATURE* _____

Figure 7.6 Person profile for selecting a salesperson

Applicant's Name Home Address Phone							S C O R E
AGE	25 to 33	4	FROM 22 TO 37	2	UNDER 22 OR OVER 37	0	
LOCATION	BRISTOL	4	WITHIN 5 MILE RADIUS OF BRISTOL	2	OUTSIDE 5 MILE RADIUS OF BRISTOL	0	
MARITAL STATUS	MARRIED WITH CHILDREN	4	SINGLE OR MARRIED WITH NO CHILDREN	2	DIVORCED OR SEPARATED	0	
FINANCIAL SITUATION	ASSETS AND REASONABLE MORTGAGE	4	NO DEBTS AND NO MORTGAGE	2	NO ASSETS AND DEBTS	0	
EDUCATION	O LEVELS OR CSEs + FURTHER TRAINING	4	CSEs WITH NO FURTHER TRAINING	2	NO QUALIFICATIONS	0	
EXPERIENCE IN SELLING	WELL TRAINED IN SELLING	4	SOME SALES HISTORY	2	NO SALES HISTORY	0	
EXPERIENCE IN MARKETS	COMPREHENSIVE EXPERIENCE	4	SOME EXPERIENCE	2	NO EXPERIENCE	0	
KNOWLEDGE OF PRODUCTS	FULL KNOWLEDGE	4	SOME KNOWLEDGE	2	NO KNOWLEDGE	0	
MOTIVATION	HIGHLY FINANCIALLY MOTIVATED	4	STATUS CONSCIOUS	2	WANTS CAR AND FREEDOM	0	
ASPIRATIONS	KEEN TO DEVELOP AS A SALESPERSON	4	MOVE INTO MANAGEMENT	2	NO VIEWS HELD	0	
HEALTH	EXTREMELY FIT	4	LOOKS IN GOOD HEALTH	2	WEAK AND UNFIT	0	
					TOTAL SCORE		

In sum, the research suggests that whilst some women may be recruited as sales associates, these appointments are usually restricted to the few whose family responsibilities enable them to be judged as 'honorary' male bread-winners. There is therefore little evidence that the recruitment of a small number of 'female bread-winners' will challenge the exclusionary practices of many direct-sales selectors. Indeed, these few exceptions not only conform to, but may also actually reinforce, deep-seated gendered assumptions and, thereby, job segregation.

Conversely, the vast majority of female applicants are likely to be treated in a detrimental fashion. In their defence, however, direct-sales selectors might argue that the self-employed status of associates grants immunity from the Sex Discrimination Act. But the Employment Appeal Tribunal ruling in the case of Quinnen v. Hovells (1984) suggests that self-employment is likely to be included within the parameters of the Act, particularly where there is a *personal involvement* in the 'execution of work or labour' (see Gunning v. Mirror Group Newspapers Ltd, 1983). Since sales associates receive financial support (from three months to two years),[10] technical and sales training in the early stages, a variety of company fringe benefits and since their contracts will be terminated for poor performance, it seems evident that they are personally totally responsible for the execution of work carried out in representing the company.

The legal position of sales associates is important particularly because of the increasing prevalence and influence of direct selling. Even traditional agency-based companies are introducing direct sales offshoots. Indeed, this growth will be reinforced by the emergence of the 'single European market' in 1992, which is likely to result in the rapid expansion of direct sales outlets of UK insurance companies throughout the Continent.

Conclusion

The research findings have displayed how two different approaches to the selling of life-assurance policies can shape the specific recruitment practices and labour-process control strategies adopted by companies within each of these product markets. In turn, these recruitment requirements and practices were shown to impact significantly upon the nature of sex discrimination found in the industry. Indeed, a distinct difference between the two sales approaches was discovered in the *form* of masculinity required by selectors.

Agency-based companies adopted an 'ethical' and 'professional' sales approach. This was also reflected in routine recruitment practices for high-status inspectors, who were defined as organisational bread-winners. Managerial control tended to be highly paternal. The widespread and deep-seated reluctance of selectors in this product market to appoint saleswomen was informed by the paternal and protective values that characterised the 'gentlemanly', ethical and dignified culture of the indirect sector.

In contrast, direct selling was highly aggressive, predatory and opportunistic. Recruiters sought to appoint salespeople who would bring their motivation to work with them. Managers operated an econo-mistic rather than paternalistic control strategy. Only those women who could fit in with the conventional male stereotype of the family bread-winner, working under the pressure of domestic responsibilities, would be considered for these self-employed positions.

Overall, research in the insurance-sales sector confirms the view of studies discussed in Chapter 3, that informality in recruitment practices is likely to facilitate sex discrimination. However, two amendments need to be made to their conclusions. First, in contrast to Jenkins's (1986) argument, the ILM will not necessarily be detrimental to women employees; for if the ILM of female-dominated office clerks had been used in some of the above examples, more women would have been promoted into the ranks of sales representatives. In fact, this internal and informal channel was consistently ignored by insurance-sales selectors. Earlier studies therefore tended to neglect the way in which job segregation may restrict the use of the internal labour market.[11]

Second, the extended internal labour market is not merely a preferred channel in times of recession as earlier studies imply: for in the insurance-sales industry, it was a long-standing and traditional recruit-ment practice. This was because it not only reduced costs, but also facilitated selection decision-making by providing greater information about applicants. It thereby helped to minimise the risk associated with attempts to predict candidates' future work performance.

Employers' perception of risk in recruitment was not simply an outcome of their lack of formal control over the labour market and the selling labour process, nor of the difficulties they faced in seeking to predict the future work behaviour of human beings. For what appeared to be embedded in selectors' decisions was their own symbolic sense of identity, first as men, and second as competent, shrewd and even object-ive managers and judges of acceptability criteria. Given this 'narcis-sistic' investment of self in decision-making, the 'risk' within selection decisions was magnified as personal status and even public career was felt to be at stake. Since women and ethnic minorities were often considered to be 'bad risks', these factors compounded selectors' pervasive 'knee-jerk' defensiveness against employing them, except for all but the most mundane and routine of clerical jobs in the office. Behind the rationalisations that sought to benefit or blame the victim,

blame clients and customers or protect production, selectors' commitment to recruit bread-winners like themselves rendered them highly
resistant to take the 'risk' and appoint saleswomen. Thus, in addition to
the extensive power of insurance branch managers, which is reflected in
their total discretion over recruitment, selectors' narcissistic concern to
recruit in their own likeness contributed significantly to the reproduction of job segregation in the insurance industry.

Yet this concern to avoid the 'risk' of appointing saleswomen clearly
had contradictory consequences for insurance organisations, for
although several of the companies were extremely short-staffed and
thereby losing business, they were found to be rejecting experienced and
well-qualified female candidates. There was also a widespread refusal
to promote highly skilled and knowledgeable women who had proved
their commitment and capabilities within the clerical structure, as the
next chapter will elaborate.

It is precisely such contradictions and tensions embedded in attempts
by men as managers to *control* female labour which constitute the
'motor of change' (Cockburn 1983: 211) by providing the basis for
resistance and for organisational transformation. The evidence in this
chapter has intimated that the 'individualising' effects of *external*
recruitment practices renders resistance to sex discrimination problematic and unlikely. The following chapter on the insurance industry
will now focus not only on the reproduction and rationalisation of job
segregation, but also on the extent to which women employees in the
case-studies were able to expose these contradictions, and how far they
were able to generate effective resistance to sex-discriminatory
practices.

Chapter eight

Risking women

Introduction

While the previous chapter focused on how and why men tended to be recruited into the insurance sales-force, the following analysis concentrates on the channelling of women into office clerical work. The research findings consistently suggest that the elevated status of insurance salesmen as the organisational 'bread-winners' reflects and reinforces the recruitment of women into the downgraded office equivalent of domestic work. This central theme is supported by evidence from both external and internal labour-market practices which reveals how women tend to be channelled into 'jobs' rather than 'careers'.

In seeking to explain how job segregation is reproduced, we are concerned to examine not merely the *quantity* of women recruits, but also the *quality* of work experience with which they are subsequently provided. It is not so much that women are rejected, but more that they are recruited for specific work tasks offering few career opportunities. By focusing on this process, we are able to illustrate some of the more subtle, internal practices through which job segregation is reproduced. Equally, we can examine the ways in which women are able to resist these practices. Before discussing the research findings a brief background to the historical patterns of women's employment in the insurance industry will now be presented.

The clerical labour process in insurance

The insurance industry now employs a large number of women (see Introduction). Yet it was only at the turn of the century that clerical work in insurance evolved from a well-paid and prestigious occupation for a small group of middle-class men into a devalued and subordinate position occupied largely by women (Lockwood 1958; Supple 1970). Alongside processes of deskilling, mechanisation and routinisation (Braverman 1974), insurance clerical work has been feminised (Davies

1974; Kanter 1977; Mcnally 1979). This transition reflects historical developments in clerical work generally (Lockwood 1958; Supple 1970; Silverstone 1976; Downing 1980; Morgall 1981; Bernard 1984; Vinnicombe 1980; Crompton and Jones 1984).[1]

The influx of female workers in the twentieth century to some extent reinforced the traditionally paternalistic nature of managerial practices in the insurance industry. An emphasis on personal relations, mutual dependence and the protection of the work-force had been a pervasive characteristic of the male-dominated early-nineteenth-century counting house. The recruitment of women later in the century reinforced this managerial style and displayed itself in a marked degree of occupational segregation. The Prudential Assurance Company, for example, sought to ensure that 'lady clerks' had no contact with male employees whatsoever. The ladies worked in a totally separate department, their times of arrival and departure did not coincide with those of the male staff and they entered and left the building by a separate entrance (Barker and Downing 1980: 68).

While the increasing number of clerical workers has led to the growing prevalence of bureaucratic control in white-collar settings (Lockwood 1958; Kanter 1977), the insurance industry is still character-ised by a large number of small-scale local branch operations where a paternalistic managerial style often persists in face-to-face office relations.[2] As other literature outlines (for example, Norris 1978; Lawson 1981; Freeman 1982; Lown 1983; Pollert 1983; Westwood 1984; Bradley 1986; Dick and Morgan 1987; Filby 1987; Maguire 1988), paternalism constitutes a managerial style in which a coercive approach is replaced by calls for moral co-operation, the emergence of personal trust relations and for employees' voluntary investment in their work and identification with the company. Paternalism is a form of managerial control which seeks to emphasise the intersubjective and interdependent nature of hierarchical relations. It is also a peculiarly gendered form of control which draws on the familial metaphor of the 'rule of the father', who is authoritative, benevolent, self-disciplined and wise. Although the paternal manager may exercise power in arbitrary ways, he can claim to dominate in subordinates' best interests. Paternalism therefore seeks to mobilise and channel labour agency and subjectivity.

Paternalism as a managerial practice and ideology may arise from a genuine concern to protect those believed to have less power, or from a manipulative strategy designed primarily to increase production and avoid or limit conflict. Either way, it is a control practice which is highly effective particularly because subordinates are encouraged to subscribe to the legitimacy of the personal relationship. By emphasising the moral and reciprocal relationship between superior and subordinate, managers can represent their exercise of power and discretion as one which benefits, protects and recognises an obligation to, and a dependence on, members of the work-force. Managerial control is thereby defined as positive and protective, rather than negative and constraining. As a result the social relations of the office are likely to be stable and productive with subordinates being compliant, loyal and deferential.

This comparatively relaxed and informal style of management in insurance is also a condition and consequence of the inconsistent and sporadic development of formal resistance and unionisation in the industry. Unlike Australia (see Benson and Griffin 1985), there is no independent trade union which exclusively represents the insurance-industry work-force. Representation is divided primarily between MSF and BIFU. MSF (formerly ASTMS) is the main union representing roughly 80,000 insurance employees in forty-eight companies (TUC 1986). Yet in many of these organisations, the union has failed to achieve a level of membership which could challenge the long-established staff associations or 'sweetheart unions' as they have come to be known. The latter's close links with the management of insurance companies reflect the typical paternal–deferential relationship characteristic of industrial relations in this industry. In 1985, BIFU had procedural agreements with fifteen insurance companies and represented 17,944 members.[3] Hence, together, BIFU and MSF only represent approximately 41 per cent of UK insurance workers. In addition, the Association of Professional, Executive, Clerical and Computer Staff (APEX) has some members in Commercial Union, while the Transport and General Workers' Union (TGWU) has traditionally represented CIS insurance staff (Crompton and Jones 1984: 201).

Against this background, we now turn to the empirical material which explores recruitment practices in one small and two large insurance companies. The first two organisations are 'composites' in that they sell a diverse range of products from motor, liability, life and fire policies to general and marine insurance. The third concentrates on, and is a market leader in, pension products. Job segregation was a pervasive characteristic of all three organisations. For example, the profile of company 1 (Table 8.1) reveals how women were clustered in clerical jobs below supervisory/management level (grades 9+) in the head office and branch structure.

At company 2, 54 per cent of the total work-force of 9,000 were women. The breakdown in percentage terms for insurance and technical grades demonstrates a similar pattern of segregation by sex (see Table 8.2).

Table 8.1 Company 1 work-force profile

Grades	Category	Male	Female	Total	Percentage Male	Female
1–4	Clerical	134	750	888	15.5	84.5
5–6	Junior technical	253	778	1031	24.5	75.5
7–8	Senior technical	360	449	809	44.5	55.5
9–15	Supervisory/field staff	1446	129	1575	91.8	8.2
	Management	285	2	287	99.3	0.7
Categories outside	Graduate trainees	14	3	17	82.3	17.7
mainstream career	Typing/secretarial	—	396	396	—	100.0
and job-evaluation	Data processing	137	25	162	84.5	15.5
structure	Engineering division	70	128	198	35.3	64.6
	Office services, Property, printing and stationery	243	175	418	58.1	41.9
	Part-time	28	181	209	13.4	86.6
		2970	3016	5986	49.7	50.3

Company census, July 1984

Table 8.2 Company 2 work-force profile

Grades	Category	Percentage Male	Female
36+	Executives	100	—
33–35	Senior managers	98	2.0
31–32	Specialists	100	—
28–39	Junior management	97.5	2.5
25–27	Technical/supervisory	92.7	7.3
	First-line technical/ supervisory	38.8	61.2
	Trainees	70.9	29.1
	Clerical	3.9	96.1

While companies 1 and 2 employed a comparatively large work-force of 6,000 and 9,000 respectively, company 3 was much smaller with just 1,289 employees. In the latter organisation, job segregation could also be discerned in the organisation's branch network where all 142 clerical staff were women. Of the sales inspectors, 184 were men (including nineteen trainees) and fourteen were women (including four trainees). In the first two companies, employees were free to join independent, TUC-affiliated trade unions, but in the third, there was only a management-sponsored staff association whose influence was rarely felt in the branches. The way in which job segregation can be reproduced, first, through external recruitment practices will now be examined.

Recruitment practices

This first section seeks to highlight the vicious circles that can characterise sex discrimination in the labour market. It also explores how the taken-for-granted practices of tiered recruitment, which channels women into 'jobs' and men into 'careers', can have both self-fulfilling and self-defeating consequences. Patterns of recruitment tiering by sex, age and qualifications help to explain why women in insurance remain segregated in low-grade clerical work.

The first case-study concerns routine recruitment practices in the most commercially successful of company 3's production branches. Here, the responsibility for recruitment was shared between the branch manager, who selected the sales-force, and an office manager, who recruited and supervised 'the girls in the office'. This division of labour between the two men reflected the branch work-force segregation, in which there were eleven sales 'inspectors' (all male) and seven clerical staff (all female).

The company had a nation-wide policy of 'growing their own' salespeople by appointing eighteen to twenty-four year olds, either after A levels or increasingly with a degree, to be 'groomed' by the local manager. Clerical staff were selected at the younger age of sixteen to eighteen. Required to have five O levels, but not necessarily typing skills, these recruits were usually found through word-of-mouth recommendation. The company offered a reward of £60 to any employee who recommended a successful candidate.

The practice of tiered recruitment was confirmed by the office manager. Whilst seeking to fill a clerical trainee vacancy, for which all the applicants to an advertisement in the Jobcentre were female, he conceded that sex-typing was built into the terms and conditions of the job: 'Men could do the job but the starting salary is too low (i.e. £2,900). You'd never get a bloke to do it.' The office manager stated that the job was usually filled by a female who was under twenty-five. Equally, the branch manager took for granted that the level of pay and career prospects in clerical work sex-typed the job *prior* to recruitment because he also assumed that young women were less ambitious and thus more stable for this work:

> There's girls out there who are more intelligent than anyone in the branch . . . but they've no drive, which suits us fine. We rely on people's inertia since our salaries are not very attractive. We try to

keep people coming in at the bottom so that we can train them to
our ways, get them used to the company.

Similar gendered assumptions were articulated by a senior head-
office personnel manager, who argued that women's relative absence
from the career structure was not the result of company selection
practices, but of young women's 'preference' for domestic work and
child-bearing:

They're normally not career-minded people, O level entrants with
limited potential. They're there basically to do the 'number
crunching' and 'pen pushing'. If they had been career-minded
they would have left that grade long since. The door is always
open to move into the career structure, but we've found by and
large, they're girls, who are not particularly ambitious, looking
forward to getting married, leaving and having a family and that's
about the measure of it.

Such presuppositions about the absence of female ambition or long-term
work commitment often reflect and reinforce practices of recruitment
tiering. They were also found to be common throughout the financial
sector (see Collinson 1987c). Of course, it is convenient for managers to
define these women as having a 'limited potential' when so few career
opportunities were available – as the branch manager stated, 'it suits us
fine'. Moreover, these gendered assumptions that tended to blame the
victim were characterised by a self-fulfilling vicious circle in which
women's perceived lack of ambition and higher turnover in clerical
work was explained not as a consequence of the rates of pay, low status,
tiered recruitment, tight supervision, mundane work, limited autonomy
and career opportunities, but because they were women. By focusing
solely on the consequences of the vicious circles of job segregation,
namely female turnover rates, selectors' rationalisations drew on
'partial truths' which sought to deny their own and the company's part
in reinforcing these vicious circles.

This same managerial tendency to tier recruits, stereotype women,
yet deny responsibility for the consequences, was discovered at company 1. Although recruitment was the responsibility of local management, a consistent sex imbalance was displayed in the company's
national recruitment figures. In the past four years, 64 per cent of all
clerical recruits were female and in *each* selection period more women
than men were recruited (see Table 8.3).

Between September 1985 and August 1986, the company recruited
105 males and 345 females with O-level qualifications. Yet at A-level
and graduate stage, the sex ratio changed. During the same period,
eighty-two males and sixty-nine females with A levels were appointed.

Moreover, between 1980 and 1984, 117 males and 41 female graduates were appointed. At company 2 there had been some improvement in the sex ratio of graduate entrants as shown in Table 8.4. The improvement in the 1984 figures resulted in top management insisting that more recruits be appointed from the graduate summer fair and instructing selectors that this time they 'should not go overboard recruiting women'. Consequently, all four second-round recruits were men.

Table 8.3 Clerical recruitment, 1980–4

		Male	Female	Total
February	1980–July 1980	148	289	437
August	1980–February 1981	87	123	210
March	1981–June 1981	16	61	77
July	1981–January 1982	45	76	121
February	1982–June 1982	13	18	31
July	1982–December 1982	72	109	181
January	1983–June 1983	58	145	203
July	1983–December 1983	109	150	259
January	1984–June 1984	85	140	225
Total		633	1,111	1,744

Table 8.4 Number of graduate recruits

	1978	1980	1982	1983	1984
Female	25 (30%)	18 (32%)	3 (14%)	12 (29%)	20 (44%)
Male	58	38	18	30	25

With regard to labour attrition rates, senior personnel managers at company 1 perceived organisational benefits in a relatively high female turnover. Resignations were valued because they enabled a consistent re-injection of 'new blood' into the work-force, which thereby facilitated a 'healthy work-force circulation'. Maternity leave was also viewed as having the same advantage of 'lubricating the career structure':

> It's very useful to us to have a high turnover in these lower grades because then those lower down can show their spurs. What better way to sell yourself for promotion than by saying to another manager, 'I have had nine months' experience of sitting in as section leader'? [Senior head-office personnel manager]

The higher percentage of female compared to male resignations is displayed in Table 8.5.

Table 8.5 Company 1's annual turnover figures

Male (%)		Female (%)
1978	9.1	23.6
1979	7.9	21.7
1980	7.3	14.3
1981	6.8	12.6
1982	5.7	13.5
1983	6.7	10.9

Recruitment tiering and gendered assumptions about women's non-career commitment are crucial self-fulfilling factors in the reproduction of higher female turnover. Women themselves are then blamed for their disadvantaged position, while job sex-typing and a career structure that only offers very limited opportunities is left unacknowledged. Hence, while the jobs themselves may be permanent, the women jobholders were often treated as temporary workers.

Having said that, the self-fulfilling nature of tiering and turnover is not always supported by the research evidence concerning women's resignation rates. A closer examination of the labour turnover figures in Table 8.5, for example, reveals that women's attrition rate in the 1980s fell by 54 per cent, compared to men's which dropped by 26 per cent. At one production branch of company 2, the four female clerks had impressive length-of-service records of thirty-seven, fifteen, thirteen and ten years. Equally, the complaints of the office manager at company 3 provided further confirmation that women clerical workers did not resign as often as managers adhering to gender stereotypes would expect or apparently would wish:

> The problem with this office is that too few leave. You need a fair amount of turnover to keep everybody happy. It's taken the senior pensions clerk six years to get where she is now and she can't move unless I get run over by a bus.

Because of these career blocks he declared himself to be 'delighted' when one of the seven women resigned. This response demonstrates that management might see positive advantages in a higher female turnover rate. These examples suggest that the managerial emphasis on women's higher turnover as an explanation for the latter's failure to progress within the organisation is therefore, in part, a *post-facto* rationalisation for a determination to retain a sex-segregated work-force. Despite such

170

evidence to the contrary, stereotypes about women as essentially short-term employees were pervasive in the accounts of selectors in insurance.

The recruitment of women as temporary and part-time workers reflects these assumptions. During the 1980s, insurance managements have been reluctant to recruit significant numbers of clerical staff to full-time permanent work because they anticipated that new technology would reduce jobs. However, partly because of the falling wastage rates, but largely as a result of business 'booms' in 1982 and 1985, under-staffing in the industry has been exposed. A short-term measure common to many companies has been to recruit temporary labour on six- or twelve-month contracts. Such workers are entitled to one week's notice (with no reasons needed) and no paid sick leave. From these 'short-term contract' (STC) staff, only the few whose performance is completely satisfactory will be appointed to permanent work. At company 2, for example, 225 STC staff had been recruited by 1982 and this figure rose to 307 in June 1984. Of these, 85 per cent were women. Since recruitment for these vacancies was largely informal through word-of-mouth contacts and waiting-lists, the exclusion of male candidates could constitute unlawful sex discrimination.

The employment of part-time staff in insurance has also increased in the past decade. In March 1985, there were 19,000 women working part-time in the UK insurance industry with another 15,000 in auxiliary sectors (Department of Employment 1985). Company 1 employed 210 part-timers, 81 per cent of whom were women. Recruitment tiering was indicated by the limited benefits available to part-timers in contrast to full-time staff:

- reduced pension entitlement;
- no Permanent Health Insurance;
- non-entitlement to the subsidised BUPA scheme;
- non-admission to the staff house-purchase scheme since 'a part-time salary could not service a mortgage'.

(management document)

Similar exemptions and limitations were to be found at company 2, where more part-time staff were employed and more of these were women. There were 376 (98 per cent women) part-timers in insurance and technical work and 105 (91 per cent women) in house and catering. Since the vast majority of these part-time workers were women, their non-entitlement to company benefits constitutes a prima-facie case of indirect discrimination.[4]

Tiered recruitment practices, then, reflect and reinforce a self-fulfilling vicious circle in which managers assume a stereotype of women as unambitious and/or likely to leave, yet provide employment conditions that preclude most other responses. While managers may blame women for resigning, they will continue to appoint them, not least because they recognise organisational benefits in the perceived lack of ambition, high turnover and replaceability of females. This is particularly so in a context where the large-scale introduction of computerised office machinery is reducing much of insurance clerical work to little more than a series of 'punching' tasks (Crompton and Jones 1984). Women's numerical domination of keyboard work is often rationalised as a consequence of their 'natural' suitability for mundane jobs that primarily require dexterity skills. Yet paradoxically, despite managers' rationalisations, high female turnover inevitably results in a recurrent need to select, socialise and train female clerical recruits, which is costly in terms of finance and labour time.

The extent to which women resist by resigning also contradicts the actual dependence of some managers on the high quality of work of many female employees. Indeed, during the research some managers informally acknowledged their extensive reliance on women's contribution to office practices. One branch manager, for example, was full of praise for the organisational skills of the female office adminis- tration manager: 'If she left it would be an absolute disaster, because she's superb. She does a better job and has more knowledge than 90 per cent of supervisors in other branches.' Yet he felt unable to promote her to office supervisor because this had always been a man's role.[5] At another company, the regional manager acknowledged a wide-ranging reliance upon his personal secretary to organise and make decisions, not just in his absence, but even when he was present: 'I rely on Jackie a great deal. I need someone I can trust because I am out of the office so much. She has a lot to do for me.' This secretary contributed to recruitment decisions either formally, as a member of the interview panel, or more informally by evaluating candidates whilst serving them coffee. The manager valued her judgement because 'They come across differently to her than they do to me. You see a woman notices things about a guy . . . and they adopt a different attitude, their true self comes across out there, . . . when they're more relaxed.' Furthermore, she also organised the whole administration behind the recruitment process, accepting levels of responsibility more usually attributed to managers, as she complained: 'I do a lot of jobs here that I don't get paid for.' Although the regional manager acknowledged the secretary's contribution, her classification as part-time meant that she was not even entitled to a discounted mortgage with the company.

The 'womanly qualities' of female clerical workers were also required in their role of sales support staff. It was expected in several companies that women clerk/typists would work past their job descriptions. In the absence of sales inspectors, female clerks usually maintained important telephone relations with clients, dealing with all their complaints and queries on an individual basis. Women were also called upon to act as 'office wives' (Kanter 1977: 89) in 'massaging' the bruised egos of sales inspectors when they returned to the office dejected after a fruitless day selling. Accordingly, insurance clerical work can be seen to be undertaken by the 'office wife' who awaits the return of the 'male provider'.

Although sometimes acknowledged informally, many of the tasks that women performed in the everyday running of insurance companies were not recognised in formal job descriptions. Such jobs in insurance can be said to be 'gendered' (Davies and Rosser 1986), since they capitalise and depend on the experience and capabilities of women at particular stages of their life cycle. These skills are not 'natural endowments' but are learnt socially as part of the process of becoming and being a woman. The failure of insurance companies and job-evaluation systems to acknowledge certain tasks which are undertaken, for example, in the gendered job of management secretary is illustrated by the contrast between the job description from company 1 in Figure 8.1 and the account by one management secretary of her routine work tasks set out in Figure 8.2.

The foregoing examples illustrate how women's skills, often learnt as wives and mothers in the home (see Crompton and Jones 1984: 146), can become essential to the everyday running of insurance companies. The research therefore reveals the contradiction of managerial practices and rationalisations, which on the one hand welcome female resignations, yet on the other, acknowledge a dependence on their gendered skills and extensive work commitment.

To summarise, women in insurance are usually recruited for specific low-status jobs, that, it is believed, they can perform better than men. This pervasive practice of recruitment tiering is characterised by a vicious circle which contains self-fulfilling as well as self-defeating consequences. Facing extensive barriers to their progress women may opt to resist by resigning; an individualistic practice which, paradoxically, can provide a partial truth on which selectors' gendered assumptions are then based. In the next section we will now explore several internal barriers to women's progress.

Promotion practices

The conventional career path in the industry can take a route that is internal or external to the office. Progress can be made either through supervisory positions – for example, in the accounts or actuarial departments as section leaders and superintendents – or via the field-force as surveyors, sales and claims inspectors. Decisions concerning training and promotion are largely the prerogative of local management

Figure 8.1 Job description of manager's secretary

JOB DESCRIPTION	JOB CODE:	
JOB TITLE: MANAGER'S SECRETARY	**LOCATION:**	HEAD OFFICE/ REGIONAL OFFICE/ MAIN BRANCH

REPORTING STRUCTURE:

REGIONAL/ DEPARTMENTAL/ ASSISTANT GENERAL MANAGER
MANAGER'S SECRETARY

JOB OBJECTIVE:

To provide an efficient secretarial and typing service to the Manager.

NOTE: THIS JOB DESCRIPTION SHOULD BE READ IN CONJUNCTION WITH THE SECTION ON JOB DESCRIPTIONS IN THE STAFF HANDBOOK

1. DUTIES AND RESPONSIBILITIES

Opens morning's post, connects to relevant files and passes to Manager.

Types dictation received from Manager.

Maintains filing Systems for Manager.

Keeps a diary of the Manager's engagements, makes appointments, travel arrangements and hotel reservations.

Answers the telephone, takes messages or redirects calls to regional staff when the Manager is not available.

Receives visitors to Regional/Head Office Management.

Assists other Managers' secretaries or undertakes routine copy typing in the Manager's absence.

2. CONTACTS

CONTACT	FREQUENCY	REASON
H.O. and Regional departmental staff	Daily	
Local Directors Brokers/Agents/Insureds	As necessary	In course of duties.
Visitors to Regional/H.O. Management	Daily	

3. SUPERVISION

No supervisory responsibility

4. KNOWLEDGE

Typing 50 wpm.
Requires knowledge of Group Organisation and Personnel

5. ENVIRONMENT

Normal office conditions.

Figure 8.2 Actual duties and responsibilities of a manager's secretary

A high standard of typing.

The ability to compose correspondence, to relieve the manager of routine work.

A reliable and neat filing system.

An excellent memory.

A range of local contacts, e.g. in catering, travel, accommodation, the local Insurance Institute, other local insurance managers and their secretaries, major clients, etc.

The ability to plan and keep an efficient diary of appointments and to make appropriate arrangements.

A knowledge of all work undertaken by Management, in order to appreciate the significance of any particular matter, to be able to grasp the situation with the minimum explanation, to take and understand messages in a sensible and impressive manner without the need for questions. This includes a general knowledge of insurance, the ability to analyse and interpret statistics, a knowledge of personnel and administrative procedures and other Management functions, e.g. Local Board.

The knowledge to identify head-office managers and other senior personnel of the group.

The ability to communicate effectively at all levels, ranging from junior female staff (in a welfare capacity) to the most senior head-office officials and including local directors, important direct clients, brokers and other representatives.

The ability to handle complainants in the absence of management – a good impression and tact are essential here.

The ability to use initiative when dealing with superintendents in the absence of management. Delay can sometimes arise if the 'grade-gap' is not crossed carefully and politely.

The ability to deal with counter enquiries when the receptionist requires assistance. These enquiries are normally of a non-insurance nature and do not fall within routine categories.

The ability to handle the routine work of the administration superintendent in his absence.

An absolute reliability with regard to the confidential information in her possession. Such information is extremely wide and includes internal management decisions, personal details of all staff, including those senior to herself, private problems of staff disclosed to management and personal matters of the management.

WORK

Type all correspondence dictated by management.

Type correspondence dictated by administrative superintendent.

Deal with correspondence on own.

Deal with correspondence on own initiative in manager's absence.

Type all agency appointments, all documents relating to such appointments and all correspondence relating thereto.

Type credit-control minutes and correspondence relating thereto, from development manager.

Maintain filing system of all management files.

Maintain all relevant management statistics.

Analyse statistics as required, e.g. field-staff performance against target, agency results, group schemes etc.

Answer managers' telephones (2) and administrative superintendent's telephone in their absence – take message or deal, as appropriate.

Keep management diary of appointments and other matters. Make travel arrangements and book accommodation as required.

Deal with routine work of administrative superintendent in his absence, including all personnel matters, company cars, forward accounts for payment etc.

Stationery.

Maintain group-scheme register.

Prepare board report

Maintain register of complaints.

Keep a record of the premium income of one very large direct client.

Catering.

Maintain special records in connection with Isle of Man Companies Act/registration of companies.

Receive managers' visitors.

Assist with training of Youth Training Scheme trainees (commencing 1985).

Assist typing department in spare time.

Keep record of holidays/sickness/flexitime of staff under direct supervision of Management.

---

in insurance with the personnel function tending to be located at corporate level. Consequently, decisions taken at local level can become unaccountable, unsystematic and potentially unlawful.

In addition to the recruitment tiering of candidates by sex and pre-entry qualifications, three key formal conditions for career progress in insurance tend to impact negatively on women's advancement. These are the requirements to be fully trained and professionally qualified, geographically mobile and to have continuous service. We will now illustrate how each of these prerequisites can impinge upon women's progress.

Training and professional qualifications

If women are not selected to participate on training courses, they are unlikely to be considered for promotion. Conversely, if women are not considered for promotion, then they are unlikely to be selected for essential training programmes. At the head office of company 1, forty-eight training courses were conducted between September 1985 and June 1986. Of the 577 staff who participated on these courses, 398 (i.e. 69 per cent) were men. Of the women participants, 63 per cent went on just four of the courses. These constituted basic training in: claims (19 per cent); data processing (13 per cent); fire and accident (11 per cent); and customer relations (20 per cent). There were no women at all on courses concerning: fire surveying (twelve men); claims inspection (eighteen men); general inspection (sixty-six men); branch managers (twenty-eight men); and only three on training for life sales inspectors (forty-two men).

At company 2, a similar sex imbalance on trainee manager courses in 1984 was displayed as set out in Table 8.6. The assistant personnel manager at company 2 complained that with regard to informal training in the work-force, women were not given the sort, or the variety, of tasks that would ensure their promotion. Consequently, they gained neither the breadth of organisational experience and technical knowledge, nor the confidence to accept the responsibility for decision-making on high-risk insurance policies. In the fire and accident department, for example, working on the insurance of fire-related high risks and claims is much more prestigious, technical and therefore valuable in career terms than concentrating on accident business.

Table 8.6 Sex balance on trainee manager courses

Course title	Females	Males
(1) Initial development	8	46
(2) Effective leadership	3	25
(3) UK special course	—	24
(4) International special course	1	38
Total	12	133

Equally, in both companies 1 and 2, women constituted a small minority of those entering for and holding external professional qualifications. At company 2, although significantly fewer women entered for the ordinary Chartered Insurance Institute examinations (CII), their pass rate was consistently better than that of men (see Table 8.7). In 1984, only 26 per cent (i.e. 294) of the 1,144 successful candidates of the *Associateship* of the CII were female (Crompton and Sanderson 1985). Equally, women made up a meagre 3, 5 and 17 per cent of the Fellows, Associates and student members respectively of the Institute of Actuaries (ibid.). By 1986, there were 7,042 female members of the CII out of a total of 57,903 (*Post Magazine* 1986). Of the 9,163 Fellows, 448 were women and of the 22,792 Associates, 1,945 were women. This sex imbalance on in-house and professional training programmes is not merely a reflection of, but also reinforces, job segregation in the insurance industry.

Table 8.7 CII examination results

		Number entered	Percentage pass rate	Number of distinctions
1982	Female	122	55.4	19
	Male	262	42.8	13
1983	Female	105	56.5	17
	Male	224	56.3	13
1984	Female	76	61.1	4
	Male	208	48.4	8

Crompton and Jones (1984) identify a pattern of increasing 'credentialism' or accumulation of professional qualifications by career-orientated women in insurance. And yet despite their apparent optimism that some women are challenging this particular block to career progress, these authors are less optimistic about the possibility of women being able to comply with the next two requirements for career progress: geographical mobility and unbroken service.

Geographical mobility

The geographical mobility condition is usually a formal requirement to progress into the technical/supervisory career structure. The following three case-studies illustrate how the need for mobility can be exaggerated and applied in inconsistent ways that are detrimental to women's career progress. The first case-study is drawn from company 1. In June 1985, three grade-nine claims-department section leaders applied for an advertised trainee-claims-inspector vacancy. Without even considering the two women, however, the male was interviewed and appointed. The first woman was fully qualified. She was told that her rejection was due to her lack of mobility. The second woman was fully mobile. The reason given for her rejection was that she was not sitting her professional insurance examinations (despite her intention to do so). There were a number of inconsistencies in these decisions.

First, since the job was based at the same branch, the mobility requirement appeared to be unnecessary and could certainly have been applied in a more relaxed fashion. Second, the stipulation for insurance qualifications was contradicted by the appointment, nine months earlier, of an unqualified male section leader to claims inspector in another section. Third, management ignored the willingness of both women to stand in temporarily while the job was vacant. Finally, as section leaders for five and six years respectively, the two women were much more experienced than the man, who had only been in the job for twelve months. Although the women had not even been offered an interview, they decided not to appeal formally. Whilst the union offered them strong support, the women preferred not to 'rock the boat'. Despite fully recognising the contradictory nature of the managers' rationalisations, they did not want to be labelled as 'trouble-makers'.

Their reluctance was also partly a result of routine promotion procedures at company 1, which required candidates to apply for vacancies 'via their manager'. This paternalistic procedure enabled local managers to enjoy extensive autonomy and discretion in scrutinising all applications. The resulting informality and absence of accountability facilitated inconsistent and potentially discriminatory decision-making. It also inhibited the expression of genuine grievances, particularly since the women were concerned to protect their working relationship with their male superior. Another barrier to effective resistance against such ILM practices was the national procedure agreement in which it was stated that the union could not take a grievance on behalf of a member if this had not been instigated by the aggrieved employee him- or herself. Within twelve months of this decision, one of the women had left to start a family.

The second case-study demonstrates that trade-union recruitment practices may also contain inconsistencies and contradictions with regard to gender and geographical mobility. In 1984, a vacancy for a seconded representative was advertised at company 1. This was a full-time three-year post designed to represent union members at union level within the Southern region. The advertisement emphasised the need for geographical mobility and a driving licence. Applications were received from three men and one woman, all of whom were interviewed.

Although the woman could drive, had a car and was totally mobile, and performed extremely well at the interview, the job was given to a man who lived 120 miles from London, was not mobile and could not drive. Despite the mobility requirement being disregarded in the case of the successful male applicant, it was the central factor dominating the female candidate's interview, as she stated: 'The emphasis was on mobility right from the start. There was no mention at all of the rep. being moved outside London. There was certainly no mention of changing areas to meet people's personal requirements.' The actual conduct of the interview provided further evidence to confirm that underlying this inconsistency was a specific intention by the all-male selection panel to appoint a man. The following questions were asked of the female interviewee but were not put to the men;

- 'Did I have any ties or commitments because the hours that I worked would mean nights away and sometimes long days?' (answer: no ties, no commitments, no mortgage and completely mobile)
- 'Did I feel that being a woman rep. I would meet with problems with management?'
- 'How would I deal with a manger who refused to let me in to see the members?'
- 'Are you actually divorced yet?' (answer: yes)
- 'So it's not just a separation?'
- 'Do you have any children?'

While these discriminatory questions may have been intended to examine the woman's capacity to be mobile, the irrelevance of such personal enquiries was exposed by the final selection decision. Thus, although the female candidate performed well and could meet all the formal criteria, she was rejected in favour of a man who was less suited to these requirements. Yet despite being aware of this discriminatory practice, the woman did not take the issue further since she hoped to re-apply the following year to try to become the Division's first-ever female seconded representative.

Once again, a female candidate, who was fully aware that she had received unfair treatment on the grounds of her sex, was unwilling to pursue her grievance even though the trade union was highly committed to equal opportunities in its public statements and policy recommendations. Moreover, union representatives within the Division were encouraging her to resist these practices. Her acquiescence parallels that discussed with regard to personnel managers in Chapter 5. Indeed, it constitutes another illustration of how formal policy claims are sometimes contradicted by actual recruitment practices, where resistance is diluted by the concern to avoid conflict and protect self.

The final case-study concerning geographical mobility is drawn from the highly successful branch office of company 3. Since joining the clerical staff five years earlier, the twenty-three-year-old senior pensions clerk has been considering a transfer into the predominantly male world of sales. Discontented with the mundane nature of her clerical jobs, she had threatened to resign previously before being promoted to her present job. Indeed, two years earlier, she secured another job, but was dissuaded from accepting it by the branch manager, who refused to provide a reference because he did not want her to leave. The clerk was complimented by the manager's paternalistic acknowledgement of the degree to which he depended on her, as she stated:

> He said 'now come on, what's the problem?' and eventually I agreed to stay, on the basis that I got a decent salary rise and they send me on a course to head office. I came back thinking the company was wonderful. So, as I say, he had tried to keep me before, which I felt good about really . . . he'd never tried this with anyone before so I felt appreciated. They don't make a habit of patting you on the back and telling you how good you are, here.

As the fifth anniversary of her appointment drew close, she informed the office manager that unless she became a sales inspector in the near future, she would definitely resign. In a way which displayed the informality that can operate in the more personal and paternal treatment of internal applicants (particularly those in small branches), the manager invited her for a meal, during which he offered a variety of objections to her ambitions.

First, he highlighted the problems associated with the geographical-mobility requirement. This began to undermine her confidence because she was told that company policy prohibited trainees from returning to the same branch, as she said 'I could be sent anywhere. It just depends where there's a vacancy and he kept harping on about whether I was prepared to move.' However, it appears that the manager exaggerated the mobility requirement. A senior personnel officer at head office confirmed that the policy was operated in a relaxed and flexible fashion:

> We try to put people in the area where they are. It's not our policy to ask people to move when they've done their training. In fact I prefer, if they're living with their parents, to try and let them stay there, unless they want to move.

Yet all the female clerks believed that geographical mobility was a prerequisite for becoming a sales inspector, as another stated: 'I'd not like to go outside mainly because you have to move. That's standard company practice. I don't think any of the girls are interested in being an inspector.'

Second, the local manager emphasised the risks attached to performance-related pay systems. According to the senior pensions clerk,

> This scared the 'whatsit' out of me. It hadn't struck me before.

Having a target does worry me. Whereas now, I know, at the end
of the day I've just to get so much work done and everything's
fine.

Third, the branch manager predicted that the male-dominated and highly
competitive client market of professional intermediaries would 'not take
her seriously'. He insisted that these objections were for her own best
interests, as she stated:

Because competition is so fierce in this type of product the women
find it hard going. Some of the brokers are quite obnoxious to the
fellas. I had to admit a woman could go into a brokers and end up
in tears . . . . You've got to let it run off you like water off a duck's
back . . . . Yes, I think men are better at that.

Finally, the branch manager focused on the senior clerk's age and
personality to discourage her ambitions. He suggested that she was too
young at twenty-three to be taken seriously and that she would have
more 'credibility with brokers' if she were at least twenty-five. However, at this stage, she identified the contradictions embedded in the
manager's rationalisations:

Of course, it's not the same for the blokes. Being female, you see,
I'd have to be that bit older. What got me was why should a
flaming young 23-year-old fella know more than I do at the same
age? I was a bit peeved about that.

The manager also suggested that she was not psychologically stable
enough yet to handle 'the pressure' of the product market. Raising these
personality 'deficiencies' had a particularly strong impact on the
pensions clerk, whose commitment thereby began to waver:

It's all right saying equal opportunities, but I don't think you will
ever get employers to look at women in the same light. They will
have to take into consideration that women do have this tendency
to get married, get pregnant and have kids. So why should they go
through all this trouble of promoting her and getting her set up? In
my case it isn't true, but this is generally what happens, you can't
fault them on that. When you get the one who wants a career,
rather than just a job, they don't get recognised because everyone
puts them in the same category.

The manager's personal approach enabled him to exaggerate the
mobility requirement and overemphasise the difficulties surrounding
the target incentive scheme, male clients and especially the senior
clerk's personality. Precisely because of the 'plausibility' of these
arguments she not only deferred her application, but was also persuaded,

first, that the manager's primary concern was her own welfare and, second, of the benefits and security of the branch office, as she herself confirmed:

> At first I was a bit annoyed, then I began to realise he was only thinking of me. What if I did all that training and found out the brokers did not like young females knocking on the door?

Largely because of the manager's paternal approach, she began to internalise his doubts and to believe that she was not yet ready for an inspector position:

> I'm very temperamental, you see. This is another thing he drew to my attention. I can get very annoyed very easily and I also get strong moods. He said, 'There's no way you could go out to a broker with some of the moods you have.

Her growing fears of the market and the possibility of experiencing 'a hard time when brokers kick you out or won't see you' resulted in her accepting the manager's view that 'If I was older I'd be more calm. By the time I'm twenty-five he reckons I'll be fine. But he doesn't think that at the moment it would be right for me to start.' Despite her earlier penetrations of the contradictions in the manager's arguments, his exaggeration of the 'dangers' and insecurities of the predominantly male world of finance eroded her confidence and redirected her aspiration towards a supervisory career within the 'domestic' world of the office. This career path was more compatible with the conventional female identity:

> From a woman's point of view, she might prefer . . . if she wants a career, . . . my idea of a career would be like . . . getting high up inside. That would be my idea, a woman's idea of going higher up within the company on the inside. Ideally, that is what I'd like to do, I think.

Compliance to traditional patriarchal employment patterns held the apparent promise of psychological and economic security in contrast to the reputedly aggressive culture of selling. This same view was articulated by another pensions clerk:

> What you have to do as an inspector involves a lot of hard work and earache, which is not something for a woman. Women are always going to get married and have kids anyway. Security is what I value. In this day and age it's a must.

As she elaborated,

> The manager is right. If you're a woman going out selling insurance you've got to be that much better than your male

counterpart just to prove yourself. If a man comes round it's all right, but if a woman does, you think 'does she know what she's talking about?' I've done it myself.

Having raised these doubts and difficulties, the branch manager finally stated that if the senior pension clerk still wished to become a sales inspector, he would not stop her. Yet on the basis of his warnings and reservations and despite her long-standing ambition, she refused this 'offer' and began, instead, to criticise herself for a lack of ambition and determination:[7]

I think it's me that's the problem. I know there'll come a time when I get fed up again . . . . There's just this financial problem of the mortgage if I have to move. But if I really wanted to, it wouldn't stop me . . . . It's not the inspector's job in here that bothers me. I know the training is good and I'm confident in myself. So it boils down to the move and the finances. It's a pretty big step and I'm spoilt at home.

Despite receiving a great deal of encouragement from brokers and some inspectors, she declined the opportunity to become an inspector.

Paternalism as a form of gendered managerial control had therefore proved to be highly effective in maintaining job segregation, particularly since the senior clerk believed that it had been *her* decision not to become an inspector[8] and that the manager was primarily concerned with her own welfare. Indeed, in one sense it was true that the branch manager's paternalistic arguments were not merely 'bad faith' rationalisations. Even though he described the jobs in an exaggerated and overly onerous fashion, his arguments represented a deep-seated concern about 'risking' the employment of women in the male-dominated world of selling, as his retrospective account of these events demonstrates:

I have in fact talked her out of leaving two or three times. She backed away from it [i.e. being an inspector] a few months ago, which I didn't try and talk her out of, because I didn't think it was the right time. I still think she's got some growing up to do. She is rather vulnerable to send her out on the road. She needs the maturity to be able to call on people and take the rebuffs and advances. You need total commitment to start off with, but if she carries on to mature we'll make her an inspector . . . if she sticks it out.

Having contributed substantially to the senior clerk's doubts and uncertainties, the manager then used these as evidence of her unsuitability. The pensions clerk's awareness of the contradictory nature of the manager's rationalisations was weakened by a defensive ambivalence about her capabilities and a preference for the security of the office. However, her acquiescence did not last too long since eighteen months after the research, she resigned from the company.

The manager's total negativity to the pensions clerk contrasted with his supervisory practices in relation to male trainees. He stated that he operated a highly cautious orientation to recruitment which had established his reputation for 'picking winners'. However, the manager acknowledged that the previous trainee 'makes me cringe thinking about him. He was particularly poor at arithmetic, so I had to buy several books and school him myself . . . . I had to protect my reputation having picked a loser!'

In the context of this highly personal and contradictory form of control, paternalistic promotion practices reflect and reinforce job segregation. This is particularly so in the absence of both job advertising and an independent trade union. At company 3, employees were represented by a staff association with whom they had very little contact at local level.

These case-studies have highlighted how geographical mobility can be applied in an inconsistent and contradictory way to female employees. They illustrate the extensive power available to line management in ILM practices, while also revealing that employees are likely to have greater knowledge than external candidates of the specific promotion exercise and of the strengths and weaknesses of particular candidates. Internal candidates are therefore more likely than external applicants to suspect that a promotion exercise is characterised by sex-discriminatory practices. Under what conditions such knowledge is likely to be translated into effective resistance will be discussed below.

Continuous service

The two case-studies discussed in this final section highlight how continuous service is a promotion criterion, like professional qualifications and geographical mobility, which can impact negatively on women in the insurance industry. Both cases focus on women who are applying for promotion during a pregnancy.

The first example, from the Northern Ireland office of company 1, concerned a twenty-eight-year-old married woman who had worked at the company for nine years. She had seven O levels and three A levels. During the past six years, she had been employed as a senior claims correspondence clerk (grade seven). On 28 October 1985, a current claims-section leader (grade nine) was offered an inspector vacancy, to commence on 3 February 1986. This left a grade-nine vacancy for which the female senior clerk was ideally suited. When the section leader had been on holiday, ill or attending a course, she had always carried out the extra duties. Equally, she had been told that she would be in a strong position, should a section-leader vacancy arise. There were, however, two other grade-sevens who could be considered for the vacancy. One man was professionally qualified (ACII), but had been at grade-seven level for only six months. The other man did not hold professional examinations and had worked as a grade-seven for six years.

Although the claims-inspector vacancy was offered and accepted in October, a delay occurred in filling the section-leader post. It became clear to the female candidate that this delay was due to her pregnancy. She began her maternity leave at the beginning of January but the interviews for the section-leader post were not conducted until 3 February 1986. Her suspicion that the management was merely waiting until she was absent from the office was confirmed by comments which she received. Shortly after the claims' inspector was appointed, for example, she had been introduced to the regional manager by the claims superintendent as follows: 'This is Dorothy, one of our best workers, but unfortunately she has got herself into trouble.' The 'trouble' to which he referred was Dorothy's pregnancy. The regional manager asked if she intended to return to work after maternity, and she stated that she definitely did. In the two months before commencing her maternity leave, several similar comments were passed by the claims superintendent, such as 'It's a pity your timing was wrong.' This woman complained to her local trade-union representative, who informed the chairman of the national equal-opportunities subcommittee. She, in turn, took up the case with corporate personnel managers, who were unaware that closed promotion procedures, rather than open internal advertising of vacancies, were custom and practice in Northern Ireland. They ensured that the decision to fill the vacancy was delayed. Yet largely as a consequence of her detrimental treatment, the female clerk decided not to return to work after maternity.

The final case-study documents a more effective form of resistance to sex-discriminatory promotion practices. It is drawn from the motor department of another branch of company 1 and again demonstrates managerial opposition to the promotion of a pregnant woman. At the beginning of March 1987, a woman grade-six motor clerk informed the company that she was pregnant, and soon afterwards, two grade-seven vacancies were advertised. The female clerk applied but was rejected. She was informed by her superintendent that he could not support her application. Yet at her assessment in the previous February he had stated that her performance was very satisfactory. The year before, she had been told that she was next in line for a grade-seven post. In October 1986, she had been seriously considered and interviewed for another grade-seven vacancy. Moreover, she was totally mobile, the only applicant with A levels and the only person in the department who had received an A for her work performance in both the previous years. A woman who was not mobile and who had been rejected outright for the October vacancy and a man who had received a warning after being criticised by clients were appointed.

Because the superintendent could give no clear reason for her outright rejection, the clerk, who was a local union representative, contacted a senior official of the trade union. At a meeting between the clerk, the trade-union representative and the administration manager, the latter stated that selection decisions were largely the responsibility of the superintendent. The manager had great difficulty in explaining why, although the clerk had been a serious contender for the previous vacancy in October, she could not even be recommended in the following March. The meeting was adjourned to allow the administration manager time to consult with the superintendent. When it was reconvened, five points were outlined to justify her rejection. First, the superintendent believed that she did not 'demonstrate the personality to take on the job'. She 'needed to display a greater desire to move beyond grade seven'. Second, she had never been fully committed and 'allowed personal issues to interfere with her work'. Third, she was reputed to have made a critical comment about the company to a colleague. Fourth, she had shown no commitment to work overtime, and finally, she had not begun to sit her professional insurance examinations.

Apart from exposing the highly vague, impressionistic and superficial nature of these rationalisations, the senior union official was able to argue that they were also largely incorrect and inconsistent. The first point concerning personality was contradicted by the complimentary reports received from insurance brokers concerning her work performance and communication skills. She had also displayed supervisory qualities in motivating and guiding young trainee inspectors. This was supported with written evidence. Second, the view that she was not fully committed was contradicted by excellent assessment reports. Third, the union representative argued that it was completely untenable to base promotion decisions on hearsay. In addition, the particular comments attributed to the grade-five clerk were denied. Fourth, it was stressed that the statements concerning the clerk's overtime record were incorrect since she had worked an extra ten hours in both January and February. Regardless of this discrepancy, it was again pointed out that overtime was not a criterion for promotion. Finally, that the clerk had not begun to sit her professional examinations (although she had always stated her intention to do so) was completely irrelevant anyway since neither had the two appointees.

Against this background of highly inconsistent and contradictory promotion decision-making, the senior national official of the trade-union executive took the case to the company's head-office personnel department. As a result, 'discreet' pressure was put on the local management to resolve the matter informally by upgrading the clerk regardless of whether a vacancy actually existed. At this point, the local branch manager (who is senior to the administration manager) intervened in the dispute. He informed the union representative that another grade-seven vacancy in the motor department was to be advertised. Although the grade-six clerk would be considered, '80 per cent' of this job consisted of VDU work. Since she had requested not to use the VDU during her pregnancy, the manager doubted that she would be appointed because of the difficulty, as he put it, with her 'health problem'. The union representative criticised this alternative proposal as a way of sidetracking from the main issue of the potentially discriminatory practices against a pregnant member of staff. She reminded the manager that there was a procedure agreement between the union and the company that any pregnant woman could ask to be taken off the VDU work during pregnancy without loss of grade.

As a result of the resilience of the clerk, the persistence of the trade-union representative and her ability to expose the contradictions of the managers' rationalisations combined with the informal pressure by corporate personnel, it was agreed that the clerk would be upgraded. The woman took maternity leave and subsequently returned to work after the minimum period of absence. This example illustrates that even after sex-discriminatory promotion decisions have been made, they can still be challenged and overturned when resistance is able to expose the contradictory nature of decisions and to mobilise the necessary power and influence to ensure their reversal. In sum, these two case-studies illustrate how women's domestic responsibilities and the ideology surrounding them can constitute a barrier to women's career progress in insurance.[9]

Conclusion

This chapter has drawn on the research findings to explore how far and why women are recruited into the insurance industry. Only by examining internal selection practices, in addition to external recruitment procedures, can the specific reasons for the appointment of women be fully analysed. Barriers to women's progress can emerge in recruitment tiering and managers' contradictory dependence on female gendered skills, in the allocation of post-entry training on in-house and professional courses and in relation to the requirements of geographical mobility and unbroken service.[10] In short, while men are often channelled into relatively autonomous field-force vacancies, women in insurance tend to be recruited for, and restricted to, the office equivalent of domestic work.

A consistent pattern emerging from the case-studies was that female employees were highly reluctant to challenge decisions, either individually or collectively, that quite clearly appeared to discriminate against them on the grounds of sex. Women tended to avoid conflict through either acquiescence or individualistic and self-defensive forms of informal resistance – for example, by resigning, either to look for a job elsewhere or to raise a family. The paradox, of course, is that these informal modes of resistance usually had the effect of reinforcing the likelihood of further sex-discriminatory practices. They therefore contributed to the reproduction of a vicious circle of sex discrimination in recruitment. Underlying these forms of defensive indifference and disenchantment was a concern to protect identity by distancing self mentally or physically from sex-discriminatory practices. Accordingly, the formal articulation of resistance was often perceived by the women to constitute a threat to material and symbolic security grounded in routine office practices.

This sense of security in conformity was partly the outcome of the paternal approach of local line managers, whose claims to be acting in the women's best interests appeared plausible and at least partially true. Paternalism is an effective mode of managing the contradictions of control since it draws on, rather than undermines, labour agency. Its emphasis on the human and moral face of management reassures staff that the employer can be trusted since their 'best interests' will be protected. This paternalistic strategy reflected and reinforced the formal organisational power structure, which also impacted on the women's defensive preference for the apparent security of compliance, in contrast to the perceived insecurity of resisting those in authority and power.

Yet the case-studies also reveal that women *employees* often had extensive knowledge on which to base a judgement about whether they were the victims of sex discrimination. They knew about the particular selectors, the relative merit of other candidates and of the outcome of promotion decisions. In this sense, they were able to 'partially penetrate' (Willis 1977: 119) the contradictions embedded in sex-discriminatory practices. Yet the foregoing evidence reveals that these partial penetrations were limited in particular by the concern to preserve gender and hierarchical identity and material security. Indeed, the concern to secure identity emerged in the data as a consistently crucial factor in the reproduction of the vicious circles of job segregation. The women's avoidance of conflict and/or their expression of resistance through distancing and self-defensive practices reflected a preoccupation with maintaining a highly conventional self-definition of gender identity. One consequence of this preoccupation was the women's perception of subordination as a form of security. This was evidenced, for example, at company 3 in women's preference for office work since a 'job inside' was believed to be more compatible with the conventional definitions of female identity. Hence, subordinates may also collude in rationalising and normalising the reproduction of job segregation. The 'individualistic strategies' (Walsgrove 1987: 52) which they adopt in coping with their subordination results in the dilution of resistance since employees thereby control or 'police' (ibid.) themselves.

The women's perceptions about gender identity were reinforced by the concern of male sales staff to project a 'professional image' and to manage a confident air of competence. As the previous chapter outlined, this presentation of self reflected a particularly masculine preoccupation with being dominant and assertive, while constructing an appearance of self-control and resilience to 'take the knocks' in the 'aggressive financial market-place'. The women's primary concern, to maintain economic and psychological security thereby contributed to the reproduction of job segregation and managerial control.

Yet such individualistic forms of resistance produced contradictory consequences; for the evidence shows that, when left unchallenged, the extensive discretion and unaccountability of line managers, which facilitated an inconsistent, arbitrary and overly personal exercise of power, invariably had a detrimental impact on women. Accordingly, practices of distancing and escapism tended merely to reinforce the women's insecurity and lack of confidence as clerical workers with little organisational power, influence and status who were vulnerable to sex-discriminatory practices. The sense of security promised by the preservation of conventional gender and hierarchical identity was thereby shown to be illusory.

An alternative, more collective approach to resistance was outlined in the final case-study. Here, the female clerk was prepared to accept the insecurity and to risk the perceived negative consequences of resistance such as labelling and the threat to future career progress. Encouraged by the trade union, she was able to penetrate and expose the contradictions of the formal rationalisations given by management to legitimise their sex-discriminatory promotion practices. The trade union, in turn, was then able to exploit the divisions within the managerial structure, isolate local-level management and thereby translate these penetrations into practices by enlisting the support of corporate personnel who were committed to upholding the company's claim to be 'an equal-opportunity employer'. As in the case-study from the banking sector discussed at the end of Chapter 6, effective resistance to sex discrimination was found to emerge where trade union and corporate personnel combined together in a way that constituted a powerful form of pressure on local line managers. The effectiveness of this opposition was all the more remarkable since it was able to reverse a decision that had already been made.

Conclusion:
the vicious circles of job segregation

Overall, the research findings reveal that despite anti-discrimination legislation in the mid-1970s, a substantial number of employers, many of whom publicly subscribe to equal opportunities, are still 'managing to discriminate' on the grounds of sex through a variety of recruitment practices. Accordingly, this book has sought to highlight how gender divisions often play a crucial role within the recruitment practices of capitalist organisations. The conventional sexual divisions of labour at home and in employment were shown to be both a routine condition and consequence of recruitment and a common means of legitimising sex-discriminatory practices. In addition, the analysis demonstrated that job segregation is a central, if often taken-for-granted, aspect of management's control of the labour process.

Although management's power over labour was highlighted by the research findings, the analysis also displayed how the managerial function cannot be treated as a monolithic and homogeneous force, whose control practices are the wholly determined and rational outcome of the capitalist pressure to extract surplus value. Rather, there are contradictions between capital and labour and within capital itself which may either facilitate the reproduction of job segregation or provide the conditions for the mobilisation of resistance.

In this final chapter, three objectives are pursued. First, the vicious circles of job segregation in recruitment are discussed, drawing on the empirical findings from all five industrial sectors. Second, these findings are then theorised by adding an analysis of the social construction of identity to that of power and agency in the recruitment process. Third, on the basis of this empirical and theoretical analysis, the possible organisational changes which could establish the conditions for the elimination of sex discrimination in recruitment are then outlined.

Reproduction, rationalisation and resistance

Part I of the book highlighted the failure of the available literature on sex

192

discrimination to present an adequate analysis of both power and agency in the recruitment process. On the one hand, the conventional liberal perspectives tended to subscribe to a 'power-blind' *voluntarism*. On the other hand, the more critical Marxist-feminist and sociological accounts, while providing a valuable counter to the conventional literature, adhered to an overly *deterministic* analysis of managerial and male power which neglected human agency. The critique of these two perspectives was then elaborated through the empirical analysis.

Although the importance of asymmetrical power relations was incorporated into this analysis, the primary concern was to focus on the way that sex discrimination could only be reproduced in recruitment practices through the agency of management, labour, men and women. The theoretical emphasis on power and agency resulted in an empirical examination not only of external recruitment, but also and wherever possible of ILM practices. Together, this analytical and methodological framework was able to highlight how the perpetuation of job segregation was characterised by a self-fulfilling vicious circle which incorporated the three key recruitment practices of *reproduction, rationalisation* and *resistance* (see Figure 9:1). Each of these practices will now be summarised in turn.

The research confirmed that informality in the channels, criteria and procedures of recruitment was both a common practice across the five sectors and one that facilitated the *reproduction* of job segregation.[1] With regard to recruitment sources, informality was especially likely where jobs were filled internally and particularly so where the ILM was characterised by closed procedures.[2] Yet even where jobs were filled externally, informal channels could operate not only through the recommendation of labour-force and business-community contacts, but also through the maintenance of waiting-lists, such as the 'people-bank' mechanism. The use of these informal sources had the effect, whether deliberate or inadvertent, of reproducing job segregation.

The research also uncovered extensive informality in selection criteria which, in concentrating on highly implicit and vague criteria of acceptability, contributed to the reproduction of sex discrimination. Depending on the nature and degree of job segregation, taken-for-granted beliefs about the male 'bread-winner' and female 'homemaker' informed the preference for either men or women. Such assumptions were often used as an indicator of a candidate's ability to do the job and of his or her future work performance.

Hence, preconceptions about the domestic responsibilities of both sexes were often perceived to be of central relevance to selection decision-making. For men, real, imagined or potential domestic responsibilities were usually evaluated as a positive indication of stability, flexibility, compatibility and motivation, while for women,

Figure 9.1 The '3 Rs': the vicious circles of job segregation

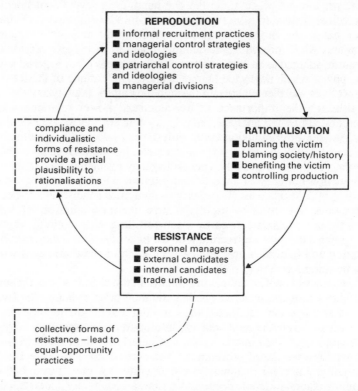

they were often viewed negatively as confirmation of unreliability and a short-term investment in work. However, these selector assumptions could be reversed, where the jobs on offer were low paying, low status and mundane with little career potential. For such jobs, it was often decided, on the basis of the stereotype of the dependent female home-maker that women would be more stable, flexible and able to 'fit in' (for detailed elaboration see Collinson 1988a). These assumptions were also embedded in tiered recruitment practices, where women were recruited at a younger age and with lower qualifications than men for poor-paying jobs, offering only mundane work, tight supervision and few career opportunities.

The research also uncovered a high degree of informality in the setting and the content of interviews. Such practices could facilitate a *hostile* approach to the interviewing of women (where men were auto-matically preferred), and lead to *inconsistent* treatment of candidates of either sex. Geographical mobility was found to be a common selection requirement that was sometimes applied both in a more relaxed fashion than formally described, and in a more onerous and hostile manner to female candidates. Similarly, the asking of 'personal' questions to female interviewees could be deemed unlawful.

All of these practices were often taken for granted and reproduced unquestioningly because they seemed to respondents to be 'normal' and 'natural'. As such, they rarely required explanation. However, in those cases where managers felt it necessary to justify sex discriminatory practices,[3] four main categories of *rationalisations* were recorded. Managers were found to deflect and deny responsibility for the reproduction of job segregation by blaming women and society or by insisting that they were merely seeking to control production. Alternatively, they were only prepared to acknowledge any responsibility as the perpetrators of sex discrimination where they could emphasise the socially beneficial consequences of their practices. These ideological rationalisations were not merely unthought-through 'excuses', for managers were often whole-heartedly convinced of the validity of their explanations. Indeed, their justifications were taken for granted precisely because they seemed to be so obviously self-evident, 'normal' and 'natural'.

It has been argued that the plausibility of these ideological rationalisations is grounded not only in vested economic interests in the perpetuation of job segregation, but also in the 'partial truths' on which these vicious circles are based. Partial truths are highly selective and exaggerated accounts of the social and material realities of production and reproduction. The capitalist managerial ideology of their exclusive right to manage and to select staff is an exaggerated partial truth of the need for some form of control and organisation within the labour process. It is also reinforced by the way in which the capitalist labour process is socially organised. Equally, the realities of biological reproduction and of its conventional social organisation constitute the 'plausible' basis for the persistence of the bread-winner and homemaker gender stereotypes.

The empirical evidence suggested that the partiality and plausibility of these interwoven ideologies crucially shaped the reproduction of sex-discriminatory recruitment practices. By recognising this partial interrelationship between ideological, social and material factors, it is possible to begin to explain why conventional gender assumptions and practices retain such a taken-for-granted grip on many male and female recruiters, jobseekers, employees and trade unionists alike.

The research therefore uncovered a variety of ways in which job segregation could be reproduced and rationalised within the recruitment process. Yet while these practices were often found to be self-fulfilling, they could also be self-defeating for managements. Informal recruitment practices could not only be inefficient and unaccountable, but might also reinforce deep-seated divisions between and within managerial functions. Attempts by personnel managers to ensure that recruitment practices were formal, consistent and lawful were often found to be undermined by divisions based on: function (between personnel and line); space (corporate/local); hierarchy (senior line manager/subordinate personnel); age; gender; control strategy; and managerial ideology. These divisions tended to emerge in all five sectors of the research. This, in turn, suggests that, although it has to be recognised that the role of personnel managers will often be shaped by the diversity of contexts in which they operate (Sisson 1989), in seeking to formalise the recruitment process these managers may also face systematic and consistent problems across different organisations.

Similarly, sex-discriminatory practices were found to be counter-productive for management where: well-qualified female candidates were rejected (even when skill shortages persisted); women's skills and experience were lost to the organisation when they resisted their subordination by resigning; and where women's abilities were under-utilised when they were refused promotion.

Moreover, many of the rationalisations uncovered in the research tended to neglect, ignore or conceal the way in which management's economic vested interests, their power over the labour market, pre-recruitment sex-typing and specific selection practices had the effect of ensuring the reproduction of job segregation, regardless of the women themselves, 'history', 'society' or the need to control production. Management's rationalisations were not so much wrong, as highly partial and entirely incomplete accounts which selectively focused on one element of the vicious circle of job segregation. The research suggests that, just as the 'common-sense' plausibility of gender and managerial ideology can be reinforced by their material grounding as exaggerated and distorted *'partial truths'*, equally and conversely resistance can emerge through the *'partial penetrations'* of the contradictions which may exist between ideology and both material realities and social practices. The partiality of ideology can therefore operate both downwards on consciousness and agency and upwards through resistance.

Hence, *resistance* can be mobilised precisely because of the discrepancies between rationalisations and recruitment practices. The emergence of resistance added a further counter-productive element to managerial practices and was particularly likely to be effective where opposition was in some sense collective in nature. For example, the combined pressure of corporate personnel, senior trade-union officials and employees was in certain cases able to challenge pregiven selection decisions. This was especially likely in promotion practices since here trade unions were sometimes able to generate a form of collective resistance which could exploit the divisions within the managerial function, penetrate the contradictory nature of sex-discriminatory rationalisations and practices and then mobilise the necessary formal power, influence and persuasion to ensure the reversal of such decisions. The combined involvement of corporate personnel managers, with their hierarchical authority, and trade-union officials, with their greater knowledge of local-level practices, sometimes facilitated the implementation of equal-opportunity policies at operational level.

Yet within the empirical material as a whole, such case-studies were rare. Indeed, just like the reproduction and rationalisation of sex discrimination, resistance was often found to be contradictory and self-defeating. The research revealed the dual character of resistance which, on the one hand, may undermine yet, on the other hand, could actually reinforce recruiters' sex-discriminatory rationalisations. Resistant practices tended to be diluted into acquiescence, compliance and disen-chantment and/or oppositional practices which were designed to 'distance' the individual from the effects of sex discrimination and from the possible conflict of challenging authority. Underlying these forms of compliance and defensive resistance was a common concern of individuals to protect their material and symbolic interests.

Junior personnel managers and internal candidates believed that sustained resistance could result in their negative labelling as a 'feminist' or 'trouble-maker', which in turn would be detrimental to their career progress. Yet compliance merely reinforced both their organisational subordination and the perpetuation of unaccountable and potentially unlawful recruitment practices. External job candidates recognised the protracted difficulties associated with taking a formal claim to an industrial tribunal and often preferred merely to look else-where for employment. Because of their marginal position outside the organisation, these candidates were likely to be more uncertain than personnel managers or employees that sex discrimination had been perpetrated.

Even where personnel managers or employees were aware that sex discrimination had been perpetrated and were able to penetrate the underlying inconsistencies in recruiters' rationalisations, resistance tended on the whole to be highly individualistic. Practices such as compliance, work indifference, inflexibility and resignation invariably generated contradictory consequences since they did not so much challenge as partially legitimise the ideological rationalisations which were a condition and consequence of the reproduction of job segreg-ation. Paradoxically, then, resistance could actually reproduce the very conditions of job segregation which it was intended either to avoid or overcome. Having highlighted the ways that job segregation can be reproduced, rationalised and resisted in recruitment, what remains to be explained is why these vicious circles continued to persist despite the organisational contradictions that were found to be embedded in each of these practices. To address this question, a closer and more critical examination of power and human agency is required.

Power, agency and identity

By focusing on the self-defeating and contradictory consequences of sex discrimination, the empirical findings eschewed overly deterministic and economistic analyses of the labour-market practices of management and men. In seeking to explain why the vicious circles of job segregation persist in spite of these inherent contradictions, the conclusions to each of the empirical chapters focused not only on the asymmetrical nature of relations in recruitment, but also on the hitherto neglected significance of individuals' concern to protect their material and symbolic security.

Thus, for example, branch managers in insurance were found to invest their identity as competent selectors in their decision-making such that the perceived risk attached to appointing a woman as a salesperson was magnified. A concern with personal status and career was also found to condition both personnel managers' compliance with line managers' informal and sex-discriminatory practices and their own reproduction and rationalisation of job segregation. Similarly, a preoccupation with material and symbolic security seemed to be a crucial factor in constraining women clerks' resistance to sex discrimination in the insurance industry. In sum, a consistent finding highlighted by the empirical chapters was the way in which individuals in positions of both domination and subordination within the recruitment process prioritised the protection of their own security. One inevitable consequence of this defensive motivation to avoid the perceived risk of challenging sex discrimination was the reproduction of job segregation.

This recurrent empirical finding of a pervasive preoccupation with the security of self among men and women of various ages and in different hierarchical and class positions underlines the analytical importance of a critical appraisal of the conditions and contradictory consequences of human agency. The first half of the book criticised the Marxist-feminist and sociological literature for its neglect of the agency of men, management, women and labour. This critique can now be extended further to focus on the failure of these studies to theorise, rather than merely to take for granted as a pregiven, the construction of identity and its relation to both power and agency. Indeed, within these 'power-sensitive' accounts, there exists a 'theoretical black hole' between the analysis of historically derived capitalist and patriarchal structures (power) and their conditions and consequences at the level of individual action (agency). A critical examination of human agency[4] provides the possibility of contributing to the understanding of how structure is reflected in, and reproduced through, the social practices of human beings.

This approach is intended to transcend deterministic and voluntaristic perspectives by analysing and more closely representing the dynamic processes wherein domination, subordination and resistance are reproduced in recruitment practices. In so doing it is possible to reveal the way in which key participants in the recruitment process are likely to reinforce the contradictions of control and resistance if they are preoccupied with maintaining material and symbolic security for themselves in a gender- and class-divided competitive world. While the struggle for material and symbolic status encouraged by capitalist and patriarchal structures serves to reproduce class- and gender-based forms of domination and insecurity, these outcomes are also conditioned by attempts to secure objectified images of self.

Such attempts to objectify identity seek to remove that which cannot be denied, namely the ambiguity of self in the 'lived through flow of experience' (Merleau Ponty 1962). This irreducible ambiguity is based primarily on the inherently dual nature of self (Collinson and Knights 1986) wherein human beings experience themselves as both active *subjects* and passive *objects* of self and others' evaluations. Given the inevitably dual nature of self, the concern to secure an objectified identity in the eyes of self and others is contradictory. This is because the objectification of identity constitutes a denial of both self and other as subjects with the creative power to transform social relations. Typically, attempts are made in such cases to use others in the embellishment of personal identity and the overcoming of insecurity. Others are thereby reduced to the status of objects, who have to be controlled for the preservation of self-image. Accordingly, the preoccupation with securing identity is highly destructive of social relations. Attempts to sustain the coherence of identity through objective validations are also contradictory because it is invariably impossible to predict, let alone control, others' judgements and evaluations on which objective images of self depend. Paradoxically, then, attempts to retain a stable identity tend to reinforce the very existential insecurity they seek to transcend.

In order to explain the resilience of the vicious circles of job segregation, it is therefore necessary to examine not only the asymmetrical nature of power in the labour market, but also the agency and, in particular, the identity-securing strategies of the key participants involved in the relations of domination, subordination, compliance and resistance which characterise recruitment practices. Moreover, the unintended and sometimes self-defeating consequences of the concern to secure identity reinforce the internal contradictions which characterise gender inequality in capitalist society. Contradictions at the level of structure can therefore be reflected and reinforced by those at the level of consciousness and action. These internal contradictions and divisions which characterise the reproduction of managerial and male domination provide the possibility not only for proactive resistance, but also for effective organisational change.

The failure of the Marxist-feminist literature, discussed in Part I of the book, to explore the conditions and consequences of seeking to preserve gender and hierarchical identity is reflected in the absence within this literature of a full examination of the contradictory nature of male domination in class society. It is also revealed by a failure to theorise fully the counter-productive consequences of some forms of women's resistance. Whilst a thorough explication of the central contradictions of men's domination in capitalist society has yet to be articulated, it is nevertheless true that certain studies have gone further than Walby (1986, 1989) in exposing some of the self-defeating consequences for men of their position of power within class society (for example, Sennett and Cobb 1977; Tolson 1977; Willis 1977; Barrett 1980; Cockburn 1983; Metcalf and Humphries 1985; Hearn 1987; Kaufman 1987; Brittan 1989). A brief discussion of the major themes of these studies facilitates the elaboration of a theory of power inequality in the labour market which is sensitive to gender identity and its self-defeating conditions and consequences.

Barrett (1980: 216) has highlighted some of the contradictory consequences of the family-bread-winner role for working-class men. She argues that this role in practice locks men into wage labour because the control systems of capitalist employment pressurise them into acquiescence in order to protect both their jobs and family. She concludes that the material and symbolic benefits enjoyed by male bread-winners should not be overstated.

This point is illustrated very well by the foregoing research findings in Chapter 7 which highlighted the male sex-typing of insurance sales. Here, selectors believed that as family bread-winners, men would be in a position of domestic authority and therefore stability. To the extent that this is so, men's domestic control is thereby converted into their employment discipline and subordination since this is used as a key aspect of management's motivation and control over individual sales representatives. In addition, men in insurance sales face the paradox that, although they might benefit from sex discrimination at the beginning of their careers, they could become victims of age discrimination at a later stage. Although the bread-winner identity may be perceived *positively* by individual men since it provides them with some employment opportunity and security, the pressures of mortgage and family dependants can become a severe burden when individuals' productivity begins to fall as they grow older and companies look for younger bread-winners to replace them.

Sennett and Cobb (1977) point to the paradox that family bread-winners are often unable to enjoy the full satisfactions of family life because of their preoccupation with providing for dependants. They argue that the US class system and its dominant ideology of individualism, personal success and the 'American Dream' creates a doubt about the self (ibid.: 171) which shapes manual workers' feelings of inadequacy and social failure. In taking their position within the social hierarchy as an indication of their personal character and skill, male workers begin to see themselves as 'failures' who must not only provide, but also sacrifice for their wife and children (see also Collinson 1981). Working longer and longer hours, they have less time to spend with their families.

Hence, underlying men's domination of women may be self-criticism, denial and doubt, which in turn conditions their sacrifice for the next generation. In the face of a class structure which threatens the dignity of manual workers (Collinson 1981, 1988b), male bread-winners may perceive an opportunity to validate self as a man worthy of dignity in the role of sacrificial provider; as Sennett and Cobb write: 'Sacrifice is the last resource for individualism, the last demonstration of competence. . .It is the final demonstration of virtue when all else fails' (1977: 140).

These two studies reveal that the typical male role of family bread-winner and men's narrow investment in the rational, instrumental world of work condition their distance from, and inability to relate to, those for whom they provide. Trapped in the 'responsible' roles of provider and employee, men's belief in the dignity of self-sacrifice often leads only to bitterness and emptiness in later years. Equally, it ensures that men are locked into wage labour and the control systems of employment. Paradoxically, then, men's domination over women may reflect and reinforce their subordination not only within the labour process, but also to their children's future. While men clearly benefit from their dominant position within a class society, a closer examination reveals that this invariably generates unintended and contradictory consequences for them, both in paid work and in the domestic sphere.

In contrast with the *individualistic* ideal of the privatised bread-winner, men's power in employment, particularly in manual work, is often characterised by a *collective* celebration of exaggerated masculinity or machismo (for an elaboration see Collinson 1988b). Willis's analysis of school counter-culture displays how a group of 'lads' constructed an oppositional culture, based on pisstaking, swearing, skiving, sexism and racism which established a sense of masculine identity and of freedom and independence from the authority of the school. Yet he demonstrates how this culture paradoxically prepares these working-class lads for the very subordinated manual jobs which offer so little freedom and independence and from which there was no escape.[5]

Cockburn (1983) explores the shop-floor contradictions of working-class men's preoccupation with competitive masculinity – as she points out: 'Second only to warfare, work is the arena in which men wrestle each other for status and survival' (ibid.: 133). She shows how male printers' preoccupation with a masculine self-image reinforces internal class divisions, conflict and competition between skilled and unskilled, men and women and different trade unions in the printing industry. In consequence, union opposition to management often carries the contradiction of being built upon the reproduction of internal working-class divisions. Moreover, the compositors' image of tough masculinity is inconsistent with both the history and the reality of organisational power. The men's ideology and exclusionary practices suppressed the historical evidence of women's presence as compositors. Cockburn highlights the contemporary dangers of printers' investment of masculine identity in their skills when the introduction of new technology is leading to their replacement by women with keyboard skills; as she observes, 'There is always a fragility in men's reliance on work as a prop for their masculine identity' (ibid.: 135).

Yet the precariousness of masculine identities, men's concern to prove their virility and masculinity and their insistence on personal independence and control is not merely conditioned by the threat of technological innovation and feminisation; for it is also a result of the preoccupation with securing self in gender identity.

The contradictory conditions and consequences of this concern are neglected in the foregoing studies. In the absence of a critical analysis of the preoccupation with gender and hierarchical identity it is difficult to explain why job segregation and men's domination are reproduced despite their inherent contradictory consequences. Like Cockburn, Brittan (1989) recognises the precariousness of masculine identity. Arguing that gender is not static since it is always subject to redefinition and renegotiation, he contends that gender identity has to be continually accomplished and constructed. Accordingly, Brittan highlights the problems of identity faced by unemployed men, whose sense of dignity based on the bread-winner role is undermined (ibid.: 189). In addition, Brittan focuses on the way in which women's objectification and trivialisation by men and their routine exclusion from power has the effect of negating women's dignity and 'respect-worthiness' (ibid.: 157). Yet despite this concentration on dignity and identity, Brittan fails to explore fully the conditions and consequences of the search for dignity through objectified social images of self, whether based on gender, class, age and so on. In particular, Brittan does not examine why and with what consequences men seek to purchase a sense of security in a solid and validated self at the cost of denying the status-worthiness of women.

Other literature has explored the way that conventional male identity, in its individualist or collective forms, appears to be the outcome of deeper, existential anxieties about the body, sexuality and biological reproduction. As such, male domination could be interpreted not simply as a form of economic exploitation, as Walby (1986) proposes, but also as a consequence of seeking to overcome these existential anxieties. Connell (1983), for example, highlights the relationship between men's consciousness, the body and class inequality. He displays how the hegemonic masculine sense of self, particularly in working-class settings, often rests on a deep-seated anxiety with the size and shape of the male body. This 'narcissism in men's preoccupation with their bodies' (ibid.: 20), which comes to symbolise power, strength, male superiority and domination, remains a central preoccupation of many men in their work, their sexual relations and as fathers.

In exploring the dialectic of reproduction, O'Brien (1981) argues that once men's seed has been discharged, they are alienated from the reproductive process and thereby from nature. This genetic alienation and loss of control generates uncertainties, tensions and contradictions which men seek to resolve through an ideology of male supremacy based on potency. This can take a variety of social and historical forms; as she writes (1981: 49): 'Potency is a masculine triumph over man's natural alienation from the process of reproduction.' In seeking to resist the genetic alienation of paternity through the ideology of potency, men will attempt to control mother and child in order to possess women's reproductive labour power in a similar way to the capitalist appropriation of labour power.

Like O'Brien, Hartsock (1983) has also argued that because men tend to experience themselves as separate, distinct and discontinuous from nature, a preoccupation with virility often emerges. Control and domination are men's routine defensive strategies in overcoming their fear of ceasing to exist as a separate being.

Hearn (1987) draws on the work of O'Brien and Hartsock to explore how men's alienated relationship to the social organisation of biological reproduction (i.e. conception, pregnancy, birth, dependent child-rearing) conditions their concern to control and appropriate. He also criticises O'Brien's exclusive focus on biological reproduction to the neglect of both sexuality and men's social distance from child-rearing.

Hollway (1983, 1984b) does explore men's sexuality. She shows how their 'desire for the other' can generate intense feelings of vulnerability because such displays of desire are perceived by men to risk the possibility of rejection and therefore to transfer power to the woman. Equally, Hollway (1984b: 232) argues that men often see women's sexuality as rabid, dangerous and needing to be controlled. In order to deal with their subsequent feelings of insecurity, men seek to deny that women do have sexual power over them by adopting defensive strategies of resistance which emphasise their own independence, autonomy and invulnerability. Their consequent appearance of strength and self-sufficiency is therefore precisely the opposite of what men are actually experiencing. Hollway argues that women often misrecognise this peculiarly male way of coping with the experience of insecurity and fail to see the vulnerability underlying this façade.

Kaufman (1987) also highlights the ambiguity for men between their actual experience of being male and the conventional social identity of masculinity. He contends that men's violence against women, other men and themselves is the outcome of their attempts to deal with the 'ambivalent feelings' (ibid.: 14) and 'great doubts' (ibid.: 15) about the precariousness, artificiality and fragility of masculine identity as it is socially constructed. One result of this is the perpetuation of divisions between men based on class, race and sexual preference (ibid.: xv).

The focus on male insecurity in the work of Connell, O'Brien, Hartsock, Hollway and Kaufman suggests that men's preoccupation with gender identity (for example, machismo or bread-winner) may be particularly acute because of its partial grounding in physical and material conditions. Hence, whilst the concern to protect identity might have been common to many of the men and women in the research, its basis in specifically physical realities is likely to shape manifestations of gender identity which have a sex-specific character. The experience of self is inevitably mediated through physical and material realities. However, whilst these realities crucially impact on the consciousness of self and of other, the experience of identity can only be understood socially by the use of symbols through which it is constituted.

The foregoing studies examine either the conditions which reinforce problems of identity for men *or* the contradictory consequences of different manifestations of masculinity. In their sensitivity to identity, they demonstrate that male domination is rarely complete either at home or in paid work. Nevertheless, these accounts fail to theorise *both* the contradictory conditions and consequences of seeking to secure gender and/or hierarchical identity. The investment of self in an objectified masculine identity is a contradictory condition and consequence of men's defensive attempts to retain control and remain independent and invulnerable within organisational, domestic, gender and class relations that are ultimately characterised by interdependence (Rowbotham 1982;

Grieco and Whipp 1986). While the literature recognises that this insecurity about self is a *consequence* of gender and class inequality, managerial and male control and biological reproduction and sexuality, it fails to theorise how the concern with gender and hierarchical identity is also a condition of, and thereby central to, the reproduction of gender divisions.

The contradictory nature of men's domination is also underlined by the incidence of women's agency and resistance in employment as several empirical studies have highlighted (for example, Purcell 1979; Barker and Downing 1980; Pollert 1981, 1983; Cavendish 1982; Wajcman 1983; Westwood 1984; Grieco and Whipp 1986).

Grieco and Whipp (ibid.), for example, disclose women's crucial contribution to informal recruitment practices in the pottery and fishing industries. Using detailed empirical evidence, they reveal the import- ance of women's active role as 'employment brokers'. Here, women were able to influence the recruitment and training of both sexes to specific trades and skills by drawing upon kinship networks both inside and outside the work-place. Women also directed their husbands towards higher-paying vacancies, acted as the main bread-winner when needed, and usually maintained control over the domestic budget. Grieco and Whipp conclude by rejecting the view that male dominance is ever complete either at work or at home. While valuably demon- strating the interstitial and informal social power exercised by working- class women within the home and in specific labour markets, this study fails to theorise the contradictions of women's brokerage role. More specifically, it neglects to consider how the reproduction of job segreg- ation in these industries was a condition and consequence of women's concern to ensure material and symbolic security within the family.

Other ethnographies *have* concentrated on the contradictions for women arising from their resistance to the power of men through various mechanisms that trade on traditional stereotypes of 'femininity'. Thus, for example, Barker and Downing (1980) point to an informal collective work culture created by women secretaries, which cannot be penetrated by 'masculine work standards' (ibid.: 83). This culture reflects and reinforces an 'escape' from mundane and routinised work as women concentrate their conversations and interactions on domestic topics related to their personal lives (and often preferred identities) as wives and mothers. Likewise, Pollert (1981) shows how female manual workers 'switched off' (ibid.: 31) from their mundane work, preferring to engage in informal discussions with other women workers about topics such as domestic life, marriage, health, television and so on. They also avoided work by 'getting out the back' to the toilets which constituted a refuge and a place to smoke and chat. 'Having a laugh' (ibid.:138) was another crucial element of the oppositional shop-floor culture (Collinson 1988b). Women used their humour and sexual innuendo to poke fun at, flirt with and sometimes to retaliate against, the authority of male supervisors. In her study of women workers in a hosiery factory, Westwood (1984: 22) documents a similar oppositional 'culture of femininity' which in various ways brought domestic concerns into the factory. Motherhood in particular was celebrated as the 'final stage in the process of becoming a woman' (ibid.: 228). These celebrations reinforced relations between the women on the shop-floor and strengthened their resistance to managerial control.

Each of these authors recognises how women's resistance can be counter-productive in that it reinforces many of the gender stereotypes which fuel men's practices of domination and discrimination. And yet, here again, as in the case of the foregoing studies of men's domination, these authors do not attend to the self-defeating character of seeking to secure identity. Accordingly, while the contradictory nature of women's resistance is recognised, it is not fully theorised. Beechey (1983, 1984) has argued that the theorisation of women's work consciousness in these empirical studies still tends to retain a 'curiously deterministic feel' since women are often represented as 'victims of domestic oppression and familial ideology' (Beechey 1984: 32). Both Pollert (1981: 87, 107) and Westwood (1984: 89) draw on Gramsci's notion of 'fragmented common sense' to explain the women's contradictory consciousness as it was shaped in the 'collision of bourgeois ideology and working class experience' (Pollert 1983: 14). While this is a valuable counter to those arguments which view women as the passive recipients of dominant ideologies and therefore as harbouring 'false consciousness', the reasons why women remain attached to specifically 'feminine' self-definitions as sources of positive personal power and security, and the consequence of so doing, remain underexplored.

In sum, the preoccupation with identity in the context of asymmetrical power relations is a crucial but often neglected factor which contributes to the reproduction of job segregation. The persistence of the contradictory vicious circles of job segregation is therefore based in particular on the partial truths embedded in gender and managerial ideology and the preoccupation with gender and hierarchical identity which they reflect and reinforce. In order to explain the way in which job segregation is routinely reproduced, rationalised and resisted in the recruitment process, we have been concerned to develop the analysis of power inequalities in the labour market, by focusing on human agency and the subjective preoccupation with the security of self. While a stable identity may be pursued because it appears to provide a positive source of personal security and power for individual men and women in positions of both domination and subordination, contradictory consequences almost inevitably result. Given these empirical and theoretical conclusions, what measures could be implemented in order to create the conditions for the elimination of sex discrimination in the recruitment process?

Prescriptions: A gender agenda

An implicit assumption throughout this book has been that an adequate solution to sex discrimination and gender inequality in recruitment cannot be advanced independently of an analysis of how these processes are produced and reproduced in routine practices. In this concluding section, we now seek to indicate how the foregoing empirical and theoretical analysis of power and identity can be translated into prescriptions which have the potential to break down the vicious circles of sex discrimination in the recruitment process. The first part highlights what is valuable in conventional liberal recommendations, while the second considers the additional measures necessary to challenge the taken-for-granted reproduction of sex discrimination.

The EOC's Code of Practice (1985b) recommends that recruitment practices be *monitored* and made more consistent and *formal* and that employees be *trained* in the provision of the 1975 and 1986 Sex Discrimination Acts. Yet it was clear from the research that many companies were still not operating formalised selection practices, training staff and monitoring the consequences. The EOC (ibid.) recommends that companies monitor their practices and work-force profile in order to identify the extent and location of any barriers to equal opportunities. While it also advocates that companies should conduct periodic reviews to assess the impact of strategies designed to reduce job segregation, the research found that many organisations retained only the most basic of work-force information. This was even true of some companies that claimed to be equal-opportunity employers, such as one head-office complex where the work-force profile had to be especially formulated for the research because a detailed breakdown by sex was not maintained.

The EOC (ibid.) also stresses that training is particularly important because the sex-discriminatory practices of staff remain the responsibility of the employer. However, equal-opportunity training of staff involved in assessing applications and evaluating candidates was largely absent in the organisations where research took place. This was the case for both line and personnel managers. In addition, even many personnel managers had not been trained in selection and interviewing methods. Several personnel managers were actually line managers who had been transferred (without training) from other managerial functions.

It is partly for these reasons that the research uncovered considerable confusion about the 1975 SDA. Recruiters were sometimes unaware that discrimination against *men* and against *married people* of both sexes was illegal. Several companies claimed to be equal-opportunity employers on the basis that they recruited a substantial number of women. Yet such claims often disregarded the specific jobs and prospects afforded these women. Hence, by heightening awareness of marital discrimination, it is possible that employers will be more likely to embrace the spirit of the SDA, since improvements to practices can then be shown to have beneficial consequences for the whole work-force.[6]

The research suggests that an important underlying reason for the continued failure to implement EOC guidelines concerns the orientation of personnel managers to selection and equal opportunities and their relationship with line managers. In practice, line managers across all five sections of the research often held the balance of power in recruitment decision-making, claiming to be the organisational bread-winners as producers of wealth and profit, while downgrading personnel as an unproductive welfare function best confined to administration. Moreover, the research found that some personnel managers of both sexes were indifferent and even hostile to ensuring that recruitment practices were both formal and lawful.

And yet, informal recruitment practices were usually vague, impressionistic and unaccountable. This often resulted in decisions which, first, were inconsistent, for example with selection criteria being changed according to the qualities of favoured candidates, and second, were sometimes unlawful, for example where gender was interpreted as a key aspect of the ability to 'fit in'.

The introduction of more systematic and formalised practices in the channels, criteria and procedures of recruitment is likely to depend on the greater organisational visibility, influence and commitment of professional personnel managers. This in turn will require the personnel function to challenge and eradicate decision-making based on bread-winner and homemaker stereotypes, not only in relation to gender, but also in the context of their own organisational identity and status. Such a challenge would focus on the inefficiencies, inconsistencies and unaccountability that characterise many recruitment exercises dominated by line management. Within the managerial structure of companies, it is the personnel department that remains the most likely function to promote the implementation and monitoring of formal and fair selection practices.

The joint management of job interviews, in particular, might facilitate more consistent practices within a highly subjective process. If personnel specialists were present at interviews, this would enable practices to be more closely monitored and systematic. Line managers' technical experience does not qualify them as effective interviewers and does not justify their domination of recruitment. Conversely, line managers' expertise would be particularly valuable at the application-form screening stage, which tends to be the exclusive responsibility of the personnel department. Joint management could therefore increase the degree of consistency and formalisation in the recruitment process, not least by overcoming the tendency for selectors to rationalise unlawful practices.

Having said that, formalisation can only ever be a *necessary* framework for the elimination of sex discrimination in recruitment. It is not, in itself, *sufficient*. Formalisation can facilitate recruitment by rendering practices more structured, visible and accountable. It cannot predetermine in a mechanical and uniform fashion the implementation of consistent recruitment practices at local level. The need to judge and evaluate candidates will always afford selectors a substantial element of discretion regardless of the degree of bureaucracy and formality present in the selection process.

The interactional nature of the interview process, in particular, is not fully amenable to formalisation. Equally, it is difficult to imagine firms, such as those in the insurance sales industry, abandoning their traditional use of informal recruitment channels, which are both relatively inexpensive and efficient to administer. Likewise, the reliance on informal acceptability criteria is unlikely to be eliminated, not least because such behavioural qualities cannot be completely divorced from job performance. The assumption that job-related criteria can be separated from the individual's whole personality has been questioned by Hollway, who asks, 'Is it not the person in entirety whose relation to the job (which includes a relation to the organisation and the social relations in and outside work) determines performance?' (1984a: 45). In sum, while formalisation can facilitate more systematic and consistent practices, particularly in the early stages of recruitment, it is highly unlikely that informality in the channels, criteria and procedures of selection could ever be eliminated either through legislation or the 'advisory' or even coercive interventions of the EOC or the personnel department. In certain cases, real practical organisational advantages of speed, cost and control may result from informal recruitment practices.

The inevitable persistence of informality and subjective interpretation has two major implications. First, it underlines the importance of training. In addition to outlining the formal provisions of equal-opportunities legislation, training would focus on the informal vicious circles of job segregation outlined earlier in this chapter, and highlight the self-fulfilling and self-defeating consequences of patriarchal assumptions, identities and practices. Training should concentrate on women as well as men by providing the technical 'bridging skills' that would facilitate their entry into male-dominated occupations. Second, the persistence of informality suggests that further measures are required to eliminate sex-discriminatory recruitment practices. Indeed, it is unlikely that the foregoing liberal prescriptions would be able to undermine the vicious circles of job segregation, for the practices of reproduction, rationalisation and resistance have been shown to be deeply grounded in material, social, and existential realities which are a historical condition and consequence of capitalist and gendered practices and ideologies. Accordingly, in the absence of other measures, liberal prescriptions are likely to be accommodated within the prevailing norms of conventional power relations and identities.

The liberal literature implicitly assumes that if recruitment practices were rendered meritocratic, then 'equal opportunities' would be established. Yet this neglects the ideological partial truths and the existential, social and material realities contributing to the vicious circles of job segregation and women's domestic subordination. The principles of gender equality cannot be reduced to mean that women should be trained to be more like men; for even *if* women were provided with full access to the labour market, this would merely reinforce their dual responsibilities of home and employment. Rather, positive and deliberate improvements to organisational practices, arrangements and requirements are needed.

In short, what is required is a fundamental re-examination of child-care arrangements and their relationship to paid employment. For only when domestic responsibilities are no longer treated negatively and are rendered compatible in *practice* with full-time employment will the ideological partial truths and conventional gender identities which underpin men's domination of the labour market be undermined. At minimum, this requires, first, the development and extension of *career-break schemes*; second, increased opportunities for *flexible working patterns*; and third, the provision of *crèche facilities*, available to the children of all employees.

Together, these initiatives could eliminate many of the problems associated with child-rearing which in male-dominated society remains primarily 'women's work'. More particularly, it is the introduction of crèche or work-place nursery facilities which potentially has the most far-reaching implications for the elimination of sex discrimination. This initiative could undermine the ideological basis of sex-discriminatory recruitment practices which impact not only on those job candidates with children, but also on young single men and women whose futures as bread-winners and homemakers are often mapped out by recruiters well in advance.

Moreover, since this step would require senior management

approval, it would also highlight the company's serious commitment to equal-opportunity policies and practices. Indeed, the provision of child-care facilities, the cost of which would be shared between the user and employer, would be compatible with the growing concern of companies to nurture a 'happy family' community of interests within the organisation. Paradoxically, similar initiatives, such as the funding of sports and leisure facilities for employees, not only exclude many women whose interests are ignored, but also draw men further away from domestic responsibilities. In so far as the organisational ideal of the 'happy family' is established, it is only purchased, ironically, at the cost of reinforcing men's distance from domestic responsibilities. Alternatively, were men to recognise the negative consequences of their attachment to the bread-winner identity and to demand a better balance between home life and work, this would constitute a very significant pressure on organisations, particularly since men usually predominate in positions of hierarchical power. In such a climate, crèche facilities could help to establish and reinforce a wider understanding that domestic responsibilities can be shared between both sexes and are not merely the province of women, while also generating precisely the co-operation and flexibility of labour which employers are seeking.

More than any other measure, the socialisation of child care would establish the conditions whereby good equal-opportunity practices could be taken for granted as the 'normal', 'natural' and self-evident way to manage the recruitment process. For against this background, recruiters, jobseekers and employees could be treated and treat themselves primarily as human beings who may be *parents*, rather than primarily as men and women who will inevitably conform to the stereotype identities of bread-winner and homemaker. The introduction of crèche facilities for the children of male and female employees is a crucial factor in undermining the defensive retreat into conventional gender identities which reflects and reinforces organisational power inequalities, unlawful treatment and the material and psychological pressures of privatised child-rearing.

Crèche facilities could thereby provide the conditions for a radical transformation in conventional gender identities and power relations. This proposal not only recognises the mutually reinforcing nature of women's subordination in paid and unpaid work, but also fundamentally challenges conventional assumptions and practices in capitalist organisations. It would involve labour and administrative costs, especially in the short run, and would require a critical appraisal of gender and class divisions in employment and at home. The position of working-class women in particular would be dramatically enhanced by attempts to facilitate the integration of paid employment and child-care arrangements.

It is precisely because crèche facilities and career breaks constitute a fundamental challenge to conventional power and identities that contemporary developments on both these issues need to be treated with caution. The danger of the current interest in both schemes is that, like the liberal recommendations discussed earlier, they will be incorporated into the prevailing norms of a male-dominated culture and distorted by a highly stratified and demand-led labour market. The result would be the dilution of career-break schemes and crèche facilities into forms of elitism and opportunism respectively.

The former tendency is already exemplified by the career-breaks schemes currently operating in the major banks. These initiatives display a willingness to recognise the importance of child-bearing and child-rearing as an integral part of employment practices. As a positive step forward, they demonstrate how companies must take deliberate and specific steps in order to ensure equal opportunities for all staff. And yet, while these initiatives provide greater *opportunities* for some, they could hardly be said to encompass all staff *equally*.

To be eligible for one of the schemes, candidates must be judged to have 'middle or senior management potential'. While there are 33,000 women in the company, of which 900 will be on maternity leave at any one time, the scheme had only thirty-five participants three years after its inception. In another scheme, those staff with at least five years' 'satisfactory' service are entitled to one unpaid career break to fulfil pre-school child-care responsibilities. They must also be 'career staff', i.e. managers, appointed officers, management trainees (with professional banking examinations) or special-grade staff. At this bank in 1983, the vast majority of women who took maternity leave and then resigned worked in grades that were excluded by the returner's scheme. They also tended to be long-standing employees with extensive working knowledge and experience. Equally, women in these same lower clerical grades formed the bulk of those returning from maternity (for elaboration see Collinson 1987c).

Thus, not only is this scheme aimed at a minute proportion of those who could potentially benefit, but it also perpetuates the loss of long-standing, highly experienced staff who might otherwise return if they were assisted by the bank. Paradoxically, the scheme excludes the vast majority of women, while it *includes* the very staff who are most able to pay for private child care. By contrast, at Lombard North Central Finance company, a return-to-work scheme was introduced in 1986 which was open to *all* staff. This scheme allows participants to work part-time and is backdated to include all maternity leavers since 1981.[7]

With regard to crèche facilities, demographic changes and the future pressure on companies to recruit *and* retain women staff are currently receiving a high profile. The result is that child-care provision is increasingly on the agenda of many companies. Yet this appears to be the outcome of opportunism rather than employer enlightenment as to the intrinsic merits of equal opportunities. The turnaround in employer attitude has been triggered primarily by the labour shortages which are anticipated from the dramatic drop in the number of teenagers expected to enter the labour market in the 1990s. As the experience of the Second World War illustrates, the danger is that in times of labour shortage the means of bringing women into the labour market may be found, only to be dismantled again when the required number of men are available for employment. The growing interest in child-care facilities may well represent not so much a fundamental rethinking on sex discrimination, but rather constitute an opportunistic initiative designed to overcome short-run fluctuations in the supply of labour.

Given the market-led nature of private industry, the provision of child care facilities may require state intervention. Legislation geared to stimulating the provision of child-care facilities would enable the organisational benefits accruing from equal-opportunity practices to become evident, even to the most hostile and sceptical of managers. [8] Equally, by ensuring that child care was available to all parents, whether in paid work or not, the state would enable women in particular to experience themselves as individuals apart from their domestic responsibilities, thereby helping to free them from the constraints of conventional gender identities.

To conclude, despite the potential problems of elitism and opportunism associated with career-break schemes and the provision of crèche facilities respectively, the EOC research suggests that the integration of the child-rearing process with the recruitment and employment process is a precondition for the establishment of equal-opportunity practices. Indeed, the social organisation of child care and its integration with paid work constitute the key issues which must be addressed if the conditions are to be created in which employers no longer manage to discriminate.

Appendix

The project was carried out, primarily in the North West of England, over a two-year period commencing in September 1983. The research objectives required that access be secured to the *whole* of the recruitment process. This involved observing the following routine practices:

(1) the identification of a vacancy;
(2) the job description and person specification;
(3) the sources of labour supply and advertising;
(4) the screening process;
(5) the decision-making process;
(6) induction and other training;
(7) employee appraisal and promotion.

Four main stages of securing access had to be negotiated, namely: contacting the companies; interviewing managers; observing job interviews; and interviewing other participants. Each of these will now be elaborated in turn.

Stage one: contacting the companies

As Table A1 outlines, vacancies in sixty-four work-places of forty-five private-sector companies were explored. Table A2 reveals that 215 research respondents were interviewed, some on more than one occasion. In total, 328 research interviews were conducted.

The sensitive nature of the project made it essential that confidentiality and anonymity be guaranteed to all participating companies and individuals. This assurance in large part alleviated managers' suspicion and defensiveness about the project. Managers were also told that the research was seeking to 'enlist their help' to explore issues of recruitment and equal opportunities in a 'practical way' rather than to stand in critical judgement over their recruitment practices. Appealing to managerial priorities proved to be a successful method of establishing their confidence in the project. For the same reason it was decided not to raise the issue of the Commission's involvement in the research, although if respondents asked, this was not deliberately concealed. Assurances of confidentiality seemed to contribute significantly to managers' willingness to co-operate in the project. While the ethical dilemmas of semi-concealed interests persisted throughout the project, they were somewhat reduced by the knowledge that assurances of confidentiality have not been broken and so no individual or organisation has suffered any negative consequences from the research.

Table A1 Scope of research access

Industry	Number of companies	Total number of work-sites visited	Number of head offices visited	Number of 'equal-opportunity employers'
Mail order	4	6	2	3
Banking	4	7	4	3
Insurance	20	31	6	7
Hi-tech	14	15	5	4
Food manufacture	3	5	2	2
Total	45	64	19	19

Table A2 Scope of research interviews

Industry	Total number of interviewees	Average per company	Total number of interviews	Average per company
Mail order	27	7	34	8
Banking	31	8	48	12
Insurance	86	4	125	6
Hi-tech	30	2	39	3
Food manufacture	41	14	82	27
Total	215	—	328	—

Two primary contact strategies were adopted. First, thirty-five private-sector companies in the North West of England, who were known to be declared 'equal-opportunity employers', were sent a letter outlining the project. A follow-up telephone call was then made within a week to arrange a meeting. Although it was found that ten companies were not recruiting, and six others refused to participate, this method proved to be highly successful in establishing contact. Interviews took place at twenty-five companies and nineteen were selected for more detailed examination.

These nineteen companies formed the core of the project and defined four of the five sectors, namely: mail order/retail, banking, insurance and food processing. Hence, the definition of the sectors was primarily 'access driven'. This was inevitable given the ambitious objectives of the project.

At this point, it was decided that the 'hi-tech' sector might provide an interesting contrast to the more traditional industries contacted by the initial screening process. In order to pursue this research as quickly as possible, and to collect further data in the other industries, a second contact method was adopted. This approach relied on the identification of job advertisements for vacancies in local and national newspapers. Fourteen hi-tech, eleven insurance and one food manufacturing company were contacted by this method.

Stage two: Interviewing managers

Of the 328 formal research interviews, 72 per cent were conducted with personnel and line managers, who also constituted 61 per cent of the 215 research respondents, as Table A3 indicates.

Table A3 Total number of interviews with managers

Status of interviewee	Interviewees	Interviews
Personnel Managers	67	127
Line Managers	64	110
Total	131	237

All research interviews were tape-recorded and then transcribed. Personnel managers were the key 'brokers' of the research project since they usually approved access, held much of the information concerning specific recruitment exercises and introduced the researcher to other members of the organisation. Having secured the support of senior personnel managers, most of the research was conducted with the help of assistant personnel managers. An important aspect of the research methodology was to conduct return interviews. Of the 113 repeat sessions, 94 per cent were undertaken with personnel and line managers. This more intensive interviewing had several advantages.

First, it established greater levels of trust between researcher and respondents. Second, return interviews enabled respondents' accounts and actions to be examined over time for consistency. This was particularly important because recruitment exercises usually extended over several weeks. An exclusive reliance on *post-hoc* accounts (see, for example, Curran 1986) would be vulnerable to the tendency of recruiters to reread previous selection practices and decisions so as to reinforce their validity and rationality. Moreover, some managers were prone to exaggerate their impartiality and consistency when interviewing candidates, preferring to deny responsibility for their intention to discriminate by blaming the prejudice of others. A combination of repeat interviews and observation usually revealed the underlying prejudice of these selectors. Finally, repeat sessions facilitated the acquisition of company literature and records on annual turnover rates, job descriptions, application forms and recruitment, training and promotion patterns.

Stage three: Observing job interviews

In addition to repeat sessions, an important source of data verification was to observe job-interview practices. As Table A4 shows, evidence was collected from eighty-two job interviews.

The purpose of observation is to capture the routine and the typical in organisational practices. Paradoxically, the very presence of a researcher could undermine this objective by increasing the artificiality of the proceedings. Nevertheless, the researcher's presence did not inhibit some interviewers from treating women candidates in a detrimental way.

Table A4 Job interviews observed

Industry	Number of job interviews observed	Number of companies	Number of 'equal-opportunity' employers
Mail order	25	1	1
Banking	14	1	—
Insurance	14	5	3
Hi-tech	2	1	—
Food manufacture	27	1	1
Total	82	9	5

In most cases the candidate was asked prior to the interview whether they would object to the presence of a university researcher. None refused. Where prejudice was apparent, a follow-up interview with the candidate was usually conducted. Caution was again needed in the analysis of the views of the rejected candidates. The most common element of distortion in these responses was the interviewees' complete lack of knowledge of the organisational processes in which they were engaged. Candidates were often unaware of the number of other interviewees or the duration and content of the selection process. Where case-studies did not include observation of job interviews, this was usually because managers were reluctant to approve access.

The most prevalent justification for managers' refusal to approve access was that candidates were already 'anxious enough' and it would be 'unfair to subject them' to further pressure due to the researcher's presence. Yet it often seemed that underlying this apparent concern to protect the interests of the interviewee was managers' own reluctance to become the evaluated, rather than the evaluator, of the interview process. Another reason for the failure to observe job interviews was that in some cases the prevalence of pre-recruitment job sex-typing resulted in interviewees being all of one sex. This was the result of decisions made both by potential applicants prior to application and by selectors in defining the job and in screening the candidates. Without a comparison of interview practices by sex of candidate, the observation of interviews was usually less valuable than would otherwise have been the case. In this context, the research focus tended to shift to the sources and criteria of recruitment in order to determine how and why a single-sex supply of applicants had emerged.

Stage four: Interviewing other participants

In addition to repeat sessions and the observation of practices, a third method of data verification was to conduct semi-structured interviews with employees, trade unionists, rejected candidates and recruits. Table A5 outlines the total number of other participants interviewed.

Table A5 Number of interviews with other participants

Status of interviewee	Total number of interviewees	Total number of interviews
Employees	39	40
Trade unionists	19	24
Recruits	10	10
Candidates	10	11
Jobcentre staff	5	5
Recruitment consultants	1	1
Total	84	91

Contact with employees and trade unions proved to be the most successful method of exploring promotion practices. During the research, promotion practices had proved to be even more intangible, nebulous and difficult to explore than recruitment. The procedures involved often seemed to be ill-defined and conducted behind closed doors. Managers were difficult to 'pin down' on the subject, preferring to provide formal and generalised accounts of what they 'usually do' rather than enter into concrete discussions about recent specific case histories. By contrast, trade unionists and employees often provided more detailed information. Indeed, they usually knew more about promotion than recruitment, because these practices are internal to the organisation and have more direct impact on trade-union members. As Table A6 outlines, trade-union representatives were interviewed in four of the five sectors.

Table A6 Number of trade unionists interviewed

Industry	Full-time official	Lay officials
Mail order/retail	1	1
Banking	4	2
Insurance	2	6
Hi-tech	—	—
Food manufacture	—	3
Total	7	12

Full-time union officials provided information concerning equal opportunities at a national level, while lay officials were able to elaborate in more detail on local promotion procedures and actual case histories. Contact with one trade union in the insurance sector was particularly valuable. As a result, a questionnaire survey of staff throughout the company on equal opportunities was jointly administered (see Collinson 1987a). This access point enabled the researcher to contact lay and full-time officials within the rest of the insurance and banking sections of the trade union. In turn, this allowed the research to penetrate beyond the formal policy statements and 'model agreements' that unions, like companies, tend to present to 'outsiders'. As a consequence of this co-operative relationship, the research was also able to infiltrate behind the superficial accounts of formalised promotion procedures offered by managers. Trade-union contacts proved to be a useful indirect method of securing company information on recruitment, promotion, labour turnover, absenteeism, length of service and equal opportunities.

Despite extensive assistance from individual union members, it would, however, be misleading to assume that there was no union resistance to this project. In particular, some female officials (both lay and full-time) limited their co-operation and expressed a scepticism about whether men could or should be involved in research on sex discrimination.

Whether the gender of the researcher was on balance advantageous to the project was difficult to establish. Clearly, 'taking gender into account' (Morgan 1981: 95) is especially problematic for male researchers: 'The male researcher needs, as it were, a small voice at his shoulder reminding him at each point that he is a man' (ibid.: 95). In particular the gender of the researcher may well have impeded the empirical focus on labour resistance to sex discrimination. Clearly, the 'immersion' in female-dominated working cultures, which would be necessary to uncover in full the informal, subtle and covert nature of (women's) resistance was all but impossible, because of the gender of the researcher and the constraints of time, money and primary research objectives. The evidence of resistance therefore relies mainly on the accounts and practices of *key* actors in specific sex-discriminatory recruitment exercises.

Having said that, much of the research concentrated on the practices of line managers because their contribution to recruitment was found to be extensive. Since approximately 85 per cent of the line managers interviewed were men, being a male researcher proved to be of no handicap. Indeed, it even became an advantage given that older line managers in particular seemed to be willing to express deep-seated and often negative opinions about female candidates that they had concealed from (women) personnel managers. Such views were often articulated as if sharing a secret between men, where one was the paternal teacher and the other was the pupil/apprentice, or 'the young lad from the university' (see Collinson 1988c, 1990 for elaboration).

Notes

Introduction

1. Because the narrow legal remit of the Commission precluded any focus on race discrimination, the following theoretical and empirical analysis is also unable to attend to the issue of ethnicity. The complexity of the questions surrounding gender analysis, the very specific requirements of the EOC and the pressure of conducting qualitative, labour-intensive research combined to make this omission largely unavoidable. However, much of the discussion remains pertinent to issues of ethnicity, and certain studies, which examine recruitment from this point of view, will be examined in detail later.

2. Although the following discussion does not constitute an exhaustive survey of this literature, it is intended to be a general overview which highlights some of the main themes within these conventional perspectives.

3. Despite its relative effectiveness, the specific investigation of the Leeds Permanent Building Society can be criticised for its failure both to include marriage discrimination within its terms of reference and to explore internal selection and training practices of present employees rather than merely concentrate on the external recruitment of prospective management trainees. Equally, its formalistic methodology, which focused upon company records and a questionnaire survey of previous applicants, was unable to capture the more subtle, informal and often most important dynamics and practices of sex discrimination. Finally, as a retrospective study, discrepancies between accounts and practices were almost impossible to avoid.

4. It could be argued that there is an inconsistency in the legislation here. Implicit in the definition of direct discrimination, for example, is the view that stereotyping is based entirely on myth and unfounded prejudice which training and education could eliminate (see also EOC 1986: 2). Indirect discrimination, by contrast, recognises the way in which conventional domestic responsibilities *can* impact on women's work contribution. The former reject stereotyping as gender ideology whilst the latter acknowledges a certain plausibility in the material realities of women's subordinate position. The relationship between gender ideology and material realities is addressed again in later chapters.

5. It is highly unlikely that the historically ingrained and culturally deep-seated

nature of gender and class inequality could be eliminated merely by the establishment of 'fair' practices. Having said that, the definition of 'sex discrimination' utilised in this book will adhere to the liberal model of meritocratic achievement, as outlined in the equal-opportunities legislation. To pursue an alternative definition would be to weaken unnecessarily the degree of conceptual clarity in what is already a highly complex field of analysis.

6. Indeed, Smith and Robertson (1986: 4) are confident enough to claim that improving recruitment techniques in the way that they recommend will lead to a 6 per cent increase in productivity. Such a specific claim seems difficult to validate. This same tension in occupational psychology between prescription and sex discrimination was revealed in a consultancy exercise with Shroeder Life Assurance by Poppleton (1980), who argued that life-history data have proved to be a highly reliable predictor of future performance in sales work. Drawing on Thayer's (1977) work, he included 'marital status' in his recommended list of required personal details of prospective candidates. Yet selection on the basis of marriage is unlawful under the 1975 SDA.

7. It would be inappropriate to consider in any greater detail Giddens's analysis of structure and action which incorporates the theory of 'structuration' and of the 'dialectic of control'. This is partly because Giddens's work remains at a highly abstract level which tends to preclude empirical issues, for example concerning recruitment. His analysis is primarily intended to produce a synthesis of the dualisms which he identifies in social science between 'structure' and 'action', 'society' and 'individual' and 'determinism' and 'voluntarism'. Whilst this central problem in social theory (see also Henriques et al. 1984) is clearly relevant to the following study, the approach adopted here is designed to elucidate the research findings from the EOC project. It is therefore more concerned to reconcile the dualism between theory and empirical research than to provide a definitive contribution to social theory which could overcome the structure/action dichotomy. The value of Giddens's work for this study is his combined focus on human agency and asymmetrical power relations.

8. However, empirical material is also used which was secured after the EOC research was formally completed in September 1985.

9. Having said that, we would acknowledge that the nature of managerial control, the intractable character of job segregation and the nebulous complexity of the recruitment process made it extremely difficult always to capture the social practices through which recruitment was conducted. Hence, although other studies have been criticised for their neglect of actual practices, internal selection processes and the nature of the job vacancy, it is not claimed here that these methodological weaknesses have been *fully* overcome by this research project. The foregoing barriers to the collection of data necessarily rendered research an imperfect process. Nevertheless, it can still be argued that these weaknesses in other studies and their impact on research findings remain largely unacknowledged by their authors and that attempts have been made either to overcome or recognise and minimise the effect of these difficulties on the present study. Equally, this is not to deny the significance of respondents' accounts of their practices. Indeed, in the

empirical chapters we are concerned both to explore how and why ideological rationalisations are invoked to 'normalise' self and the status quo and then to theorise the various ways in which sex discrimination was found to be rationalised by participants in recruitment.

1 Managing the labour market

1. Major theoretical problems of reductionism, economism and functionalism also characterised the debate (see Barrett 1980: 24). These were carried over into the female-reserve-army perspective and will be criticised later. In addition, however, within the debate biological difference and familial ideology were usually neglected. This meant that the specific responsibility of women for domestic labour remained unexplained. Equally, most contributors ignored male and female agency and resistance in their highly static and structuralist accounts. The following chapter will discuss more theoretically sophisticated and empirically informed analyses of domestic labour and gender relations.

2. Whilst the permanence of women's jobs constitutes a crucial critique of the reserve-army thesis, it should also be noted that this point fails to consider the gender-stereotyping which usually accompanies job sex-typing. For although the jobs themselves are permanent, employers' selection decisions may be based on stereotyped assumptions of women's *temporary* investment in employment based around biological realities and familial ideology. Recruiters often assume that women will *voluntarily* resign. The extent to which such preconceived assumptions may have self-fulfilling consequences will be considered in the empirical analysis later.

3. There is considerable confusion in the literature about the necessary criteria for membership of the reserve army. This is noted by Beechey and Perkins (1987: 132). In their recent review of the literature, they themselves make a clear distinction between the female reserve army and deskilling theses. Yet although there are differences between these two perspectives (for example, in recession the former suggests that women will be dispensed with, whilst the latter predicts that women will substitute for men) Beechey and Perkins's approach neglects the way in which the two perspectives overlap, particularly on the criteria of female substitutability. As Liff (1986: 79) has argued (following Connelly's (1978) application of the original Marxist concept), the claim that women are functioning as a reserve must be supported by evidence demonstrating that they have been 'real competitors for men's jobs'. Beechey and Perkins tend to exaggerate the differences between the reserve army and deskilling theses and fail to incorporate women's substitutability into their own discussions of the industrial-reserve-army thesis. This could be because of their focus on part-time jobs, which, as they show, tend to emerge in female-dominated areas of work. A somewhat similar distinction is used by Mallier and Rosser (1987: 464) between 'cyclical' and 'substitution' theory. The former concentrates on how women's availability and disposability is reflected in their fluctuating employment patterns, which vary (more sharply than men's) with changes in the business cycle, while the latter outlines the long-term tendency to

replace male labour with cheaper female workers and thereby to limit unit costs and increase profits.

4. In part, this critique is unfair since Braverman was primarily concerned to highlight how managerial control was directed towards the elimination of worker resistance. None the less, Braverman can be criticised for assuming that managerial control will inevitably overcome, rather than sometimes reinforce, labour opposition. He thereby failed to identify how managerial control through deskilling might be a condition as well as a consequence of labour resistance.

5. This argument is elaborated in Chapter 6 where a case-study is presented which examines recruitment practices for temporary and part-time workers in the mail-order industry.

6. In order to overcome the abstractions of these earlier versions, Dale (1987: 331) has recently demonstrated that age, race and domestic circumstances are equally crucial factors which combine with gender to structure the secondary labour market. In addition, Walby (1986: 86) has pointed to the importance of spatial and historical variations in labour-market segment-ation. Regional labour-market segmentation is particularly significant for gender divisions given the growing employer emphasis on workers' flexibility and geographical mobility. How this requirement can reinforce sex discrimination will be considered in the empirical analysis of the insurance sector later.

7. Storey (1985: 208) warns against the use of 'glib citations' of this study to confirm the absence of managerial strategy. This is because Rose and Jones rely on data from only six case-studies. Storey criticises Rose and Jones for demanding too coherent a policy as a definition of strategy. He argues that at corporate level at least, managers do weigh up and evaluate alternative broad paths. However, he (1985: 203) does concede that a 'centrally derived, all embracing, multifunctional and multilevel plan' is unlikely. The relationship between corporate policies and operational practices is a key question for the elimination of sex discrimination which is addressed in particular in Chapter 5 below.

8. Mcnally (1979: 188) criticises the reserve-army thesis because it presents 'an over-socialised or over-determined view of woman'. She contends that the thesis treats women as passively fulfilling the 'needs' of capitalism. For example, the growth of women's employment is treated solely as a neces-sary development of capitalist production. Yet this neglects the way in which women's work-force participation may (also) be an escape from the confines of domesticity. Similar criticisms can be levelled at segmentation theory. Women's agency will be discussed further in the following chapter.

2 Gender and the labour market

1. In a later paper (1989), Walby adds patriarchal culture as a sixth structure of patriarchy. This incorporates cultural institutions such as religion, the media and education. Similar yet different 'spheres' of patriarchy have recently

been outlined by Hearn (1987: 89) and Connell (1987: 109). Hearn identifies the following 'institutions' of male domination of women's reproductive labour powers and their products:

- hierarchic heterosexuality,
- fatherhood,
- the professions, and
- the state.

Interestingly, despite this coalescence on the spheres of patriarchy, the perspectives of Hearn and Walby also diverge considerably. While the latter contends that women have to be analysed in relation to production, the former is arguing that men (as well as women) have to be theorised in relation to reproduction.

Connell also asserts that it is possible to identify a 'core' in which the power of men and the authority of masculinity are concentrated. In the advanced capitalist countries, four components of this core are discernible:

- the hierarchies and work-forces of institutionalised violence – for example, military police, prisons;
- the hierarchy and labour force of heavy industry and the hierarchy of high-technology industry;
- the planning and control machinery of the central state;
- the working-class milieux which emphasise physical toughness and men's association with machinery.

2. Strangely, although Walby (1986: 22) discusses Barrett's analysis of the family-household system, she makes no attempt to criticise it from her own economistic perspective. This is despite the fact that Barrett is highly critical of Delphy's materialist analysis, on which Walby draws heavily.

3. The issue of the complex relationship between familial ideology and biological reproduction is addressed again in the conclusion. At this point, it is sufficient to recognise that both factors are of importance for the analysis of sex discrimination in the recruitment process.

4. Walby's insistence that all domestic tasks can be bought as a service or goods on the market and should be seen as production illustrates her under-estimation of the impact of familial ideology and biological reproduction in shaping the social relations and practices of both sexes in the home and in employment. Moreover, as Pat Armstrong (1984: 34) has argued, for theorists to categorise domestic labour as production does not change the way that it is evaluated by men and women in empirical contexts.

5. Although Barrett (for example, 1980: 110) addresses the question of human agency more directly than Brenner and Ramas, she still fails to explain how gender ideology and identity are socially constructed in a way that is distinct from, yet related to, the concrete organisation of the household.

6. Moreover, there are several ethnographic studies which display women's agency and resistance in the work-place (for example, Purcell 1979; Barker and Downing 1980; Pollert 1981, 1983; Cavendish 1982; Wajcman 1983;

Westwood 1984). Yet none of these very important studies for the understanding of both patriarchy and capitalism is discussed by Walby. This again reflects her narrow focus on structure which precludes a theoretical consideration of agency, consciousness and resistance.

7. In proposing this perspective, Connell is also criticising attempts to resolve once and for all the origins of women's oppression. This objective lies at the heart of the debate between Barrett and Brenner and Ramas. Yet the concern with the analytical primacy of capitalism and patriarchy leads down the murky and highly selective path of historical analyses. Questions of origin are impossible to answer, because, as Connell (1983: 34) argues:

    > Both gender and class divisions can be traced through a complete evolution and interaction since the 'Palaeolithic'. It is this evolution and interaction that is the object of real historical knowledge. What concerns us is the dynamic, not its largely unknowable point of departure. Only myth, not history, makes determinations out of origins.

    While contemporary practices cannot be fully understood without a historical perspective, a major reliance on historical evidence, as in the case of Barrett, Brenner and Ramas and Walby, makes it difficult to explore social practices; for this methodology must inevitably rely on secondary accounts of practices which are unable to examine possible discrepancies between formal accounts and informal practices and 'public' rationalisations and 'private' intentions.

8. Again in a later paper, Walby (1989) begins to incorporate practices into her analysis. However, her dual-systems approach prevents a full development of an analytical focus on the interwoven nature of gender and class in social practices. This is because dual-systems theory must inevitably treat gender relations and capitalism as somehow outside each other, or as Acker argues, this approach, 'leaves intact the patriarchal assumptions buried in theories about the other systems to which patriarchy is related' (Acker 1989: 237). By pointing to analytically independent structures it is difficult, if not impossible to capture the way that 'gender is implicated in the fundamental constitution of all social life' (ibid.: 238).

9. Interestingly, Barrett's (1980) argument that the demand of nineteenth-century male craft unions for the family wage crucially shaped women's subordination has been criticised from two opposing perspectives. Walby (1986) believes that this seriously underestimates the importance of trade-union practices. Yet Brenner and Ramas (1984) argue that Barrett overestimates the power even of craft unions to reinforce job segregation. They emphasise that union resistance to female entry was a well-grounded and rational strategy designed primarily to defend against the erosion of skilled wages rather than a deliberate attempt to exclude women *per se*. Brenner and Ramas further argue that since craft unions only represented a small percentage of the labour force, their contribution to the reproduction of the widespread and persistent nature of job segregation must inevitably be limited.

3 Controlling recruitment

1. Although most of the studies discussed in this chapter do not focus explicitly on gender issues but rather concentrate on the ethnic and/or class dimensions of recruitment, their empirically based findings are of value for this analysis.
2. The critique of segmentation theory in Chapter 1 focused on the questions of managerial intentionality and labour agency and resistance. It did not deny the existence of labour-market segmentation and gender divisions. Rather, it criticised the thesis advocated by Edwards (1979) and Reich et al. (1980) where it was argued that segmentation was intentionally designed by an omnipotent management to 'divide and rule' the work-force.
3. There is a dearth of research on actual case-studies of internal labour-market *practices*. This reflects the way in which these markets are insulated from all 'outsiders', whether jobseekers or researchers.
4. Of particular interest in Curran's data, although perhaps left underexplored, is the way in which selectors' generalised preconceptions about candidates' domestic responsibilities were often informed by projections from personal experience. Curran argues that selectors' views concerning family commitments were most often influenced by experiences within their own household. Thus, for example, one respondent's 'allergy' to married women with young children was found to be shaped primarily by the fact that, if his own children were ill, it would be his wife who would take time off work to care for them. The way in which selectors may project their own specific and narrow experiences and self image on to their general evaluation of candidates will be considered in more detail later.
5. Equally this assertion cannot allow for the possibility that, whilst selection criteria might shape practices, practices can also feed back into and even transform initial selection criteria. Case-studies presented in Part II of the book will illustrate how initial criteria might change over time in accordance with the perceived qualities of actual candidates.
6. Jenkins proposes to understand human agency through the notion of 'cognitive practice' (1986: 15) and what he calls the individual's 'egocentric cognitive framework' (ibid.: 18), which consists of a number of available identities (or what he terms 'subject models'). Suffice it to say here that this approach to theorising consciousness produces, at best, ideal-typical *descriptions* of human agency and at worst fails to capture the dynamic and shifting nature of social life since these models tend to be ascribed a reified status.

   Jenkins is unwilling to theorise the subjective processes which underpin the racist stereotypes held by many recruiters. In his concern to avoid the 'epistemological arrogance' (ibid.: 5) of derogating the understanding of 'fully competent' (ibid.: 235) individuals and their skilled contributions to social reproduction, Jenkins insists that motives are 'ultimately mysterious' (ibid.: 113), 'unknowable and opaque' (ibid.: 240). This proposition is unacceptable given that Jenkins's empirical data largely focus on consciousness. It is also problematic because there is now a growing body of literature which discusses the way in which discrimination against 'outsiders' may be informed by the concern to secure self identity through the identification with some and the differentiation from others (for example, Tajfel 1978; Henriques 1984; Willmott 1987). The question of selector self image is raised in the studies of agency in the interview process in the second half of this chapter. These subjective processes and their relationship to agency, power and gender in the recruitment process will be discussed in the empirical material presented later and will then be elaborated in more detail in the conclusion. As the previous chapter suggested, the issue of human agency cannot be raised without recognising and seeking to theorise its problematic and potentially contradictory nature.

7. One further study by Waddington (1982) which explores the interview process was excluded because its findings merely reinforce those rehearsed in the text. For example, he found that the selection of Prison Assistant Governors was characterised by 'an almost ostentatious avoidance of occupational relevance' (ibid.: 210).

8. While women rarely apply for male-school headships, men often do for girls' schools.

9. This study therefore implies that selectors' accounts of their practices are unreliable, since they are merely context-specific rationalisations produced after the event. In presenting a theoretical and methodological critique of this study, Jenkins (1986: 241) refutes the argument by Silverman and Jones that it is impossible to 'get at' what actually produces selection decisions. He rejects their proposition that rationalisations of acceptability criteria are merely a *consequence* of decision-making. Jenkins argues that this underestimates the knowledgeability of respondents. Recruiters understand a great deal of what they are doing, hence their accounts must also be, to some extent, a *condition* of their decisions. He therefore reasserts his view that the selection criteria which he records do in fact shape managerial practice. While supporting this argument, it is argued here that Jenkins is unable to show *how* these criteria might shape practices and equally *how* these practices might then feed back into and redefine criteria as the selection process progresses.

4 Formalising recruitment

1. The case in the European Court of Justice of Bilka v. Weber (1986) and the House of Lords decision in Rainey v. Greater Glasgow Health Board (1986) suggest that the definition of justifiability as the 'sound reasons of right-thinking people' is in the process of being replaced by 'objectively justifiable grounds'. The decision of the European Court indicates that in order to establish justifiability, 'the means chosen to achieve an objective that corresponds to a real need on the part of the undertaking 'have to be' appropriate to achieving the objective in question and be necessary to that end'. The EOC (1988) has recently submitted proposals for strengthening the anti-discrimination legislation. In particular, it has been argued that the test of justifiability as elaborated by the European Court of Justice in Bilka should be incorporated in the Sex Discrimination Act. This is part of a proposal designed to simplify and strengthen the existing laws by drawing

together the two SDAs, the Equal Pay Act and European Court laws under the umbrella of an Equal Treatment Act.

2. The arguments in support of formalisation outlined by Jenkins also mirror many of the recommendations proposed by Morgan et al. (1983) for the selection of secondary-school headteachers. They advocated the introduction of a formalised *technical* and job-related assessment of candidates, which included: a detailed job description specifying the job-related competencies required; the use of systematic and consistent procedures to evaluate candidates' skills (the elimination of informal practices such as 'trial by sherry'); a detailed outline of structured interview techniques as well as of the methods for securing the necessary evidence and for reaching a final decision; the greater priority placed on job-simulation analogous tests; and the clear designation of the responsibilities of the different interest groups on the selection panel.

3. We propose two additional conclusions from the study by Silverman and Jones. First, it confirms the methodological value of observing selection practices as opposed to relying on managerial accounts. Second, the ethnographical data underline the complexity of human agency and the need to go further than Jenkins in examining the conditions and consequences of consciousness and agency.

4. There remains a tension between Jenkins's prescriptions and his analysis here; for although he asserts the managerial weakness and impotence of the personnel function (1986: 249), he does not prescribe *how* formalisation is to be achieved or *who* is responsible for it, if it is not to be sponsored by personnel specialists. This failure to be more specific reflects Jenkins's neglect of the possible form, content and extent of resistance when outlining his recommendations for positive action.

5. It should be noted, however, that Jenkins and Jewson and Mason appear to interpret formalisation somewhat differently. Whilst the former treats the exclusive use of the ILM as a relatively informal practice, the latter see this as an example of a formalised procedure where a written agreement has been made between management and trade union. At least part of the disagreement between the authors can be attributed to their different definitions of formalisation. The disagreement can be partly reconciled by recognising a distinction between negotiated agreements and organisational practices. While in the case of the ILM the former may be formalised, the latter is likely to be much more informal.

6. The methodology of this study was somewhat unusual within the literature on recruitment because it examined processes from *within* the organisation, which facilitated the observation of internal organisational practices. The empirical sections in the second half of the book will present data on recruitment practices from inside as well as outside the organisation. Hence, whilst studies by Jenkins and Jewson and Mason each represent one side of this methodological coin, this study seeks to encompass both.

7. In a later work, Tyson and Fell (1986) refer to these three distinctive categories of personnel manager as 'Clerk of the Works', 'Contracts Manager' and 'Architects' respectively.

8. It could be argued that the interdependent nature of organisations is likely to

impair attempts to isolate and quantify the contribution of *any* individual function.

9. Empirical material which develops Armstrong's point by revealing divisions within the personnel function itself, based on the conflict between 'managerial' and 'professional' models of recruitment, will be outlined in Part II of the book.

10. A recent survey of personnel managers suggests that their organisational contribution is presently being further eroded by the increasing use of consultants to undertake traditional personnel-management tasks (Torrington and Mackay 1986).

5 Managing to recruit

1. The bread-winner ideology is compatible to some extent with the 'managerial model' outlined by Jenkins (1986), particularly in the preference for informal practices. However, his notion of 'model' is too static and fails to capture the way in which gender imagery is embedded in managerial control strategies and ideology. In addition, Jenkins's highly descriptive concept is unable to incorporate the crucial discrepancies that might arise between ideological accounts, material realities and social practices. It thereby omits a consideration of contradiction.

   In brief, the definition of ideology, in either or both its managerial and patriarchal forms adhered to here, follows that outlined by Giddens (1979: 193–5). He argues that domination is concealed as domination through ideologies which: represent sectional interests as universal ones; deny or transmute contradictions and naturalise or reify the present. Hence, it can be seen that ideologies define and prescribe how things are and how they should be in ways that legitimise vested interests and reify the status quo as 'natural' and 'inevitable', or as Fox (1980: 124) outlined in his (albeit gender-blind) analysis of ideology in industrial relations,

   > Ideology is a resource in the struggle for power, since it shapes the ways in which men perceive, think, feel and act. Management seeks to propagate an ideology which justifies its behaviour, legitimizes its rule, evokes loyalty and commitment on the part of lower as well as higher participants, and serves as a support for those norms and values which are congruent for its goals.

   The following chapter reveals how this managerial ideology can be used within intramanagerial relations.

2. These three organisations were all small companies within the hi-tech sector. In the absence of a personnel input and the presence of a strong entrepreneurial ideology articulated by each of their owners, these three companies were found to be characterised by recruitment practices that were inconsistent with formalised and meritocratic principles. For example, word-of-mouth practices were the most common source of recruits for the two computer sales companies. This included a routine practice of 'poaching' staff from the larger computer firms. When this source was exhausted, both companies used recruitment agencies. In one case during

the research, a female candidate, sent by an agency, was rejected simply because it stated on her CV that she was engaged. Strong reservations about women's ability to sell and about the possibility of their leaving to have children was expressed by owner/recruiters at both companies.

In contrast, the third small firm was a data-processing company that employed fifteen 'key-to-disc operators' who were all women. The owner of the company believed that the job was only appropriate for females because it was so 'boring, tedious and monotonous'. He likened it to work in the cotton mills of the nineteenth century. On the odd occasion when men applied, he would simply increase the minimum number of required key depressions per hour to prohibitive levels. When the issue of equal-opportunities' legislation was raised, he responded, aggressively: 'I'm the gaffer here. It's my choice who works for me, not these equal-opportunity women.' Each of these owner-selectors believed that the sex segregation of work was highly compatible with both efficient production and their personal control of the labour process.

3. The following selected examples are representative, without being exhaustive, of the available research material on this issue. The case-studies discussed provided the most detailed evidence on which to illustrate the overall argument.

4. At this company, corporate personnel's 'respect' for line managers' autonomy had led to difficulties in securing the implementation of a national equal-pay-for-work-of-equal-value agreement. Some line managers who were antagonistic to the principles involved were able to withstand the pressure from corporate personnel to implement the agreement for over two years after the claim had been settled. Another indication of line managers' confidence in opposing the company's equal-opportunities policy was revealed in the reported statement of a line manager at one head-office training course on recruitment techniques: 'I don't mind employing women, but not blacks, never!' Although corporate personnel enjoyed the hierarchical status, as well as the backing of formal company policy, the ambiguity in their relations with line managers often shaped their reluctance to intervene and to use their hierarchical power.

5. She stated that, as a line manager, the senior personnel officer had asked one female job candidate during a job interview whether she was on the pill.

6. At a computer manufacturer within the same multinational organisation, the local personnel team did conduct the first interview. Yet the personnel manager, who recruited the manual workers, preferred to leave the responsibility for the final selection decision with the line manager concerned. She explained this defensive stance as follows:

> If a manager says I want that person, then even when I've put my objections, if he still says the same, then that's the person he'll get. I'm here to recruit the people he wants. They're working for him not for me.

7. This quotation illustrates that in practice, acceptability and suitability criteria often become entangled when specific candidates are evaluated. Only by relying on *post-facto* accounts (for example, Jenkins) is it possible

to present such a clear distinction between the two sets of criteria.

8. Since she had argued very strongly for the inclusion of Janet H. who had then withdrawn, it was now more difficult to argue for a female candidate. Indeed, she had been teased by the managers as the assistant confirmed: 'I had to laugh when Lyn said Janet H. was not coming. I felt like blowing a raspberry down the phone.'

9. Somewhat ironically, the assistant personnel manager resigned from the company less then twelve months after this recruitment exercise, primarily because she was frustrated at her lack of career progress.

6 Rationalising discrimination

1. Similar waiting-lists, albeit less formal and lacking the participation of the Jobcentre, were discovered at the bakery, in certain banks and in the hi-tech sector (see Collinson 1988a: 44–5 for an elaboration). Equally, Maguire (1988: 78) described how in a Northern Ireland electronics factory, foremen used a special 'pink slip' to record their evaluation of the performance of those who resigned. When a vacancy arose, those who had performed well in the past would be contacted.

2. The labour-intensive nature of warehouse work was a particularly important factor contributing to the power and status of the personnel function within the mill. The only other senior manager was responsible for production. Within the personnel function, the manager had four assistants, all of whom were women.

3. The equal pay for work of equal value case of Pickstone v. Freemans Mail Order Company (1987) has strong similarities with this example. A female packer claimed that her work was of equal value to that of a warehouse 'checker', who was responsible for dealing with the arrival of goods at the loading bay. The difference in pay between the tasks was also £4.

4. Employers' concern about the impact on production of women's domestic responsibilities is also reflected in the company's application forms. Here, questions pertaining to marital status and family commitments were asked routinely – for example: 'marital status', 'number of children' – 'specify male or female', 'their ages', 'have you any other dependants?' This supports Curran's (1986) findings that at interviews and on application forms, employers consider that child-care arrangements are a legitimate area of enquiry. A similar finding specifically related to part-time workers is documented by Beechey and Perkins (1987: 113) who conclude that recruiters 'definitely saw the question of childcare as being within their sphere of concern'.

5. Indeed, the research discovered little overt resistance by trade-union representatives, employees or jobseekers to the reproduction of these patri-archal practices. Picking and packing were widely assumed to be 'women's work' and many of the women considered themselves to be beneficiaries of these practices. Hence, while the perpetrators of sex discrimination (i.e. management) claimed to be its victims, the victims perceived themselves to be its beneficiaries (see Collinson 1987: 380, 384 for an elaboration).

6. A similar rationalisation by a bakery manager, who argued that part-time

work for women was 'therapeutic', is also noted by Beechey and Perkins (1987: 116).

7. The evidence therefore suggests that the female-reserve-army thesis (Chapter 5) retains some theoretical validity where: management enjoys extensive power over a sex-segregated labour market and labour process; women are used as cheap and disposable temporary and part-time labour; and where the issue of women's substitution for men is omitted from the analysis.

8. It also resulted in the rejection of the best-qualified male candidate. Although he scored the highest on the selection tests, he was rejected because, as a practising Jew, he would be unable to work on Saturdays.

9. Informal comments by the personnel manager suggested that her preconceived antagonism to young women reflected her own domestic difficulties with her teenage daughter.

10. It was a consistent finding in the five sectors that older women were considered highly reliable and stable employees for specific jobs (Collinson 1988c). This point undermines the assumption found in human-capital and dual-labour-market theories that women are essentially temporary workers who will leave employment on starting a family.

11. Having said that, corporate personnel at this bank have not managed to challenge the informal promotion practice of closed procedures throughout the organisation. Indeed, these managers themselves were appointed through such closed procedures. An experiment of advertising vacancies internally at the head-office complex was initiated during the research. For a discussion of recent initiatives in the banking industry (for example, equal-opportunity managers, career-break schemes, management 'fast-track' training programmes, see Collinson 1987c).

12. This rationalisation displays how the concern to control the labour process is not merely a managerial strategy that informs practices, but is also a *post-facto* ideological justification which is designed to legitimise both these practices and their discrepancies with formal policy. In the literature, this distinction between managerial strategy and ideology is sometimes neglected. Extensive criticism has been levelled at Braverman, for example, for exaggerating the extent to which Taylor's principles of 'scientific management' have been translated into practice (for example, Wood 1982). This critique, however, has deflected attention away from the important ideological impact of scientific management in legitimising both managerial prerogative and the technical and elite status of the function. Management's assertion of its professional 'right to manage' is legitimised by its claim to expertise in controlling the organisation and its responsibility for safeguarding profit and the survival of the organisation. This justification neglects the extent to which managers must in practice depend on workers' voluntary co-operation.

13. The pressure to rationalise or explain practices was also reinforced by the research methodology deployed in this study. Interviewing recruiters is to some extent an artificial exercise which requires respondents to provide accounts of practices that might otherwise be taken for granted. Equally, because the project was specifically designed to get as close as possible to

actual practices and therefore to examine any discrepancy between formal policy and informal practice, the pressure on recruiters to downplay the significance of informal or unlawful practices was again that much greater.

14. Beechey and Perkins (1987: 103) confirm this finding in their research on part-time workers. With regard to the criticisms of the feminist literature for its neglect of management outlined earlier, this study is an exception which tends to prove the rule. This is because it is more concerned with managers' 'attitudes' than with their practices. Moreover, these attitudes are described rather than fully analysed. This reflects an exclusive concentration by these writers on asymmetrical power relations and a failure to theorise human agency.

15. Moreover, even when ideology is examined, feminist attention concentrates on gender to the neglect of managerial ideology and its interrelationship with male domination.

7 Males for sales

1. A third approach to selling insurance, known as the 'ordinary' or 'industrial' branch method, has been excluded from this analysis. Selling in this sector is conducted on a door-to-door basis, while premiums are collected personally by the representative weekly, monthly or annually at the residence of the insured.

2. Companies 1–10 sell insurance through intermediaries, whereas companies 11–20 go direct to the public.

3. Having said that, a recent recruit at company 5 claimed that word-of-mouth recruitment at his previous insurance company was specifically intended to subvert equal opportunities: 'They don't like to advertise in case they get the wrong sort. No Jews, Catholics, or Negroes and particularly no women.'

4. Sex-typed assumptions were also found in agency-based company recruitment documents. At company 5, 'the interview guide for new salesmen', although produced by outside consultants, assumed a male applicant throughout. Likewise, a very similar guide at company 4 talked of a 'Man Profile' and took for granted that interviewees were always male. These gendered assumptions were found in the employee appraisal assessment form for inspectors, where, for example, the interviewer had to answer 'Is he [i.e. the employee] willing to move?' Hence, it can be seen that attempts to formalise interview practices may themselves reflect and reinforce taken-for-granted patriarchal selection criteria.

5. This is a depressed inner city area of Manchester.

6. Ironically, this particular candidate was seeking other job opportunities precisely because her career was being restricted by the sex-discriminatory practices of a line manager in her present company.

7. At least one insurance company has realised the commercial benefits to be gained from avoiding a sales focus exclusively upon *male* bread-winners. The 'Dorothy Genn Women's Financial Service' produces policies covering women's specific needs. By employing female representatives too, this company has begun to recognise that conventional assumptions about the inevitability of male-dominated product and labour markets in insurance

sales can have negative commercial consequences.

8. Moreover, precisely because of their self-employed status, women would not be entitled to maternity-leave protection.

9. Yet this manager disclosed later that he was even antagonistic to women working in the office and would prefer to replace female labour with advanced information technology, as he outlined: 'I want the paperless office. The route to go is the technological route. The problem with women is that they answer back, they have bloody periods . . . . they get pre-menstrual . . . . Well machines just don't do that.'

10. This is formally presented as a loan, but in practice is usually not returned and no interest is charged.

11. Indeed, at one food manufacturer during the research, closed promotion practices were used for more senior ILM vacancies which were almost exclusively male-dominated, whilst in lower-grade jobs that were largely female-dominated, the open advertising of vacancies was the consistent ILM practice (for elaboration see Collinson 1988a: 35).

8 Risking women

1. Some writers (for example, Thompson 1983) have argued that feminisation and its accompanying gendered ideology is a direct consequence of deskilling, the introduction of new technology and capital's concern to cheapen the price of labour. In contrast, Phillips and Taylor (1980) argue that the degraded status of clerical work was not so much a product of actual task deskilling and/or the replacement of men by women, but of the pregiven inferior status of the women who perform this largely new work. They assert that socially constructed definitions of skilled status are always 'sex saturated'. Yet as Chapter 2 commented, the debate over the relative historical priority of capitalist appropriation and patriarchal domination is in danger of disappearing down a theoretical black hole. Suffice it to say here that it is important to recognise the combined analytical significance of the social and historical subordination of women, particularly in segregated work; and the introduction of new technology with its accompanying gendered ideology as well as the cheapness and flexibility of female labour for employers concerned with production, control and the accumulation of capital.

2. The paternalistic nature of management in insurance is also illustrated by the fact that many full-time employees in the finance sector still enjoy the considerable benefit of subsidised mortgages. This perk, which was introduced to attract labour in times of scarcity, constitutes an effective means of tying the worker to the organisation. Recently, at one insurance company where research took place, the eligibility criteria for mortgages (for example, length of service and hierarchical position) have been tightened. This change is likely to have a disproportionately severe impact on female employees. Before the amendment male staff comprised 70 per cent of those taking up the concessionary mortgage scheme.

3. BIFU's presence in insurance has been severely weakened by the decision of the Eagle Star Division to break away, which has 'cost' the parent

organisation around 4,500 members. This action seems to confirm a general trend in insurance begun in 1986 when the Sun Alliance staff union was formed during the takeover of Phoenix Insurance Company by the Sun Alliance. This staff union was created out of ex-BIFU members in Phoenix and ASTMS members and staff association members in Sun Alliance.

4. That employers may not be able to treat part-timers differently is suggested by the recent cases of Bilka v. Weber (1986) and ASTMS v. Norwich Union Insurance Group (1987). In the former case, the European Court concluded that on the basis of Article 119 of the Treaty of Rome, it may be unlawful to exclude part-timers from pensions schemes. In the latter case, the Central Arbitration Committee decided that exclusion of part-timers from company mortgage allowance schemes constituted indirect discrimination against women.

5. Instead, he filled this vacancy by advertising in the local newspaper. Having received 104 replies, the office manager screened out all married applicants. This was because he considered that geographical mobility was an essential requirement and one that married people could not meet. Hence, married candidates were excluded prior to interview even though they had applied to an advertisement which clearly specified the need to be mobile at short notice. 'I hope there isn't a marital discrimination board, is there?' asked the office manager (see Collinson 1988a for further details).

6. Despite taking this view, most of the women were critical of the senior pensions clerk for her indecision and change of mind. They thereby colluded in 'blaming the victim'. The exercise therefore had the effect of reinforcing divisions between the women. Resistance that did emerge between them tended to remain at the level of humour, flirtation with the office manager and 'skiving' by leaving the office on the pretext of doing an errand.

7. Her self-criticism parallels the findings of Sennett and Cobb (1977) who describe how their working-class male respondents in the US took the class system 'personally' and subsequently criticised themselves for their lack of 'success'. Clearly, this manager's focus on the clerk's so-called personality 'defects' penetrates right to the heart of the individual's sense of identity, and in this very process reinforces its own legitimacy, as Sennett and Cobb (1977: 156) again write: 'Power in the organisation, like the God of Weber's early Protestants, knows about you what you do not know about yourself.'

8. As Burawoy's (1979: 27) work clearly demonstrates, where workers believe that they have 'freely chosen' their particular work practices, they are likely to be committed to them.

9. These case-studies reinforce the criticism of Walby (1986) outlined in Chapter 2 where it was argued that she underestimates the significance of gender ideology and biology. As Crompton and Jones (1984: 142) and Dale (1987: 327) contend, women's domestic responsibilities often have a crucially negative impact on their career progress.

10. A more informal practice which has the same effect of excluding women from consideration for promotion concerned the practice of linking personal prestige with the playing of sport. As Crompton and Jones (1984) found, the sports and social club is often of central significance for individuals seeking to fit into the social requirements of insurance organisations. At company 1

the predominant sports tended to be male-orientated (for example, football, snooker, cricket, darts). Employees' involvement in organising and playing were often valuable in enhancing prestige since participation became synonymous in the eyes of authority with 'character', 'honesty' and 'integrity'. The social importance of the sports and social club at company 1 was exemplified by the provision of time off for committee members to attend their monthly meetings which paradoxically were held more regularly than those of the local union committee! This 'sacrifice' of 'personal time' for the 'good of others' in the company was an important factor influencing promotion recommendations. With regard to promotion decisions, involvement in sports activities was treated as a key aspect of 'fitting in'.

Conclusion: the vicious circles of job segregation

1. For a discussion of the legal case precedents relevant to these findings, see Collinson 1988a.
2. The research suggests that where trade unions were present, the likelihood of internal advertising of vacancies was increased.
3. For one or more of the following reasons these practices sometimes had to be legitimised. As participants in the research, managers were either directly questioned about their practices or they recognised how such practices contradicted their professional occupational responsibility, the organisation's formal policy or current legislation. Indeed, a closer examination of the quotations justifying sex-discriminatory practices in the foregoing chapters suggests in a mildly optimistic way that some managers are at least *aware* that such assumptions do contradict the legislation. This is illustrated by statements that commence by insisting, for example, 'It may sound sexist but . . . . '; 'It's not for anti-feminist reasons . . . . '; 'Although I shouldn't say this, it has to be a woman'; 'Obviously it is technically illegal to discriminate but this time I want a man.' The organisations for whom these managers worked had all declared themselves to be 'equal-opportunity employers'.
4. This critical appraisal of human agency is based primarily on the empirical evidence. However, other literature has drawn attention to the contradictory nature of self-consciousness and insecurity, such as Trungpa (1973), Watts (1973), Fromm (1977), Laing (1977), Becker (1980) and Henriques et al. (1984). The deconstructions of Henriques et al. of the 'unitary, rational and coherent subject' assumed by psychology is an analysis which is particularly useful and compatible with the one outlined here. Indeed, the work of Hollway and Henriques is referred to throughout this book. However, because their analysis of gender concentrates exclusively on sexuality and also because of the constraints of space, further consideration of their work has not been possible.
5. Whilst providing a valuable contribution to the analysis of the contradictory nature of male resistance and domination, Willis's analysis also tends to romanticise the lads' oppositional culture (see also Collinson 1981, 1988b). This is because of a failure to explore the way in which the concern with masculine identity has not only collective, but also individualising effects on

the members of the group. Willis neglects to examine the deep-seated social and psychological insecurities which reflect and reinforce the lads' defensive concern to embellish gender and class identity that, in turn, conditions divisions within the culture.

6. A large-scale survey of staff in one insurance company revealed that the vast majority of respondents (71 per cent of men and 67 per cent of women) who were constrained by the company's mobility requirement were married. These figures illustrate that the conventional male role of family bread-winner also includes domestic responsibilities which may be incompatible with a totally flexible commitment to the company (for further details see Collinson 1987a).

7. If the eligibility criterion for career-break schemes was length of service rather than grade, this measure could have a much greater impact on job segregation.

8. Indeed, with regard to equal opportunities, the present government appears to be primarily concerned with the labour-market practices of trade unions, to the neglect of those perpetrated by employers. Paradoxically, there exists an 'unholy alliance' between the political objectives of the Conservative government and the analytical focus of some feminist theorists of patriarchy who concentrate on trade-union exclusionary practices. The overwhelming finding of the research reported here, however, is that future legislation and the promotional activities of the EOC should intensify their focus on managerial practices, for it is *primarily* through these routine recruitment procedures that job segregation continues to be reproduced.

References

Acker, J. (1989) 'The problem with patriarchy', *Sociology* 23 (2): 235–40.

Althauser, R.P. and Kalleberg, A.L. (1981) 'Firms, occupations, and the structure of labour markets: a conceptual analysis', in I. Berg (ed.) *Sociological Perspectives on Labour Markets*, New York: Academic Press, 119–45.

Amsden, A.H. (ed.) (1980) *The Economics of Women and Work*, Harmondsworth: Penguin.

Anderson, N. and Shackleton, V. (1986) 'Recruitment and selection: a review of developments in the 1980s', *Personnel Review* 15(4): 19–26.

Anthias, F. (1980) 'Women and the reserve army of labour: a critique of Veronica Beechey', *Capital and Class* 10: 50–63.

Armstrong, P. (1984) *Labour Pains*, Toronto: Women's Educational Press.

Armstrong, P. and Armstrong, H. (1985a) 'Beyond sexless class and classless sex: towards feminist Marxism', in P. Armstrong, H. Armstrong, P. Connelly and A. Miles, *'Feminist Marxism or Marxist Feminism: A Debate*, Toronto: Garamond Press.

—— (1985b) 'More on Marxism and Feminism. A response to Patricia Connelly', in Armstrong et al. (eds) *Feminist Marxism or Marxist Feminism: A Debate*, Toronto: Garamond Press.

—— (1986) 'More for the money: redefining and intensifying work in Canada', paper presented at Conference on Work and Politics, Harvard University Centre for European Studies.

—— Armstrong, Peter (1986) 'Management control strategies and interprofessional competition: the cases of accountancy and personnel management', in D. Knights and H. Willmott (eds) *Managing the Labour Process*, Aldershot: Gower, 19–43.

Armstrong, Peter, Goodman, J.F.B. and Hyman, G. (1981) *Ideology and Shopfloor Industrial Relations*, London: Croom Helm.

Arvey, R.D. (1979) 'Unfair discrimination in the employment interview: legal and psychological aspects', *Psychological Bulletin* 86(4): 736–65.

—— and Campion, J. (1982) 'The employment interview: a survey and review of recent research', *Personnel Psychology* 35: 281–322.

ASTMS v. Norwich Union Insurance Group (1987) *Central Arbitration Committee* Award no. 87/2.

Barker, J. and Downing, H. (1980) 'Word processing and the transformation of patriarchal relations of control in the office', *Capital and Class* 10: 64–99.

Baron, A. (1987) 'Technology and the crisis of masculinity: the social construction of gender and skill in the U.S. printing industry, 1850–1920', paper presented at the 5th UMIST–ASTON Organisation and Control of the Labour Process Conference, Manchester, April.

Barrett, M. (1980) *Women's Oppression Today: Problems in Marxist Feminist Analysis*, London: Verso and New Left Books.

Barron, R.D. and Norris, G.M. (1976) 'Sexual divisions and the dual labour market', in D.L. Barker and S. Allen (eds) *Dependence and Exploitation in Work and Marriage*, London: Longman, 47–69.

Becker, E. (1980) *The Birth and Death of Meaning*, New York: Free Press.

Becker, G.S. (1957) *The Economics of Discrimination*, Chicago: Chicago University Press.

Beechey, V. (1977) 'Some notes on female wage labour in capitalist production', *Capital and Class* 3: 45–66.

—— (1978) 'Women and production', in A. Kuhn and A.M. Wolpe (eds) *Feminism and Materialism*, London: Routledge & Kegan Paul.

—— (1979) 'On patriarchy', *Feminist Review* 3: 66–82.

—— (1982) 'The sexual division of labour and the labour process: a critical assessment of Braverman', in S. Wood (ed.) *The Degradation of Work?*, London: Hutchinson, 54–73.

—— (1983) 'What's so special about women's employment? A review of some recent studies of women's paid work', *Feminist Review* 15 (November): 23–45.

—— (1984) 'Women's employment in contemporary Britain', paper presented at British Sociological Association Conference, Bradford, April.

Beechey, V. and Perkins, T. (1987) *A Matter of Hours: Women, Part-Time Work and the Labour Market*, Cambridge: Polity Press.

Benson, J. and Griffin, G. (1985) 'Women at work: a case study of the insurance industry', *Industrial Relations Journal* 16(4): 75–84.

Benston, M. (1969) 'The political economy of women's liberation', *Monthly Review* 21(4): 13–27.

Bernard, E. (1984) 'Science, technology and progress: lessons from the history of the typewriter', *Canadian Woman Studies* 5(4): 12–14.

Beynon, H. (1973) *Working for Ford*, Harmondsworth: Penguin.

BIFU (Banking, Insurance, Finance Union) (1985) *Jobs for the Girls*, London: BIFU.

Bilka Kaufhaus GmbH v. Karin Weber von Hartz (1986) *The European Court of Justice* case 170/84, 13 May.

Blackburn, R.M. and Mann, M. (1979) *The Working Class in the Labour Market*, London: Macmillan.

Bradley, H. (1986) 'Technological change, management strategies, and the development of gender-based job segregation in the labour process', in D. Knights and H. Willmott (eds) *Gender and the Labour Process*, Aldershot: Gower, 54–73.

Braverman, H. (1974) *Labour and Monopoly Capital*, New York: Monthly Review Press.

Brenner, J. and Ramas, M. (1984) 'Rethinking women's oppression', *New Left Review* 144: 33–71.

Bresnen, M.J., Wray, K., Bryman, A., Beardsworth, A.D., Ford, J.R. and Keil, E.T. (1985) 'The flexibility of recruitment in the construction industry: formalisation or re-casualisation?' *Sociology* 19(1): 108–24.

Brittan, A. (1989) *Masculinity and Power*, Oxford: Basil Blackwell.

Brown, R.K. (1976) 'Women as employees: some comments on research in industrial sociology', in D.L. Barker and S. Allen (eds) *Dependence and Exploitation in Work and Marriage*, London: Longman, 21–46.

Brown, R.K. (1984) 'Working on work', *Sociology* 18(3): 311–23.

Bruegel, I. (1979) 'Women as a reserve army of labour: a note on recent British experience', *Feminist Review* 3: 12–23.

Burawoy, M. (1979) *Manufacturing Consent*, Chicago: Chicago University Press.

Burrell, G. (1984) 'Sex and organisational analysis', *Organisation Studies* 5(2): 97–118.

Burton, C. (1985) *Subordination: Feminism and Social Theory*, Sydney: Allen & Unwin.

Cash, T.F., Gillen, B. and Burns, D.S. (1977) 'Sexism and "beautyism" in personnel consultant decision making', *Journal of Applied Psychology* 62: 301–7.

Cavendish, R. (1982) *On the Line*, London: Routledge & Kegan Paul.

Chaney, J. (1981) *Social Networks and Job Information: The Situation of Women Who Return to Work*, Manchester: EOC/SSRC.

Child, J. (1985) 'Managerial strategies, new technology and the labour process', in D. Knights, H. Willmott and D. Collinson (eds) *Job Redesign*, 107–41.

Childs, P. (1985) 'Work and career expectations of insurance company employees and the impact of unionisation', *Sociology* 19(1): 125–35.

Chiplin, B. and Sloane, P.J. (1976) *Sex Discrimination in the Labour Market*, London: Macmillan.

—— (1982) *Tackling Discrimination at the Workplace*, Cambridge, Cambridge University Press.

Cockburn, C. (1983) *Brothers*, London: Pluto Press.

—— (1985) 'Technology as a factor in occupational segregation', *EOC Research Bulletin* 9 (Spring): 45–61.

—— (1986) *Machinery of Dominance: Women, Men and Technical Know-how*, London: Pluto Press.

Collinson, D.L. (1981) 'Managing the Shopfloor', MSc thesis, Department of Management Sciences, Manchester: UMIST.

—— (1987a) 'A question of equal opportunities: a survey of staff in a large insurance company', *Personnel Review* 16(1): 19–29.

—— (1987b) 'Picking women: the recruitment of temporary workers in the mail order industry', *Work, Employment and Society* 1(3) 371–87.

—— (1987c) 'Banking on women: selection practices in the finance sector', *Personnel Review* 16(5): 12–20.

—— (1988a) *Barriers to Fair Selection: A Multi-sector Study of Recruitment Practices*, Equal Opportunities Commission Research Series, London: HMSO.

—— (1988b) 'Engineering humour: masculinity, joking and conflict in shop-floor relations', *Organization Studies* 9(2): 181–99.

—— (1988c) 'Managing to discriminate: power and agency in the recruitment process', unpublished doctoral thesis, Manchester School of Management, UMIST.

—— (1990) 'Researching recruitment', in R. Burgess (ed.) *Studies in Qualitative Methodology, Volume 3*, London: JA1 Press.

Collinson, D.L. and Knights, D. (1986) 'Men only: theories and practices of job segregation in insurance', in D. Knights and H. Willmott (eds) *Gender and the Labour Process*, 140–78.

Conference of Socialist Economists (1980) *Microelectronics, Capitalist Technology and the Working Class*, London: CSE Books.

Connell, R.W. (1983) *Which Way Is Up?*, London: Allen & Unwin.

—— (1985) 'Theorising gender', *Sociology* 19(2): 260–72.

—— (1987) *Gender and Power*, Cambridge: Polity Press.

Connelly, P. (1978) *Last Hired, First Fired: Women and the Canadian Work Force*, Toronto: The Women's Press.

Craig, C., Garnsey, E. and Rubery, J. (1985) 'Labour market segmentation and women's employment: a case study from the United Kingdom', *International Labour Review* 124: 267–80.

Cressey, P. and Macinnes, J. (1980) 'Voting For Ford: Industrial democracy and the control of labour', *Capital and Class* 11: 5–33.

Crompton, R. and Jones, G. (1984) *White Collar Proletariat: Deskilling and Gender in Clerical Work*, London: Macmillan.

Crompton, R. with Sanderson, K. (1985) 'Credentials and careers', paper presented to Segregation in Employment Symposium, University of Lancaster, July.

Crompton, R. and Sanderson, K. (1986) 'Credentials and careers: some implications of the increase in professional qualifications amongst women', *Sociology* 20(1): 25–42.

Curran, M. (1986) *Stereotypes and Selection: Gender and Family in the Recruitment Process*, EOC Research Report (unpublished version).

Dale, A. (1985) 'The role of theories of labour market segmentation in understanding the position of women in the occupational structure', University of Surrey, *Occupational Papers in Sociology and Social Policy* no. 4.

—— (1987) 'Occupational inequality, gender and life-cycle', *Work, Employment and Society* 1(3): 326–51.

Dalla Costa, M. and James S. (1972) *The Power of Women and the Subversion of the Community*, Bristol: Falling Wall Press.

Dalton, M. (1959) *Men Who Manage*, New York: John Wiley and Son.

Daniel, W.W. and Millward, N. (1983) *Workplace Industrial Relations in Britain*, London: Heinemann.

Dasey, R. (1980) 'Pin ups or pin money: the same old picture', *Computing*, October: 16–17.

Davies, M. (1974) 'Women's place is at the typewriter: the feminisation of the clerical labour force', *Radical America* 18(4).

Davies, C. and Rosser, J. (1986) 'Gendered jobs in the health service: a problem for labour process analysis', in D. Knights and H. Willmott (eds) *Gender and the Labour Process*, 94–116.

Delphy, C. (1977) *The Main Enemy: A Materialist Analysis of Women's Oppression*, London: Women's Research and Resources Centre.

Department of Employment (1985) 'Employment statistics', *Employment*

Gazette 92(4): 151–64.

—— (1986) 'Employment statistics', *Employment Gazette* 9, 7:513

Dick, B. and Morgan, G. (1987) 'Family Networks and Employment in Textiles', *Work, Employment and Society* 1(2): 225–46.

Dipboye, R.L. (1980) 'Self-fulfilling prophecies in the selection recruitment interview', unpublished manuscript (cited in Arvey and Campion 1982).

Dipboye, R.L., Arvey, R.D., and Terpstra, D.E. (1977) 'Sex and physical attractiveness of raters and applicants as determinants of resumé evaluations', *Journal of Applied Psychology* 62: 288–94.

Dipboye, R.L., Fromkin, H.L. and Wilbach, K. (1975) 'Relative importance of applicant sex, attractiveness and scholastic standing in evaluation of job application resumes', *Journal of Applied Psychology* 60: 39–43.

Doeringer, P. and Piore, M. (1971) *Internal Labour Markets and Manpower Analysis*, Mass: Lexington Books.

Downing, H. (1980) 'Word processors and the oppression of women', in T. Forester (ed.) *The Microelectronics Revolution*, Oxford: Basil Blackwell.

Dunnette, M.D. and Borman, W.C. (1979) 'Personnel selection and classification systems', *Annual Review of Psychology* 18: 477–525.

Edwards, R. (1979) *Contested Terrain: The Transformation of the Workplace in the Twentieth Century*, London: Heinemann.

Egan, A. (1982) 'Women and banking: a study of inequality', *Industrial Relations Journal* 13(3): 20–31.

Equal Opportunities Commission (1985a) *Report of the formal investigation into Leeds Permanent Building Society*, Manchester: EOC.

—— (1985b) *Code of Practice*, Manchester: EOC.

—— (1986) 'Fair and Efficient Selection', London: HMSO.

—— (1988) *Equal Treatment For Women and Men: Strengthening the Acts*, Manchester: EOC.

Evans, B. and Waites, B. (1981) *I.Q. and Mental Testing*, London: Macmillan.

Fevre, R. (1989) 'Informal practices, flexible firms and private labour markets', *Sociology*, 23(1): 91–109.

Filby, M.P. (1987) 'The Newmarket racing lad: tradition and change in a marginal occupation', *Work, Employment and Society* 1(2): 205–24.

Finnegan, J. (1983) *The Right People for the Right Jobs*, Aldershot: Gower.

Firestone, S. (1972) *The Dialectic of Sex*, London: Paladin.

Flanders, A. (1970) *Management and the Unions*, London: Faber.

Ford, J., Keil, T., Bryman, A., Beardsworth, A. and Jenkins, R. (1984) 'Internal labour market processes', *Industrial Relations Journal*, Summer: 41–9.

Ford, J.R., Bryman, A., Beardsworth, A.D., Bresnen, M. and Keil, E.T. (1986) 'Changing patterns of labour recruitment', *Personnel Review* 15(4): 14–18.

Fox, A. (1980) *A Sociology of Work and Industry*, London: Macmillan.

Fraser, J.M. (1966) *Employment Interviewing*, London: Macdonald Evans.

Freeman, C. (1982) 'The understanding employer', in J. West (ed.) *Work, Women and the Labour Market*, London: Routledge & Kegan Paul, 135–53.

Friedman, A.L. (1977) *Industry and Labour*, London: Macmillan.

—— (1987) 'The means of management control and labour process theory: a critical note on Storey', *Sociology* 21(2): May, 287–94.

Fromm, E. (1977) *The Fear of Freedom*, London: Routledge & Kegan Paul.

Gamarnikow, E., Morgan, D., Purvis, J. and Taylorson, D. (eds) (1983) *Gender,*

References

Class and Work, London: Heinemann.

Giddens, A. (1976) *New Rules of Sociological Method*, London: Hutchinson.

—— (1979) *Central Problems in Social Theory*, Cambridge: Polity Press.

Goffman, E. (1959) *The Presentation of Self in Everyday Life*, Harmondsworth: Penguin.

Gray, S. (1987) 'Sharing the shop floor', in S. Kaufman (ed.) *Beyond Patriarchy*, Oxford University Press, 216–34.

Grieco, M. (1987) 'Family networks and the closure of employment' in G. Lee and R. Loveridge (eds) *Stigma: The Manufacture of Disadvantage* 33–44.

Grieco, M. and Whipp, R. (1986) 'Women and the workplace: gender and control in the labour process', in D. Knights and H. Willmott (eds) *Gender and the Labour Process*, 117–39.

Gunning v. Mirror Group Newspapers Ltd. (1983) *Industrial Tribunal*, 6045, 22 June.

Hakim, C. (1979) 'Occupational Segregation', *Department of Employment Research Paper* no. 9.

—— (1988) 'Women at work: recent research on women's employment', *Work, Employment and Society* 2(1): March, 103–13.

Harrison, J. (1973) 'The political economy of housework', *Bulletin of the Conference of Socialist Economists*, Winter: 35–52.

Hartmann, H. (1979) 'Capitalism, patriarchy and job segregation by sex', in Z. Eisenstein (ed.) *Capitalism, Patriarchy and the Case for Socialist Feminism*, New York: Monthly Review Press, 206–47.

—— (1981) 'The Unhappy Marriage of Marxism and Feminism: Towards a More Progressive Union', in Sargent, L. (ed.), *The Unhappy Marriage of Marxism and Feminism'*, London: Pluto Press, 1–42.

Hartsock, N. (1983) *Money, Sex and Power*, New York: Longman.

Hearn, J. (1982) 'Notes on patriarchy, professionalisation and the semi-professions', *Sociology* 16(2): 184–202.

—— (1985) 'Men's sexuality at work', in A. Metcalf and M. Humphries (eds) *The Sexuality of Men*, London: Pluto Press, 110–28.

—— (1987) *The Gender of Oppression*, Brighton: Wheatsheaf.

Hearn, J. and Parkin, W. (1987) *'Sex' at 'Work'*, Brighton: Wheatsheaf.

Hearn, J., Sheppard, D.L., Tancred-Sheriff, P. and Burrell, G. (1989) *The Sexuality of Organization*, London: Sage.

Heilman, M.E. (1980) 'The impact of situational factors on personnel decisions concerning women: varying the sex composition of the applicant pool', *Organisational Behaviour and Human Performance* 26: 386–96.

Henriques, J. (1984) 'Social psychology and the politics of racism', in Henriques et al. *Changing the Subject*, 60–90.

Henriques, J., Hollway, W., Urwin, C., Venn, C. and Walkerdine, V. (1984) *Changing the Subject*, London: Methuen.

Heritage, J. (1983) 'Feminisation and unionisation: a case study from banking', in E. Gamarnikow et al. (eds) *Gender, Class and Work*, 131–48.

Hollway, W. (1983) 'Heterosexual sex: power and desire for the other', in S. Cartledge and J. Ryan (eds) *Sex and Love*, London: The Women's Press, 124–40.

—— (1984a) 'Fitting work: psychological assessment in organisations', in Henriques et al. *Changing the Subject*, 26–59.

—— (1984b) 'Gender difference and the production of subjectivity', in Henriques et al. *Changing the Subject*, 227–63.

—— (1985) 'Personnel practices and the labour process: the case of Zimbabwe', paper presented at the 3rd ASTON/UMIST Organisation and Control of the Labour Process Conference, April.

Hopper, T., Cooper, D., Lowe, T. and Capps, T. (1984) 'Financial control and the labour process in a nationalised industry', mimeo, University of Manchester.

Humphries, J. (1977) 'Class struggle and the persistence of the working class family', in A.H. Amsden (ed.) *The Economics of Women and Work*, 140–65.

Hyman, R. (1987) 'Strategy or structure? Capital, labour and control', *Work, Employment and Society* 1(1): 25–55.

Incomes Data Services (1985) 'Maternity and paternity leave', *IDS Study* 351 (December).

Institute of Personnel Management, (1986) *The IPM Equal Opportunities Code*, London: IPM.

Jenkins, R. (1986) *Racism and Recruitment*, Cambridge: Cambridge University Press.

Jenkins, R. and Parker, G. (1987) 'Organisational politics and the recruitment of black workers', in G. Lee and R. Loveridge (eds) *Stigma*, 58–70.

Jenkins R., Bryman, A., Ford, J., Keil, T. and Beardsworth, A. (1983) 'Information in the labour market: the impact of recession', *Sociology* 17(2): 260–7.

Jewson, N. and Mason, D. (1984–5) 'Equal opportunities policies at the workplace and the concept of monitoring', *New Community* 13(1) 124–36.

—— (1986a) 'The theory and practice of equal opportunities policies: liberal and radical approaches', mimeo, Department of Sociology, University of Leicester.

—— (1986b) 'Modes of discrimination in the recruitment process: formalisation, fairness and efficiency', *Sociology* 20(1): 43–63.

Jones, B. (1982) 'Destruction or redistribution of engineering skills? The case of numerical control', in S. Wood (ed.) *The Degradation of Work?*, London: Hutchinson.

Kanter, R.M. (1977) *Men and Women of the Corporation*, New York: Basic Books.

Kaufman, M.L. (1987) 'The construction of masculinity and the triad of men's violence', in M. Kaufman (ed.) *Beyond Patriarchy*, Oxford: Oxford University Press, 1–29.

Kelly, J. (1985) 'Management's redesign of work: labour process, labour markets and product markets', in D. Knights et al. (eds) *Job Redesign*, 30–1.

Khanna v. Ministry of Defence (1981) *IRLR*, 331.

Knights, D. and Collinson, D.L. (1985) 'Redesigning work on the shopfloor: a question of control or consent?', in D. Knights et al. (eds) *Job Redesign*, 197–226.

—— (1987) 'Disciplining the shopfloor: a comparison of the disciplinary effects of managerial and financial accounting', *Accounting, Organisations and Society* 12(5): 457–77.

Knights, D. and Willmott, H. (eds) (1986a) *Gender and the Labour Process*, Aldershot: Gower.

—— (eds) (1986b) *Managing the Labour Process*, Aldershot: Gower.

References

Knights, D., Willmot, H. and Collinson, D. (eds) (1985) *Job Redesign*, Aldershot: Gower.

Laing, R.D. (1977) *Self and Others*, London: Harmondsworth.

Latham, G.P. and Saarie, L.M. (1984) 'Do people do what they say? Further studies on the situational interview', *Journal of Applied Psychology* 69: 569–73.

Lawrence, B. (1987) 'The fifth dimension: gender and general practice', in A. Spencer and D. Podmore (eds) *In a Man's World*, 134–57.

Lawson, T. (1981) 'Paternalism and labour market segmentation theory', in F. Wilkinson (ed.) *The Dynamics of Labour Market Segmentation*, London: Academic Press.

Lee, G. and Loveridge, R. (eds) (1987) *Stigma: The Manufacture of Disadvantage*, Milton Keynes: Open University Press.

Legge, K. (1978) *Power, Innovation and Problem Solving in Personnel Management*, Maidenhead: McGraw-Hill.

—— (1987) 'Women in personnel management: uphill climb or downhill slide?', in A. Spencer and D. Podmore (eds) *In a Man's World*, 33–60.

Liff, S. (1986) 'Technical change and occupational sex-typing', in D. Knights and H. Willmott (eds) *Gender and the Labour Process*, 74–93.

Littler, C.R. (1982) *The Development of the Labour Process in Capitalist Societies*, London: Heinemann.

Lockwood, D. (1958) *The Blackcoated Worker*, London: Allen & Unwin.

Long, P. (1984) *The Personnel Specialists: A Comparative Study of Male and Female Careers*, London: IPM.

Loveridge, R. (1987) 'Social accommodations and technological transformations: the case of gender', in G. Lee and R. Loveridge (eds) *Stigma*, 176–98.

Lown, J. (1983) 'Not so much a factory, more a form of patriarchy: gender and class during industrialisation', in E. Gamarnikow et al. (eds) *Gender, Class and Work*, 28–45.

Luckmann, T. and Berger, P. (1964) 'Social mobility and personal identity', *Archiv. Europ. Sociology*.

Mcintyre, A. (1981) *After Virtue*, London: Duckworth.

Mackinnon, C.A. (1979) *Sexual Harassment of Working Women: A Case of Sex Discrimination*, New Haven: Yale University Press.

Mcnally, F. (1979) *Women for Hire*, London: Macmillan.

Maguire, M (1984) 'Location and recruitment as a means of control: the case of a Northern Ireland electronics factory', presented at the British Sociological Conference, Bradford, April.

—— (1988) 'Work, locality and social control', *Work, Employment and Society* 2 (1): 71–87.

Makin, P.J. and Robertson, I.T. (1983) 'Self assessment, realistic job previews and occupational decisions', *Personnel Review* 12: 21–5.

Mallier, A.T. and Rosser, M.J. (1987) 'Changes in the distribution of female employment in Great Britain, 1951–1981', *Work, Employment and Society* 1 (4) 463–86.

Manpower Services Commission (1984) *New Technology and the Demand for Skills*, Sheffield: MSC.

Manwaring, T. (1984) 'The extended internal labour market', *Cambridge Journal of Economics* 8 (2): 161–87.

—— and Wood, S. (1985) 'The ghost in the labour process', in D. Knights et al. (eds) *Job Redesign*, 171–98.

Marx, K. (1946) *Capital: A Critical Analysis of Capitalist Production*, London: Allen & Unwin.

Mayfield, E.C. (1964) 'The selection interview: a re-evaluation of published research', *Personnel Psychology* 17: 239–60.

Merleau Ponty, M. (1962) *Phenomenology of Perception*, London: Routledge & Kegan Paul.

Metcalf, A. and Humphries, M. (eds) (1985) *The Sexuality of Men*, London: Pluto Press.

Milkman, R. (1976) 'Women's work and economic crisis', *Review of Radical Political Economics* 8: 72–96.

Millett, K. (1971) *Sexual Politics*, New York: Abacus.

Mitchell, J. (1975) *Psychoanalysis and Feminism*, Harmondsworth: Penguin.

Molyneux, M. (1981) 'Women in socialist societies' in K. Young and others *Of Marriage and the Market: Women's Subordination in International Perspective*, London: CSE Books.

Morgall, J. (1981) 'Typing our way to freedom: is it true that new technology can liberate women?', *Feminist Review* 9 (October): 87–101.

Morgan, C., Hall, V. and Mackay, H. (1983) *The Selection of Secondary School Headteachers*, Milton Keynes: Open University Press.

Morgan, D.H.J. (1981) 'Men, masculinity and the process of sociological enquiry', in H. Roberts (ed.) *Doing Feminist Research*, London: Routledge & Kegan Paul, 83–113.

—— (1988) 'No more heroes? Masculinity, violence and the civilising process', presented at the British Sociological Conference, Edinburgh, April.

Morris, L. (1987) 'Constraints on gender: the family wage, social security and the labour market', *Work, Employment and Society* 1 (1): 85–106.

Nichols, T. and Beynon, H. (1977) *Living with Capitalism*, London: Routledge & Kegan Paul.

Nolan, P. and Edwards, P.K. (1983) 'Homogenise, divide and rule', *Cambridge Journal of Economics* 8: 197–215.

Norris, G.M. (1978) 'Industrial paternalist capitalism and local labour markets', *Sociology* 12: 469–89.

O'Brien, M. (1981) *The Politics of Reproduction*, London: Routledge & Kegan Paul.

Offe, C. (1976) *Industry and Inequality*, London: Edward Arnold.

Ojutiku v. Manpower Services Commission (1982) *IRLR*, 418.

Palm, G. (1977), *The Flight From Work*, Cambridge: Cambridge University Press.

Pearn, M., Kandola, R.S. and Mottram, R.D. (1987) *Selection Tests and Sex Bias*, EOC Research Series, London: HMSO.

Perkins, T. (1983) 'A new form of employment: a case study of women's part-time work in Coventry', in M. Evans and C. Ungerson (eds) *Sexual Divisions, Patterns and Processes*, London: Tavistock.

Phillips, A. and Taylor, B. (1980) 'Sex and skill: notes towards a feminist economics', *Feminist Review* 6: 79–83.

Plumbley, P.R. (1974) *Recruitment and Selection*, London: Institute of Personnel Management.

247

References

Pollert, A. (1981) *Girls, Wives, Factory Lives*, London: Macmillan.

— (1983) 'Women, gender relations and wage labour' in E. Gamarnikow et al. (eds) *Gender, Class and Work*, 96–114.

Poppleton, S.E. (1980) 'Characteristics of the effective life assurance salesman: a paper prepared for branch managers of Schroeder life assurance company', unpublished paper, July.

Purcell, J. (1985) 'Is anybody listening to the corporate personnel department?', *Personnel Management* September: 28–31.

Purcell, K. (1979) 'Miltancy and acquiescence amongst women workers', in S. Burman (ed.) *Fit Work For Women*, London: Croom Helm, 112–33.

Quinnen v. Hovells (1984) *Employment Appeal Tribunal*, 624, 13 March.

Rainey v. Greater Glasgow Health Board (1986) *House of Lords Judgment*, 27 November.

Reich, M., Gordon, D.M. and Edwards, R.C. (1980) 'A theory of labour market segmentation', in A.H. Amsden (ed.) *The Economics of Women and Work*, 232–41.

Reilly, R.R. and Chao, G.T. (1982) 'Validity and fairness of some alternative employee selection procedures', *Personnel Psychology* 35: 1–62.

Roberts, J. (1982) 'Power, freedom and identity', unpublished PhD thesis, Department of Management Sciences, UMIST.

Robertson, I. (1985) 'Approaches to the prediction of managerial performance', paper presented at Conference of Managerial Assessment, UMIST, May.

— and Kandola, R.S. (1982) 'Work sample tests: validity adverse impact and applicant reaction', *Journal of Occupational Psychology* 55: 171–83.

Rodger, A. (1974) *The Seven-Point Plan*, Windsor: NFER.

Rohstein, M. and Jackson, D.N. (1980) 'Decision making in the employment interview: an experimental approach', *Journal of Applied Psychology* 65: 271–83.

Rose, M. and Jones, B. (1985) 'Managerial strategy and trade union responses in work reorganisation schemes at establishment level', in D. Knights et al. (eds) *Job Redesign*, 81–106.

Rowbotham, S. (1982) 'The trouble with "patriarchy"', in M. Evans (ed.) *The Woman Question*, London: Fontana, 73–9.

Rubery, J. (1980) 'Structured labour markets, worker organization and low pay', in A.H. Amsden (ed.) *The Economics of Women and Work*, 242–70.

Ryan, W. (1976) *Blaming the Victim*, New York: Vintage Books.

Salaman, G. and Thompson, K. (1978) 'Class culture and the persistence of an elite. The case of army officer selection', *Sociological Review* 27: 283–304.

Schmitt, N. (1976) 'Social and situational determinants of interview decisions: implications for the employment interview', *Personnel Psychology* 29: 79–101.

— Gooding, R.Z., Noe, R.A. and Kirsch, M. (1984) 'Meta-analysis of validity studies published between 1964 and 1982 and the investigation of study characteristics', *Personnel Psychology* 37: 407–22.

Seccombe, W. (1974) 'The housewife and her labour under capitalism', *New Left Review* 83: 3–24.

Sedley, A. and Benn, M. (1984) *Sexual Harassment at Work*, London: National Council for Civil Liberties.

Sennett, R. and Cobb, J. (1977) *The Hidden Injuries of Class*, London:

Cambridge University Press.

Silverman, D. and Jones, J. (1973) 'Getting in. The managed accomplishment of "correct selection outcomes"', in J. Child (ed.) *Man and Organisation*, London: Allen & Unwin, 63–106.

—— (1976) *Organisational Work*, London: Collier Macmillan.

Silverstone, R. (1976) 'Office work for women: an historical review', *Business History* 18 (1): 98–111.

Simas, K. and McCarrey, M. (1979) 'Impact of recruiter authoritarianism and applicant sex on evaluation and selection decisions in a recruitment interview analogue study', *Journal of Applied Psychology* 64: 483–91.

Simons, G. (1981) *Women in Computing*, Manchester: National Computing Centre.

Sisson, K. (1989) 'Personnel management in perspective', in K. Sisson (ed.) *Personnel Management in Britain*, Oxford: Basil Blackwell.

Smith, M. and Robertson, I.T. (1986) *The Theory and Practice of Systematic Staff Selection*, London: Macmillan.

Spencer, A. and Podmore, D. (1986) 'Gender in the labour process: the case of women and men lawyers', in D. Knights and H. Willmott (eds) *Gender and the Labour Process*, 36–53.

—— (eds) (1987) *In a Man's World*, London: Tavistock.

Storey, J. (1985) 'The means of management control, *Sociology* 19 (2): 193–211.

—— (1986) 'The phoney war? New office technology: organisation and control', in D. Knights and H. Willmott (eds) *Managing the Labour Process*, 44–66.

Supple, B. (1970) *The Royal Exchange Assurance: A History of British Insurance, 1720–1970*, Cambridge: Cambridge University Press.

Tajfel, H. (1978) *The Social Psychology of Minorities*, London: Minority Rights Group, 38.

Taylor, F. (1947) *Scientific Management*, New York: Harper & Row.

Thayer, P.W. (1977) 'Something's old, something's new', *Personnel Psychology* 30: 513–25.

Thomason, G. (1978) *A Textbook of Personnel Management*, London: Institute of Personnel Management.

Thompson, P. (1983) *The Nature of Work*, London: Macmillan.

Thompson, P. and Bannon, E. (1985) *Working the System*, London: Pluto Press.

Tolson, A. (1977) *The Limits of Masculinity*, London: Tavistock.

Torrington, D. and Chapman, J. (1983) *Personnel Management*, Englewood Cliffs: Prentice-Hall.

Torrington, D. and Hall, J. (1987) *Personnel Management: A New Approach*, London: Prentice-Hall International.

Torrington, D. and Mackay, L. (1986) 'Will consultants take over the personnel function?', *Personnel Management* February: 34–7.

Torrington, D., Hitner, T. and Knights, D. (1982) *Management and the Multi-Racial Work Force*, Aldershot: Gower.

Trades Union Congress (1986) 'Award in the dispute between BIFU and ASTMS over negotiating rights in Sun Alliance Insurance Company', *Disputes Committee Ruling*, Case No. 85/544, March. p. 6.

Trungpa, C. (1973) *Cutting through Spiritual Materialism*, London: Routledge

References

& Kegan Paul.

Tyson, S. (1983) 'Personnel management in its organizational context', in K. Thurley and S. Wood (eds) *Industrial Relations and Management Strategy*, Cambridge: Cambridge University Press.

—— (1985) 'Is this the very model of a modern personnel manager', *Personnel Management* May: 22–5.

—— and Fell, A. (1986) *Evaluating the Personnel Function*, London: Hutchinson.

Ulrich, L. and Trumbo, D. (1965) 'The selection interview since 1949', *Psychological Bulletin* 63: 100–16.

Upton, R. (1984) 'The home office and the new homeworkers', *Personnel Management* September.

Vinnicombe, S. (1980) *Secretaries, Management and Organisations*, London: Heinemann.

Waddington, P.A.J. (1982) 'Indeterminacy in occupational recruitment: the case of prison assistant governors', *Sociology* 16 (2): 203–19.

Wajcman, J. (1983) *Women in Control*, Milton Keynes: Open University Press.

Walby, S. (1983) 'Patriarchal structures: the case of unemployment' in E. Gamarnikow et al. (eds) *Gender, Class and Work*, 149–66.

—— (1986) *Patriarchy at Work*, Cambridge: Polity Press.

—— (1989) 'Theorising patriarchy', *Sociology* 23 (2): 213–34.

Walsgrove, D. (1987) 'Policing yourself: social closure and the internalisation of stigma', in G. Lee and R. Loveridge (eds) *Stigma*, 45–57.

Walters, P.A. (1987) 'Servants of the Crown', in A. Spencer and D. Podmore (eds) *In a Man's World*, 12–32.

Watson, T. (1977) *The Personnel Managers*, London: Routledge & Kegan Paul.

Watts, A. (1973) *This Is It*, New York: Random House.

Webster, E.C. (ed.) (1964) *Decision Making in the Employment Interview*, Montreal: Eagle.

Weekes, J. (1977) *Coming Out: Homosexual Politics in Britain from the Nineteenth Century to the Present*, London: Quartet.

Westwood, S. (1984) *All Day Every Day: Factory, Family, Women's Lives*, London: Pluto Press.

Wharton, A.S. (1985) 'Blue-collar segregation and the economic organization of U.S. manufacturing industries', presented at the 3rd Organisation and Control of the Labour Process Conference, Manchester, April.

Willis, P. (1977) *Learning to Labour*, London: Saxon House.

—— (1979) 'Shopfloor culture, masculinity and the wage form', in J. Clarke, C. Critcher and R. Johnson (eds) *Working Class Culture*, London: Hutchinson, 185–98.

Willmott, H. (1987) 'Racism, politics and employment relations', in G. Lee and R. Loveridge (eds) *Stigma*, 128–43.

Wilson, E. (1984) 'I'll climb the stairway to heaven: lesbianism in the seventies', in S. Cartledge and J. Ryan (eds) *Sex and Love: New Thoughts on Old Contradictions*, London: The Woman's Press, 180–95.

Winch, G.G. (1985) 'The labour process and labour market in construction', presented at the 3rd Organisation and Control of the Labour Process Conference, Manchester, April.

Winstanley, D. (1986) 'Recruitment strategies as a means of managerial control of technological labour', presented at the 4th Organisation and Control of the Labour Process Conference, Aston, March.

Witz, A. (1986) 'Patriarchy and the labour market: occupational control strategies and the medical division of labour', in D. Knights and H. Willmott (eds) *Gender and the Labour Process*, Aldershot: Gower, 14–35.

Wood, S. (ed.) (1982) *The Degradation of Work?*, London: Hutchinson.

—— (1986) 'Personnel management and recruitment', *Personnel Review* 15 (2): 3–11.

Wright, O.R. (1969) 'Summary of research on the selection interview since 1969', *Personnel Psychology* 22: 391–413.

Yanz, L. and Smith, D. (1983) 'Women as a reserve army of labour: a critique', *Review of Radical Political Economics* 15 (1): 92–106.

Zikmund, W.G., Hitt, M.A. and Pickens, B.A. (1978) 'Influence of sex and scholastic performance on reactions of job applicant resumes', *Journal of Applied Psychology* 63: 252–5.

Name index

Subject index